Kitchener's Sword-Arm

Destroying a Boer gun on a night sortie from Ladysmith
(Author's collection)

KITCHENER'S SWORD-ARM

The Life and Campaigns of
General Sir Archibald Hunter

G.C.B., G.C.V.O., D.S.O.

by

Archie Hunter

SARPEDON
New York

To Mirabel, Archie and Clare

Published in the United States by
SARPEDON

First published in the UK in 1996 by
Spellmount Ltd
The Old Rectory, Staplehurst, Kent TN12 0AZ

Library of Congress Cataloging-in-Publication Data available.

ISBN 1-885119-29-1

Manufactured in Great Britain.

10 9 8 7 6 5 4 3 2 1

Contents

List of Maps

Maps drawn by the author. Computer enhancement by Tim Boyden

Abbreviations

BOD	Bodleian Library, University of Oxford
IWM	Imperial War Museum, London
LHC	Liddell Hart Centre for Military Archives, King's College, University of London
NAM	National Army Museum, London
NR	Nicol Russel Collection, Swanage, Dorset
OIO BL	Oriental and India Office Collections, British Library, London
PRO	Public Record Office, Kew, Surrey
RA	Royal Archives, Windsor
RCSAW	Royal Commission on the South African War
SAD	Sudan Archive, University of Durham Library
OH	*Official History of the War in South Africa 1899–1902*
TH	*The Times History of the War in South Africa*
AHd	Archibald Hunter's Diary
DHD	Duncan Doolittle – *A Soldier's Hero: General Sir Archibald Hunter*

List of Plates

Introduction and Acknowledgements

My great-uncle Archie, the subject of this book, has, I believe, been neglected by military historians. In family circles he was disinclined to talk about his exploits. As a soldier he shunned publicity and, according to tradition, ordered his batman to burn his private papers. Until quite recently it was thought that he had left no letters or other material behind him which might shed light on his career.

Some ten years ago some of Hunter's great-nephews in the United States came to be curious about him. They wondered how he, with his once awesome reputation as a fighting General, had remained on the sidelines during World War I, and why historians were, with the odd exception, silent about him. During the second half of the 1980s my cousin Duncan Doolittle of Rhode Island began digging around for any surviving material that there might be on Hunter.

His energy and persistence were rewarded. A fine haul of letters which Hunter had written over a long period to his younger brother Duncan, who settled in the United States, and to his American sister-in-law Abby were unearthed in family trunks and attics in New England and elsewhere. A revealing picture of Hunter, both the man and the soldier, emerged. The material was put to good use and Doolittle published privately in 1991 in the USA a book on Hunter based on these letters.

Another rich seam of material was struck more recently when Nicol Russel, also a cousin of mine and whose father was Hunter's executor, found in his attic – but this time it was one in Dorset – a cache of Hunter's papers including a weighty diary with entries in it collated over a 50 year period. Family legend about that bonfire of Hunter's papers had, happily, proved to be wrong.

The cup for any would-be biographer now looked to be overflowing.

In writing this book I was granted access to papers in the Royal Archives at Windsor. I wish to acknowledge with gratitude that I have had the gracious permission of Her Majesty the Queen to make use of this material and to quote from it. I am indebted for the help I received at the Royal Archives from Miss Pamela Clark, the Deputy Registrar.

I have been allowed to use and reproduce Crown copyright material from the Public Record Office and from the Oriental and India Office Collections, British Library, by the Controller of Her Majesty's Stationery Office. I am grateful to the following who have given me permission to quote from unpublished copyright and other material in their care: Mrs Diana Acland, Durham University Library, the Hon. Mrs E. A. Gascoigne

(Lord Harcourt papers), the Earl Haig, Lady Patricia Kingsbury (the papers of the Earl of Ypres), the trustees of the Imperial War Museum (Field-Marshal Sir Henry Wilson's Diary), the trustees of the Liddell Hart Centre for Military Studies (Maj-General Sir Frederick Maurice and General Sir Ian Hamilton papers), A. J. Maxse Esq., the trustees of the National Library of Scotland, Lord Mottistone, the Marquess of Salisbury (Lord Edward Cecil's Diary and The Leisure of an Egyptian Official), and Mrs Josephine Street (General Sir Reginald Wingate's Diary).

I owe a special debt to my cousins Duncan Doolittle and Nicol Russel who allowed me to use and quote extensively from their material, both published and unpublished. This material provided the basis on which my story is founded. I also wish to record the great help I had in my research from Jane Hogan of the Durham University Library.

I should like to thank for their help the staff of the following museums, libraries, institutions and organisations: Ardrossan Library, Bodleian Library, British Library, Carnegie Library Ayr, Churchill Archives Centre Churchill College, James Hunter Dick Institute Kilmarnock, University of Durham Library, Hatfield House Library, Headquarters Southern District Aldershot, House of Commons Public Information Office, Hove Central Library, Imperial War Museum, Lancaster Central Library, Liddell Hart Centre for Military Studies, London Library, National Army Museum reading-room, National Library of Scotland, Public Record Office Kew, Central Library Royal Military Academy Sandhurst, Scottish Record Office, Wellcome Institute, West Kilbride Museum and the West Sussex Record Office Chichester. I also received help from Stuart Eastwood, Curator of the Regimental Museum of the Border Regiment and the King's Own Royal Border Regiment, Carlisle, Peter Donnelly, Assistant Keeper at the King's Own Royal Regiment Museum, Lancaster, T. J. Finlayson, the Gibraltar Government Archivist, and from C. W. Turner the Rector of the Glasgow Academy.

Most valuable recollections of my subject were provided by Hugo von Dumreicher, Sheila Grahame, Lt-Col Anthony Hunter and Lt-Col James Robertson McIsaac. My brother David Hunter, Roger Montague and Nicol Russel all read the manuscript and offered much good advice and support. Henry Keown-Boyd allowed me to quote from a letter he wrote to the *Sunday Telegraph* and helped enormously with his knowledge of the Egyptian army. Michael Ponting gave invaluable help, especially over the Notes and Index. Tim Boyden made a vital contribution in the production of the maps.

Others who helped – and I am sorry if I have not named them all – were: Dorothy Almack, Ken Atherton, Dr Ian Beckett, Imbert Bourdillon, Dr Peter Boyden, Alan and Betty Burbage, Christopher Chapman, William Colfer, Judith Davenport, Lesley Forbes, June Freeman, Adrienne Gleeson, Robin Harcourt-Williams, Marjorie Heron together with Maureen

Richards and Elizabeth Spirit all of the Ladysmith Historical Society, Rebecca Hunter, General Sir William Jackson, Dame Elaine Kellett-Bowman MP, I. M. McNaught, Joan Robins, Simon Robbins, Jack Smithers, John Stewart, Dr T. H. E. Travers and Susan Wilson. I am grateful to them all.

I have been fortunate in my editor, John Walton, and thank him for his wise guidance.

This work would hardly have seen the light of day had it not been for Lorna Kingdon, who miraculously produced a typescript from my hand-written manuscript. My sincere thanks go to her for all she achieved.

Finally I thank my wife, Mirabel, who patiently shouldered with me the burdens of aspiring authorship in a hundred and one different ways. Her advice was always perceptive and her encouragement unflagging.

Dorset, England
April 1996

A. A. de C. H.

CHAPTER 1

The Early Years

The storming party of 200 men led by a stocky figure scrambled up the boulder-strewn hill. It was nearly 2 a.m. The night was very dark. Most of the men were in stockinged feet to keep the noise down for fear of alerting enemy pickets. As they neared the summit they heard a voice from above calling out: 'Wie daar?' This was repeated several times. Suddenly the defenders realised what was happening and began to fire wildly. Their fire was returned and for a moment all was chaos. The commander of the assault force seized a trumpet and, perhaps for the first time in British army history, a General sounded the cease-fire. It was correct, they said, but quavery.[1] Anyhow it did the trick. In a moment the firing both to the rear and in front stopped. The attackers pressed desperately on. An order now rang out: 'Fix bayonets and give the buggers cold steel'. There were no bayonets. But rifle butts were banged on rocks to produce the sound of fixing bayonets. With their commander at their head the men charged towards the skyline and the guns they had come to destroy. Unwilling to face what they thought was cold steel the defenders fled. The gun pits reached, the sappers at once went to work. Gun-cotton charges were inserted in the breeches and muzzles of the 'Long Tom' Creusot gun and the 4.7 inch howitzer, while the commander, lantern in hand, watched proceedings. Explosions quickly followed. As trophies breech blocks, a gun sight and a Maxim machine gun also found on the summit were all carried back down the hill. But not before the commander had called for three cheers for the Queen.

But what was the occasion just described and who was the commander of the assault party? It was a sortie to Gun Hill from the town of Ladysmith in South Africa which was besieged in the Boer war. The attack took place on the night of 7/8 December 1899. The commander was Archie Hunter, then aged 43, the Chief of Staff and second in command of the 13,500 troops at Ladysmith.

But who today has heard of Archie Hunter? Yet at the end of the nineteenth century as a dashing Major-General, the youngest man to reach that rank since Wellington, he captured the imagination of the public with his exploits in Africa. He was tough, brave, almost reckless. But he was compassionate too, a man who cared deeply for the well-being of his soldiers. The young Winston Churchill called him at the end of the Sudan campaign 'the darling of the Egyptian army'. G. W. Steevens, *The Daily Mail* war correspondent writing at the time, described him as 'a true knight-errant', and above all a man who could captivate and lead men. Journalists on their way to the Boer War wishing to be at the scene of the

1

fighting were all asking 'where will Hunter be?' The Prime Minister, Herbert Asquith, said of him in 1916, that 'he had won the Battle of Omdurman in spite of Kitchener, and defended Ladysmith in spite of White'.[2] For a time he was a household name, his character ideally fitting him for the role of a schoolboy hero. A full General at 49 and well regarded as an administrator, he seemed destined for the very top. But, always out-spoken, he was forced to resign as Governor of Gibraltar for injudicious remarks. In World War I his powers of leadership were neglected and to his chagrin he spent the war on the side-lines. He is now forgotten and the history books scarcely mention him. This is unjust as the following pages aim to show.

On 6 September 1856 twins were born in London to a Scottish couple Archibald and Mary Jane Hunter. The elder, the first boy in their family, was named after his father, and was always known as Archie. The Hunter parents were comfortably off and lived in Kilburn in an unassuming but quite handsome semi-detached house built of dark London brick with cornerstones and windowsills of white Portland stone. Archibald Hunter was a merchant in the cloth trade, and had a calico printing business. His office was in Cannon Street. As he travelled to it by horse-drawn omnibus he would read from the New Testament in Greek. He was inclined, in politics, to be radical and was a friend of Richard Cobden, the free trade advocate, who was also a calico printer.

Almost a confirmed bachelor, Archibald had surprised his family by suddenly at the age of 48 becoming engaged to his 20-year-old first cousin Mary Jane Grahame. Pretty and vivacious, she was proving a bit of a handful to her widower father Major Duncan Grahame, late of the Sixth Foot. He had just decided to pack her off on a sea voyage when she received a letter from Archibald proposing marriage. At the time she was actually on board ship at Greenock awaiting a fair wind. She accepted him and they were married in 1853. They settled in London and soon were starting a family. First there was a daughter, Mary Jane and then the twins Archie and Nellie. They were followed by three more girls, Janet, Ann and Marion. In July 1863 came Duncan, and the next year on Christmas Day, George, the author's grandfather, was born. Finally there was Florence, the only member of this family not to reach adulthood.

Archibald Hunter's business career was successful until it was cruelly interrupted by a lawsuit. It all seems to have started when he backed some trader's bill. The affair may have been connected with the well-known failure of the City of Glasgow Bank, the crash of which caused widespread ruin. Hunter, deeply aggrieved, took the case to court. The judge, while sympathising, found Hunter liable, with the result that he lost all he had, over £10,000. He reacted to this catastrophe with spirit, determined to recover his lost wealth. He must have been an able business man, for he succeeded. By the time of his death in 1868, attributable to overwork, this typical Victorian *paterfamilias* had sufficiently restored his financial situation to be able to leave his children enough money to provide each with some measure of independence.

Not a lot is known about Archibald Hunter's forebears. His father, also confusingly Archibald Hunter, was born in 1768 and was a tailor burgess in Glasgow who, by the beginning of the nineteenth century, was becoming reasonably well-to-do. He married a Helen Grahame of Glenny, Port of Menteith. The Grahames were landowners and had a tradition of soldiering. Duncan, Helen's brother, and the grandfather of our subject, was a regular officer in the army and fought through the Peninsular War. He was one of Sir John Moore's pall-bearers at Corunna, and is believed to have been the last man to leave the city, locking the gatehouse door behind him and taking the key. On retiring from the army Duncan left Glenny and built himself a house at Ardrossan, Castle Craig, which still stands today. His four sons all became soldiers.

When she was widowed Mary Jane Hunter returned with her brood to her native roots in Scotland. First she went to the small tartan weaving town of Kilbarchan, some 11 miles west of Glasgow, where her brother Robert Grahame lived. Soon she moved into a house in St George's Road in the middle of Glasgow. There she was well placed to send Archie, now 12 years old, in January 1869 to a fee-paying school, The Glasgow Academy nearby. During his four years at the Academy Archie proved himself intelligent and hard-working. He learned, too, to write well; his orders, as a soldier, would always be a model of brevity and clarity. At various times he won first prizes in Latin, Geometry, Ancient History and Geography, and in English, and scored near misses in Religious Knowledge, Arithmetic and Algebra.[3] In the summer holiday task set for 1872, which was devoted to Caesar, Virgil and Roman history he was placed first with James Grierson, also destined to make a great career for himself in the army.

In 1871 Mary Jane remarried and moved to Whitefield House at Govan, just down the Clyde. Her second husband, Robert Robertson, by whom she had two children, Robert and Clemence, was the laird of a small property there and a shrewd business man. He imported rum from the West Indies and then exported the casks, filled this time with coal, back whence they came.

In the holidays Mary Jane went with her children to Seamill, a tiny village on the Ayrshire coast west of West Kilbride. Here they stayed in a thatched cottage overlooking the sea and the island of Arran. The cottage, though no longer thatched, still stands, on the main coast road. This was familiar territory to Mary Jane, for she had been brought up only a few miles away. With the nearby green and unspoilt hills of Ayrshire to explore, it must have been a grand place for children. Young Archie as often as not was out with the Ayrshire hounds.

On the death of her second husband, Mary Jane sold the house at Govan to good advantage, and went to live at Crosbie House, an ancient country house a mile or so out of West Kilbride nestling at the foot of the hills. She had a happy-go-lucky streak in her and this led Archie to feel at an early age a strong sense of responsibility for his brothers and sisters. There is no doubt that he saw himself as the family leader. He was once asked as an old man, when in his life he had been most frightened. His questioner expected to hear about some fascinating moment during a great battle in the Sudan campaigns or in the Boer War. The reply was unexpected. He said, 'Well, in battle one is not frightened. There is too much to do and think about. Perhaps the worst time was when I was with all my brothers and sisters in Scotland by the sea and we were very nearly cut off by the rising tide. As eldest I was responsible for them all and this was a terrible time for me. I never forgot it'.

With the blood of the Grahames flowing strongly in his veins Archie, even as a boy, always wanted to be a soldier. He was taught by his grandfather Duncan, who died when he was five, to repeat the poem 'The burial of Sir John Moore' by Charles Wolfe. It was the first thing he learnt, and he used to say the poem as if it were the Lord's Prayer. When a year or two later the truth was broken to him he thought he was being fooled.[4]

In his late teens Archie accompanied his mother to the funeral of one of his Grahame uncles, who was reputed to be the tallest man in the British army. As a Grahame of Glenny he was entitled to be buried at the Old Priory on the island of Inchmahome in the Lake of Menteith in Perthshire. As the funeral service was about to begin a heavy thunderstorm broke over the lake and many of the mourners were drenched before they reached the church. The boatmen detailed to take the coffin across the lake to the island resting place had, while they waited in the storm, been drinking too much, no doubt to ward off the chill effects of the cold and rain, and to prevent the onset of pneumonia and rheumatism. The service over, they somehow managed to get the coffin on board the small boat, and then set off on an uncertain course for the island. When they reached the landing-stage the befuddled men succeeded in dropping the coffin between the boat and the jetty. Unseemly salvage operations ensued. When the grave was finally reached it was found the gravediggers had made inadequate provision for the height of the deceased. There was a distressing interval while a party of willing but inebriated men enlarged the grave. But nothing was going right. Their clumsy efforts broke open the side of the next-door coffin, from which rolled forth a skull. Poor Mary Jane, Archie by her side, recognised it by its teeth. 'It's my father', she shrieked and fainted in her son's arms!

Archie had one more task on that macabre day. The coffin had come up to Stirling by train from London. There it had been put into a horse-drawn hearse and driven the 15 miles to the Port of Menteith with the coachmen and undertaker's men. All these had been making the most of their time partaking liberally while the cortège was on the island. When the mourners' party returned from the burial, the undertaker's men were found to be completely prostrate. Young Archie rose quickly to the occasion, showing that military decisiveness to be expected from a future General. He took the drunks and unceremoniously bundled them all, bar one, into the hearse. He who was least tight was propped by Archie on the box with the reins at his feet. Then Archie led the horse on to the road, and, with a few well-placed whacks, sent the whole apparatus off into the blue in the general direction of Stirling![5]

Archie Hunter left school in the summer of 1873 aged not quite 17. His sights were now fairly set on the army. But what kind of life and career could be expected for an officer in the army in the last quarter of the 19th century, and in particular for one such as Hunter, keen and serious though he might be, who had no influence? Certainly the life was congenial. Soldiering in those days was not so strenuous as it was to become. Young officers pursued their field sports with vigour, played polo and other games, raced, gambled, and enjoyed themselves socially. Slow promotion did not matter too much as only a minority of officers took their profession seriously.

Happily, the archaic system of purchasing both a commission and promotion had been abolished in 1871 by the Cardwell reforms. In course of time these reforms would lead to promotion becoming more dependent on merit and would contribute towards making the army a more attractive career for a young man. But in the meantime ambitious officers, and Hunter would always number himself among these, would usually have to seek advancement by going overseas on active service or to India.

Britain in the mid 1870s had been at peace in Europe, the Crimean War apart, for 60 years. Until the Boer War at the end of the century, Victorian wars were essentially colonial in character. These minor wars at the outposts of the Empire were often challenging and sometimes bloody. Campaigning in them called for qualities of leadership, endurance and courage. The opportunity therefore for excitement and possibly glory existed in far off lands, provided of course the young soldier could somehow reach the scene of the action.

Hunter had originally been destined for the artillery. But he decided in April 1874 to sit the competitive examination that had become the usual way of obtaining a regular commission in the infantry.

There were two compulsory subjects, elementary mathematics and English, as well as three optional ones. Marks were weighted in favour of the classics and this must have suited Hunter. He had a good brain and had no difficulty in passing. Courses at the Royal Military College Sandhurst were in a severe state of flux at this time. In 1870 it had been decided to close down Sandhurst and abolish the cadet system. Instead, direct commissions to regiments were to be granted to candidates successful in the exams. But this scheme did not find favour. So as Sandhurst was empty, it was decided to offer successful candidates the option of a year's course at the Royal Military College. As an incentive, those who passed out in the first class, would have their commissions antedated by two years and in the second class by one year. These men would be known as unattached Sub-Lieutenants. Hunter chose to go to Sandhurst under this scheme.

Due to administrative and other problems being experienced while Hunter was there, the Sandhurst records provide little information about his time at the Royal Military College. Strangely, he is recorded as having both arrived and departed on 13 June 1874! He certainly arrived on this date, but left about a year later at the conclusion of his course. The only annotation on his record shows he obtained a First Class certificate, which enabled him to claim the extra seniority due when he became a Lieutenant in 1876.

During Hunter's year at Sandhurst the authorities faced difficulties as to how they should treat students who were entitled to their officer's pay as Sub-Lieutenants (£100 a year) and to salutes from their drill sergeants. At the time the students objected to having to answer roll call at 10 p.m., with lights out an hour later, and to not being allowed to keep their dogs at the College.[6] Consequently the Commandant nearly had a rebellion on his hands. Hunter's fellow students came from a mixture of the aristocracy, the landed gentry and the middle classes. Almost all of them had some private means. Just occasionally, according to Repington, the distinguished military journalist who went to Sandhurst soon after Hunter, 'dreadful outsiders' got into the College. He recalls three or four students who had gone so far as to dine with the Commandant's cook. This was discovered and they were all taken down to the lake and thrown in.[7] Officially the Commandant gave the culprits responsible a strong dressing-down, but unofficially he applauded what they had done.

On 27 August 1875 Hunter was gazetted a Sub-Lieutenant in the King's Own Royal Regiment of Foot (also known as the 4th Regiment of Foot). How he came to join this English regiment, famous as it was, rather than a Scottish one, is not known. It may simply have been that there was an early vacancy available in it. The King's Own Royal Regiment with its long list of battle honours going back to 1680 was to mean a good deal to Hunter. In later years he was to be Colonel of the regiment for 13 years. He was not, however, destined to serve more than nine and a half years as a regimental officer. In that time he gained varied experience at home and abroad, but there was no campaigning.

At the end of September 1875 Hunter sailed from Southampton to join the 1st battalion of his regiment which was stationed in Gibraltar. He remained there, with one break, for a little over three years. On arrival he was put under the charge of a senior subaltern, John Edward Troyte (who changed his name to Acland after he left the army). The two became life-long friends and corresponded over many years.

Gibraltar had been a British fortress since Admiral Rooke seized it in 1704, an operation in which the King's Own Regiment had been involved against a small Spanish garrison. By the treaty of Utrecht in 1713 the Rock was ceded to Britain and ever since had remained an important base, both naval and military. It survived repeated attacks and a $3\frac{1}{2}$-year siege during the American War of Independence, just under 100 years before Hunter's arrival. It stood at the entrance of the Mediterranean as a symbol of British supremacy.

In 1875 Gibraltar was garrisoned by five army battalions, considerably fewer men than the 7,000 soldiers and sailors needed to defend it during the famous siege. It must, however, have been a cramping place in which to be stationed, especially at the start of a military career; the promontory is, after all, only three miles long by $\frac{3}{4}$ mile wide, even if it does rise to its angular 1,400 foot peak. Consequently there is little room on the Rock for manoeuvres or recreation. The men obtained what exercise they could by sea-bathing and athletic sports, while the officers, according to the regimental history,[8] were prominent in the hunting field, on the cricket ground and race-course, and in the ball-room. Hunting had been introduced to Spain by Wellington during the Peninsular War, and subsequently Gibraltar's own Royal Calpe Hunt had been established when a fox-hunting parson arrived with a pack of hounds. Somehow the Hunt thrived, pink coats and all! It must have been meat and drink to Hunter whose favourite sports were always hunting and shooting.

Hunter, a Lieutenant from the previous August, obtained some leave in 1877 and spent four months at home. May and June he spent on a course at the School of Musketry at Hythe, where he took a 'First Class Extra' certificate.[9] FM Sir William Robertson, the remarkable soldier who rose from the ranks to become CIGS in World War I, in his autobiography described the curriculum as 'unpractical and wearisome' with 'little or no attention paid to the art of shooting in the field'.[10] Nonetheless, Hunter always attached the greatest importance to efficiency in musketry, and insisted that the troops under him achieved the highest standards.

Hunter joined his family in Scotland during his leave and he appears in a family photograph taken probably in March or April of that year. Archie, 20 years old at the time, is looking somewhat stern and as yet he has no moustache. Among his womenfolk and younger brothers he looks taller than his 5ft 8in. On his return to Gibraltar an event occurred which Hunter regarded as important. He was admitted to the Freemasons. Throughout his life he remained an active Mason.

Gibraltar, once considered an unhealthy post, must have been a popular station with the regiment because all ranks left it with regret. In January 1879 the 1st battalion embarked for the West Indies. Here in the Caribbean the regiment found itself living in very different surroundings from those at Gibraltar. As a start the battalion was split up. Three companies went to Jamaica, where they were stationed in the cool hills, 4,000 feet up. Another company went to Trinidad, the hottest station, while Headquarters with Hunter attached to it, and the remaining four companies, were posted to Barbados. Trinidad, despite its hotter climate, was the most popular posting, for it was well away from the sharp eyes of Headquarters. But the life led in Barbados, a Crown Colony since 1652, was not without its charms. The people in this fertile and beautiful island were friendly and the climate was mild. The officers' mess was housed in a new bungalow with a long and attractive verandah running its length, and there were quarters for bachelor officers. On Sunday mornings the band played 'church call', the regiment paraded and marched smartly to the wooden church down the road for Matins. The Orderly Officer regularly went his rounds, cutting up the meat ration in the mornings and later visiting the married quarters, knocking on each door to ask if the wives had any complaint. It may not have been the rude rough soldiering that Archie Hunter had joined the army for – that would come later – but nonetheless it must have been a pleasant and civilised existence, even if a trifle uneventful.

On arrival in the West Indies Hunter was appointed musketry instructor, a job he held for rather more than a year until in April 1880 he was appointed Adjutant. A year later the tranquil life of Barbados was shattered when an epidemic of yellow fever swept through the island. There had been several deaths from fever at Bridgetown among the civil population, but yellow fever was not diagnosed at once, possibly because the disease rarely appeared epidemically in Barbados. Once the disease was confirmed, British troops went under canvas. Unfortunately, this did not prevent cases of the disease occurring among the soldiers. Although momentarily checked, the disease broke out again and camp was once more moved. One of the first to succumb was Lieutenant Le Blanc who died in Hunter's room. They had joined the regiment the same day. The course of yellow fever can be swift. Sergeant Morgan was eating his dinner one day at 2 p.m. He was buried at 6 p.m. the same day. Despite all the efforts of the medical staff and others, the regiment was badly hit and no fewer than 77 officers, men, women and children died.[11] In a period of six weeks the battalion lost a tenth of its fighting strength. Some years later a monument was erected in Barbados by the regiment in memory of those who died. During the epidemic Hunter, as Adjutant, worked tirelessly day and night, often not undressing, tending to the sick and dying.[12] He was a compassionate man and as a soldier always paid the closest attention to the sick and wounded.

As a result of the depredations suffered by those stationed in Barbados it was decided to recall the regiment home. A troopship, *HMS Orontes*, was sent to Bridgetown, and Headquarters and the four companies of the garrison, including Hunter, were evacuated to England. On arrival in November 1881 they all moved into barracks at Plymouth, the rest of the battalion joining them the following May. Bowerham barracks, at Lancaster, had recently become the regimental depot and in August 1882 Hunter travelled up north to Lancashire with the battalion. They went first to Fleetwood and then to Preston. Just after this move Hunter was promoted, by selection, to Captain and obtained command of a company. Promotion, which now depended on examinations, was slow, and there had been blockages. In the circumstances Hunter did well to become a Captain just before his 26th birthday.

The prospect of continuing peacetime soldiering in Lancashire did not appeal to Hunter. The urge to go overseas was strong and so he must have watched events abroad with a critical eye. As it was, an opportunity for soldiering of a very different sort from the one he had been used to soon occurred, and his talents would be fully stretched on active service.

NOTES

1. Wilson *With the Flag to Pretoria* I 499.
2. Duff Cooper *Old Men Forget* 56.
3. Records of The Glasgow Academy.
4. DHD 322.
5. Information supplied in 1959 by the late Archie Hunter Service.
6. Mockler-Ferryman *Annals of Sandhurst* 39.
7. Repington *Vestigia* 38–9.
8. Cowper *The King's Own: The Story of a Royal Regiment* 176 et seq.
9. Hunter's diary (AHd), part of the Nicol Russel collection, entry for 1/5/77. This diary is contained in one large notebook. Each day of the year is allocated one page and on each page is annotated significant events which took place on that day, mainly over the period 1875 to 1925, the events usually being those which occurred in Hunter's own life.
10. Robertson *From Private to Field-Marshal* 23.
11. Eastwood *Lions of England: A Pictorial History of the King's Own Royal Regiment (Lancaster) 1680–1980* 41–2.
12. RA G V L521/1.

CHAPTER 2

The New Egyptian Army

In the summer of 1882 Egypt was in a state of some turmoil. The country had fallen badly into debt to the western powers, who for some years had been financing the huge programme of public works, and its chaotic finances were to an extent being supervised by Britain and France. At the same time the army, led by Colonel Arabi, an early nationalist, was in revolt against the Khedive, the title by which the ruler of Egypt was known.

As general unrest developed riots broke out in June which led to the deaths of Europeans. The British government took fright and decided on military intervention. France, however, stood aside. So the British fleet bombarded Alexandria and an expeditionary force was despatched under Sir Garnet Wolseley. In a lightning campaign, in support of Khedive Mohamed Tewfik, Wolseley defeated the Egyptians under Colonal Arabi at Tel-el-Kebir, a village some 40 miles north-east of Cairo, on 13 September 1882. The Egyptian army disintegrated and so did opposition to the Khedive and the invading British who now occupied Cairo. Tewfik, disgusted with the behaviour of his army, disbanded it by Khedival Decree which simply read 'L'armée Égyptienne est dissoute'.[1]

Lord Dufferin, the British ambassador at Constantinople, was hastily sent to Cairo to determine what should be done, now that Britain appeared to be, at least temporarily, in charge of the country. The position was awkward and politically complex because Egypt was not a fully sovereign state, the Khedive owing ultimate allegiance to the Sultan of the decaying Ottoman Empire. Quite apart from the constitutional problem, there was an immediate need to build up order in a country where government had utterly collapsed.[2] In the unusual circumstances, Britain decided to stay on in Egypt for the time being, propping up the Khedive's regime, introducing her own advisers and officials into the government machine and trying to initiate appropriate reforms. In due course, and behind the modest sounding title of Agent and Consul General, Evelyn Baring, later Lord Cromer, became the effective ruler of Egypt.

One of Dufferin's first decisions was to raise an entirely new army. The troops would be Egyptian, but all senior posts were to be filled by officers seconded from the British army. Major-General Sir Evelyn Wood VC was appointed the first Commander-in-Chief, or Sirdar (after the Indian word meaning 'leader') as the post was known. A small band of British officers, at first 25 in number, was chosen to train and lead the new army. With the deterioration of the situation in the Sudan following a revolt against Egyptian rule there was a call for a second wave of officers. Archie Hunter applied for a post and was one of 12 chosen. So in February 1884, at the age of 27, he joined the new army. Thereafter for nearly 15 years, with one long gap in his service after he had been badly wounded, he served in Egypt and in the Sudan. Almost all his time was spent in defending the southern frontiers of Egypt against the Dervishes (literally 'poor men', the name given to the Sudanese armies) and then in helping to reconquer the Sudan. Over these years he proved himself a born leader of men, fearless in action and a shrewd tactician. His natural dash was tempered with his Scottish caution. Above all he came to be revered by his troops. Hunter's military career and reputation were based on his service in the Sudan during which he rose in the space of $12\frac{1}{2}$ years from the rank of Captain to Major-General.

The old Egyptian army had had a chequered history since the start of the 19th century. Mohamed Ali, an Albanian officer of militia who had seized power in Egypt in 1811, conquered the Sudan in the early 1820s using a force of some 10,000 troops[3], who were essentially mercenaries. By the 1830s he had expanded his forces considerably and had included in them, successfully, battalions of conscripted fellahin (Egyptian peasants). When fighting victoriously in the Morea (part of Greece) and Syria, his forces, organised by French officers, were said to number 277,000 of whom 130,000 were regulars.[4] But Egyptian commitments changed, and by the 1860s the Egyptian army was small and its soldiers of poor quality. In 1876 came the Abyssinian campaign when the Egyptians were routed on several occasions with heavy losses. The decline in the army's efficiency and morale, was due as much to administrative neglect as to the inept leadership of its officers, many of whom were Turkish. By the early 1880s, as a fighting force it was regarded as useless. Wolseley's victory at Tel-el-Kebir confirmed this.

Service in the old army had been dreaded by the conscript fellahin. For that service might well mean a posting to the garrison in the Sudan from which, with its harsh climate and constant insurrections, a soldier might never return. Then his conditions of service were rudimentary. Pay, which was wretched, came at long intervals, or not at all. In the Sudan when it did come, pay could be in the form of lengths of cloth, the Egyptian officials having misappropriated the cash.[5] Barracks were filthy and there was no provision for the sick and wounded. All young men between the ages of 19 and 23 were liable for military service unless they fell into an exempted category. Thus, scripture readers, both Moslem and Coptic Christian, and sons responsible for old or infirm parents were exempted. Also service could be escaped by making a lawful payment of £100 to the government. But the ordinary fellahin could not afford this, and so resorted to all kinds of subterfuge such as cutting off the index finger of the right hand or destroying an eye to evade the draft.

Sir Evelyn Wood, the Sirdar, certainly faced a daunting task in raising and training the new army. He was, however, a man of energy. He had begun his career as a Midshipman and had seen action in the Crimean War. He transferred to the army, commanded successfully a column in the Zulu War and somehow found time to be called to the Bar. Wood was given a very good salary – £5,000 a year – for the job in hand, and allocated £200,000, a sum with which he would have to pay his officers and men and provide for rations.[6] As he clearly saw, he needed outstanding officers. So criteria set were high. Every successful applicant had to have an impeccable military record and a high standard in horsemanship and musketry. Every officer had to be capable of carrying on official correspondence in French and pass an exam in colloquial Arabic within six months and a further one in a year.[7] There would be a demand for innate intelligence and flexibility. The commissions, made out in English and Arabic, were sealed by the Khedive and all officers contracted themselves, through the Foreign Office, for two years' service, a contract that was renewable. The Egyptian government had the right to terminate an officer's contract after six months.

On arrival in Egypt all officers stepped up a rank. No officer would be inferior to a Bimbashi (Major). Pay was far better than at home. Thus a Kaimakan (Lieutenant-Colonel) commanding an infantry battalion received £750 plus the right to the courtesy title of Bey, and his second-in-command £550. There was no allowance for quarters and officers were mounted at their own expense. The Khedive insisted that British officers wore a fez. To go with it was a resplendent uniform, the gold buttons of which were embossed with the crescent and star. The Sirdar's decision was final in all matters. Wood could often be severe, especially where the code of behaviour had been infringed. For instance, one young British officer failed to pay an outstanding bill due to his Greek tailor. The tailor complained to the Sirdar. Even though the officer was talented and ready to pay, he was sacked forthwith.[8]

But most importantly for the ambitious soldier, service in Egypt with the new army carried with it the almost certain prospect of active service against the rampant Dervishes. This could mean professional advancement and must have provided a strong incentive for those bored with peacetime soldiering at home. As things turned out, service in Egypt and the Sudan did no one's career any harm. The first three Sirdars, Wood, Grenfell and Kitchener, all rose to be Field-Marshals. Of those serving in the 1880s, Wodehouse, Hunter, Rundle, Smith-Dorrien, Maxwell and Wingate all became full Generals. And this is to overlook Douglas Haig, Commander-in-Chief in France in World War I, who served in the Egyptian cavalry for a short time. Many others reached the rank of Major-General.

There were other attractions of serving on the Nile. Two months' leave a year was not ungenerous. Europe was almost on the doorstep: fast steamer to Bari, express train across Italy and France, and you were at the Channel in a matter of days. This compared favourably with the tedious journey home for those in the Indian army. Then there was Cairo, a city that was becoming the Paris of the Levant with its French style houses and flats, theatres, cafés, public baccarat and roulette tables, and houseboats on the Nile. Also army officers were in much demand in Cairo society.

Of course, there were drawbacks to service under the Khedive, though not all of these could be anticipated. First and foremost was the question of whether the experiment being conducted by Wood would succeed. No serious soldier would wish to identify himself with troops who reputedly lacked courage or were otherwise militarily inept. There was therefore this risk to be weighed. Then there was the climate, which could be harsh. Up the Nile and on the Red Sea at Suakin there was no escaping the excessive heat and discomfort. Disease too, especially cholera and dysentery, took a steady toll as did enemy action and accident. A young officer worth his salt would not of course be put off by these perils.

At first the size of the new army was limited to just 6,000 men. By the end of 1883 there were eight infantry battalions, four with British commanding officers, some artillery and a camel corps. Ten years later there were 12,500 troops with 76 British officers and some 40 NCOs. Finally at the close of the campaign against the Dervishes the strength of the army was 18,000 consisting of 19 infantry battalions, ten squadrons of cavalry, five field batteries and a camel corps of eight companies. The infantry was from the start divided into Egyptian battalions of fellahin and 'Black' battalions of Sudanese. The former had three British officers and the latter four. The remaining officers were Egyptian, usually of Turkish origin. The fellahin were mostly of exceptional physique and made patient soldiers who loved drill and were excellent at it. In fact, they loved nothing better than to practise drilling in their spare time. In their white uniform and red fezzes they looked very smart. The Sudanese were tall, loosely-knit men. They were mostly deserters from the Dervish army or former slaves, who had enlisted for life. They proved to have more initiative than the Egyptians and were exuberant and worthy fighting men. They could be wild, and needed at times to be carefully controlled on the battlefield. It was with the 9th Sudanese that Hunter did all his regimental soldiering while in the Egyptian army. Each battalion had a drum and bugle band while each brigade developed in time a full band which could play western-style music with its marches and operatic arias as well as eastern.

Pay and conditions of service of the men were radically improved. And they were paid promptly. Leave was granted periodically and travel by

13

rail and steamer was allowed at reduced rates. For those on active service medals were awarded. The army was henceforth well housed and properly cared for by its officers. Furthermore, to begin with there was no service in the Sudan. Having no settled home the Sudanese were allowed to marry and given a marriage allowance for their wives. But in due course as the army advanced up the Nile, families had to be left behind. It was said that the inconstant warriors paved their paths with expectant wives and children!

Inevitably difficulties arose in the training of the new battalions. One of these related to the language in which the work was to be carried on. Egypt was a multi-lingual country. Arabic, Turkish, French and English were all in daily use. British officers would speak French to Egyptian officers and Arabic to the NCOs and soldiers. Words of command, it was decided, would continue to be given in Turkish. The task of drilling the troops and instructing them on musketry fell to British NCOs and the part they played in training was invaluable.

A measure of the success achieved by Wood and his officers in a comparatively short space of time is reflected in the improved standing of the army in the eyes of the public. In the old days a soldier returning to his village would sneak back like a dog, and as likely as not would be struck by the local sheikh. But now under the changed order, when the soldier returned, the sheikh would invite him for coffee and beg to be told the news.[9]

The new army's role was at first purely defensive, though in course of time this changed. Thus the Egyptian army, except for a detachment of the camel corps, did not take part in the offensive operations undertaken in the Gordon Relief Expedition of 1884/85. But its troops played an increasingly active role in the rearguard as Wolseley's force withdrew down the Nile, and by the end of 1885 its soldiers had proved themselves in their first major exchange with the Dervishes at the battle of Ginnis. With the final withdrawal of British troops from the Sudan, the Egyptian army became the main bastion of defence against the Dervish army on the frontier at Wadi Halfa and in the Eastern Sudan at Suakin on the Red Sea coast (see map A, p. 16). The sturdy fellahin and the fierce Sudanese, when well led, were showing themselves to be steadfast and reliable in battle.

NOTES

1. Cromer, *Modern Egypt* II 467.
2. Milner *England in Egypt* 75.
3. Duncan *The Sudan* 6.
4. Cromer II 468.
5. Keown-Boyd *A Good Dusting: The Sudan Campaigns 1883–1899* 97.

6. Wood *From Midshipman to Field-Marshal* 154.
7. Haggard *Under Crescent and Star* 34.
8. Ibid. 35.
9. Wingate *Mahdiism and the Egyptian Sudan* 224.

CHAPTER 3

With the Gordon Relief Expedition

On 17 February 1884 Hunter left Preston at 11 p.m. by the London train en route for Egypt. Travelling via Paris, Marseilles and Alexandria he reached Cairo on 28 February, and on that day took the momentous step of joining the Egyptian army. He was posted on 1 May to the 9th Sudanese battalion, which was in the process of being transferred from Suakin in the Sudan to the Red Barracks Abbasia, just outside Cairo. As he was the senior of the five British Captains in the battalion, he was appointed second-in-command. Major Hallam Parr, the Officer Commanding, was still at Suakin and Hunter acted for him in Cairo. On his return to Cairo, Hallam Parr went on sick leave and left the battalion. The command was therefore taken by Hunter.[1] It was a lucky break and he made the most of it.

In the early 1860s, the 9th Sudanese had been stationed at Massawa (now in Ethiopia). In 1883 they were moved up the coast to Suakin. Here they proved to be in a semi-mutinous state having been continually cheated of their pay by the old Egyptian government. When Hallam Parr had gone down from Cairo to take charge of them he found on his first parade that a senior native officer had just been attacked with a bayonet. The battalion, therefore, was packed off to Cairo to be reorganised under British officers, who were told as a precaution to carry revolvers on parade.

At Abbasia four companies, each 200 strong, were formed out of 1,500 men, the rest being discharged as unfit. Included among these was a man found at the medical inspection to be a eunuch. To begin with the men resented the keenness of the British officers, for after many years of fighting in the Sudan they were hoping for a quiet time in Egypt. When they were ordered to exchange their Remington rifles for the newer Martini Henrys, they refused to give up their weapons, and even went so far as to assault Hunter. The position was serious. Plans were made to disarm the battalion on parade. An order would be given to 'pile arms' in the usual way when the men were breaking off for a ten-minute rest and smoke. The arms would then be suddenly seized by a regiment of British troops, stationed in Cairo as part of the occupation forces. This plan did not have to be

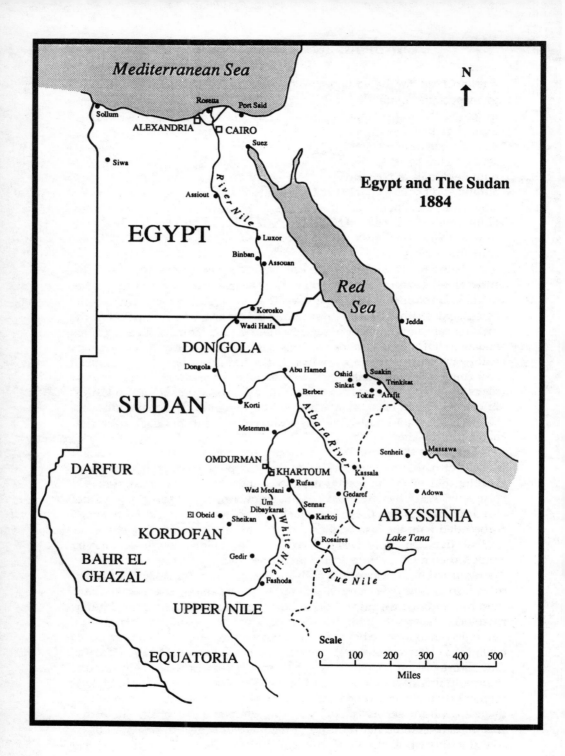

Egypt and The Sudan
1884

implemented, for the Sirdar sent a message to Hunter that he was coming to inspect the battalion. At the parade Sir Evelyn Wood lost no time in telling the troops that he would not tolerate disaffection but would immediately disband the battalion, and give each man his free discharge.[2] At the same time he would re-raise the battalion with fresh conditions of service. Those who wanted to go on serving would be treated as volunteers with new rates of pay and extra money for married men. About 100 men, Shilluk and Dinkas, all tribesmen from the southern Sudan who had stood aloof from the others, volunteered to serve, and the rest were discharged. Hunter was given power to press-gang any Sudanese in the country, and so was able to form two companies.

In those early days of the new Egyptian army disaffection was not uncommon. Once Hunter was given a gruesome task, when he had to supervise the execution of the ringleaders of a mutiny arising in a battalion of Turkish soldiers raised experimentally by the Sirdar. These men, while being sent south by train, had been shooting from the windows of the moving carriages, picking off peasants as they worked in the fields. They had also shot at the engine-driver and at two British officers. The prisoners had been court-martialled - a Turkish General presiding over the court – and condemned to death. They were to be executed at the grim hour of 5 a.m. in a disused barrack compound. The prisoners had had their last smoke. They had been blindfolded and roped to chairs. Their backs were to the firing-squad and they faced a high wall. The Sirdar and his staff had taken up their positions. The firing parties, composed of ten Turks, ten Egyptians and ten Sudanese, were ready. Suddenly Sir Evelyn Wood raised his hand and shouted 'stop'. But it was not a reprieve. Wood told Hunter that the firing parties were too close to the prisoners and would probably be hit by bits of plaster from the wall when the volleys were fired. So Hunter had the executioners moved back a few yards, and then proceeded with the task he had been given.[3]

The 9th Sudanese began to shape up to the rigorous drill and training imposed on them by Hunter. He may have been tough but he was always straightforward and fairminded. With him they knew exactly where they stood. In August 1884 orders were now given for the 9th to leave Cairo and proceed by rail and steamer to the cataract town of Assouan. Hunter had been barely six months in Cairo, and he would never again be stationed there, though during leaves he would enjoy its society and the delights it offered. At Assouan smallpox broke out in the ranks and the battalion was put in quarantine. The wives of the men did not take too kindly to this arrangement. One day Hunter was superintending the dis-embarkation of women and children from barges. A shortish man, he was standing on the shore, when a very tall woman, well over 6 feet, with a massive iron pot on her head, stopped beside him. Deliberately she tilted the pot and emptied its contents in the direction of Hunter's head. He nimbly stepped aside, but only just in time to avoid a rain of heavy objects, which, had they hit him, might have had fatal consequences.[4]

When given a clean bill of health the battalion moved up the Nile towards Dal, south of Wadi Halfa. This move was prompted by the serious situation developing in the Sudan.

A move against Egyptian rule in the Sudan had been gathering force until it amounted to a major rebellion. Its leader was Mohamed Ahmed Ibn el Sayyid Abdullah, better known as 'the Mahdi'. A powerful religious leader, he had been preaching against the moral decline of the age. But there was a political dimension to Mohamed Ahmed's teaching, and, joined by the practically minded Abdullahi Ibn el Sayyid Mohamed, a member of the important Baggara cattle-owning tribe, he raised the standard of revolt against the hated 'Turks', as the Egyptians were known in the Sudan. The people of the Sudan had been waiting for this and flocked to his banner. At first the Egyptian authorities had not taken the Mahdi seriously, underestimating the fanatical power of his movement, and suffered a series of military reverses in trying to deal with him. In January 1883 El Obeid, the chief city of Kordofan (see map A, p. 16), surrendered to the Mahdi, who was now master of the western Sudan. Ten months later Colonel William Hicks, a former Indian army soldier of no particular distinction, was chosen to lead against the Mahdi a motley Egyptian force mainly composed of those who had been dismissed from Arabi's routed army. Short of supplies and water, Hicks' force was surrounded in hostile territory and annihilated by the enemy at the battle of Sheikan in November 1883.

The way to Khartoum was now open. The Egyptian government wanted to hold that city and the Nile valley, but had to bow to British advice that their garrison numbering about 24,000 should be withdrawn to the north. This task, unwisely as it turned out, was entrusted to General Charles Gordon. This strange and unpredictable man hurriedly set out from London in January 1884 for his final spell in the Sudan. He arrived in Khartoum in February. The instructions given Gordon were just sufficiently ambiguous for him to feel justified in delaying an evacuation. This delay proved fatal.

By the end of March Gordon's communications with Cairo were disrupted by the Mahdi and two months later, at the time Hunter was assuming command of the 9th Sudanese, Berber, an important town 200 miles north of Khartoum, fell to the Dervishes. Retreat for Gordon was virtually impossible, even if he had really wanted to evacuate his garrison and its assorted followers. At the same time as these events were taking place on the Nile, the Mahdi had sent his able lieutenant, Osman Digna, of whom we shall hear more, to raise the standard of revolt in the Eastern Sudan.

It had now become abundantly clear to Baring in Cairo that if Gordon was not to be abandoned then a relief expedition of British or Indian troops would be needed to reach Khartoum and extricate him. For over four vital months the home government did nothing, except that Sir Garnet Wolseley, Adjutant-General in London, began to make plans for an expedition. Eventually Gladstone, the Prime Minister, bowed to public pressure, obtained a vote of credit of £300,000 from Parliament and appointed Wolseley on 26 August to command a relief expedition.

The problems facing the expedition, especially those involving distance, terrain, climate and health were formidable. From Cairo to Khartoum is, as the crow flies, around 1,000 miles. Measured along the length of the Nile and taking account of the river's two huge loops it is more like 1,750 miles; but this distance could be substantially reduced by striking south-east from Korti at the bottom of the first loop through the Bayuda desert to Metemma lying on the Nile north of Khartoum (see map A, p. 16). An alternative route mooted was down the Red Sea by ship to Suakin and then across the desert to Berber and so on south to Khartoum by the Nile. This way the land route would be not far short of 500 miles. In the event and against the advice of those on the spot, who favoured the Suakin route, Wolseley chose to go by the Nile. The terrain of the northern Sudan is harsh, inimical to invading troops, especially Europeans. Much of it is desert, the monotony being relieved here and there by rocky hills and defiles. The vegetation is limited to thorny scrub except alongside the Nile where fertile and cultivated land could sometimes be found.

For fighting men and their supplies to reach their distant destination immense problems of logistics would have to be faced and overcome. Navigation on the Nile south of Assouan would not be easy. Vast numbers of animals, especially camels, would be needed. As staging posts south of the frontier, the expedition would be able to use a few small towns and villages sprinkled along the route.

The climate of the Sudan is dry and the heat unrelenting. There are not many hotter places on earth, and the temperature can exact a terrible toll on man. There are places where rain is almost unheard of. Wind and sandstorms can be severe, and may arrive without warning. In the desert water is everything. Wells, unless already available, take time to dig. Campaigning troops, except where they are relying on the Nile, must carry great quantities of water with them. Finally to add to an already complex picture, there was obviously a time problem. How long could Gordon, superman that he was in the eyes of many, hold out? No one seemed to know the answer to this, and Gordon did little to supply one. For the expedition to succeed in its object of relieving Gordon, everything had to go right.

Initially, Wolseley moved fast, arriving in Cairo on 10 September 1884. Then there was a pause, for he was kept waiting until Baring was authorised to issue him with written instructions. He arrived at Wadi Halfa on 5 October, but thereafter progress was painfully slow and there were

19

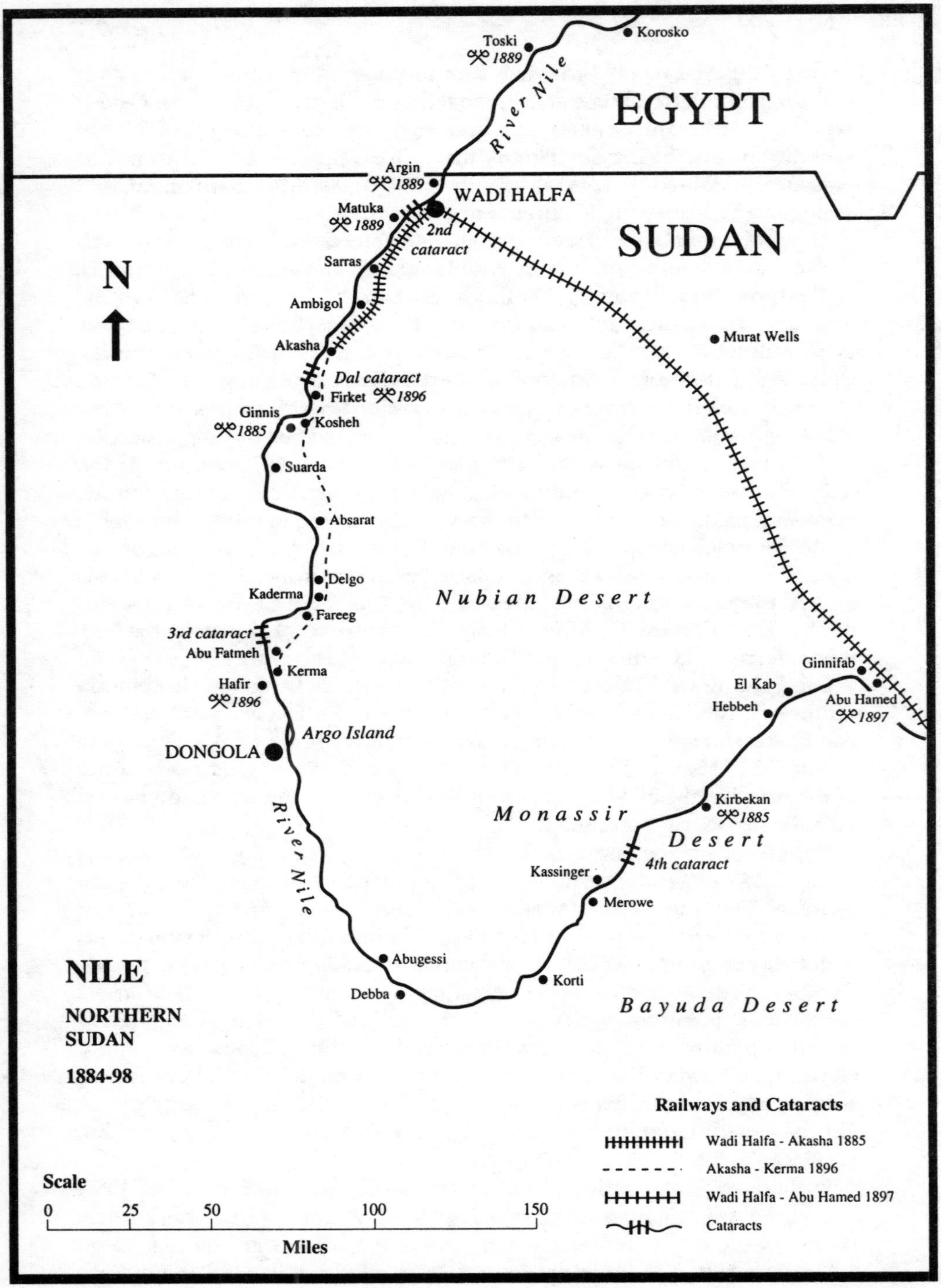

Korosko
Toski
1889
River Nile
EGYPT
Argin
1889
WADI HALFA
Matuka
1889
2nd
cataract
SUDAN
Sarras
N
Ambigol
Murat Wells
Akasha
Dal cataract
Firket
1896
Ginnis
1885
Kosheh
Suarda
Absarat
Delgo
Kaderma
Nubian Desert
Fareeg
3rd cataract
Abu Fatmeh
Kerma
Hafir
1896
Ginnifab
El Kab
Abu Hamed
Hebbeh
1897
Argo Island
DONGOLA
Kirbekan
1885
Monassir
Desert
River Nile
4th cataract
Kassinger
Merowe
Abugessi
NILE
NORTHERN
SUDAN
1884-98
Korti
Debba
Bayuda Desert
Railways and Cataracts
Wadi Halfa - Akasha 1885
Akasha - Kerma 1896
Wadi Halfa - Abu Hamed 1897
Cataracts
Scale
0
25
50
100
150
Miles

Map B

immense delays in transporting troops and supplies up the Nile. Wolseley had decided to employ English-built whalers piloted by Canadian boat-men, a form of transport successfully used by him in the Red River cam-paign in Canada in 1870. Unhappily, the whalers proved unequal to the task, their masts not being tall enough to allow their sails to catch the breeze where the river banks were high.

Wolseley's plan was to concentrate his troops at Korti and there divide them into two separate columns. A 'desert' column, under Brigadier-General Sir Herbert Stewart, would strike south-east across the Bayuda desert to Metemma on the Nile. From there it would be poised to strike at Khartoum once it had been reinforced by the 'river' column under Major-General W. Earle which would take the much longer route follow-ing the Nile all the way via Berber before going southwards. The columns would be unable to communicate with each other, and the nerve-centre of the whole operation would be at Korti directed by Wolseley.

The role to be played by the small Egyptian army, and therefore by Hunter, during the expedition was a minor one. It was to be deployed defensively and administratively on the lines of communication. Wolseley had no time for Wood's untried 'native' army to which he refers disparag-ingly in the Journal he kept during the campaign. Nor could it have helped that Wolseley disliked Wood, finding him vain.[5] Nevertheless, all that happened on the Gordon Relief expedition would be of the utmost signifi-cance to those who were to pass along the same way, including Hunter, by then a divisional commander, during Kitchener's campaign of reconquest in 1896–98.

In October 1884 in the vanguard of Wolseley's expedition, Hunter was sent forward ahead of his battalion from Assouan to the village of Abu Fatmeh, situated on the third cataract, to help set up a staging post for moving troops up to an advanced base at Korti. He travelled up the Nile in a nuggar (barge) with an Italian priest as a companion. Although not a particularly religious man, Hunter always liked the company of intelligent clergymen.

Still commanding the 9th battalion, which had by now reached Abu Fatmeh, Hunter found himself wearing two hats. In addition to his regi-mental one, he became staff officer to the Officer Commanding at Abu Fatmeh, Lieutenant-Colonel Frederick Maurice, an academically-minded soldier who later became a distinguished military historian, who wrote the Official History of the War in South Africa. Hunter admired Maurice and the two became friends. When Maurice left the Expedition, Hunter wrote and congratulated him on his promotion. In his letter he apologised for his 'boorish' behaviour, for not saying good-bye properly, explaining that on the evening in question 'my night clothing was so tattered that to put my head outside [my tent] was to render me liable for indecency'![6]

Hunter became closely involved at Abu Fatmeh with administrative matters. Having an orderly mind and an eye for detail, he proved to be good at it. Maurice delegated to him responsibility for payments to the local workforce and for keeping the accounts of the post. In addition, he was involved in transport matters, supervising the passage up the Third Cataract of the whalers and other craft. He also helped to run the postal service. Maurice appreciated Hunter's work and wrote that he was an 'exceedingly nice fellow, a good officer and man of principle'.[7]

Early in the new year Hunter, together with 134 men of the 9th Sudanese, was sent by Sir Redvers Buller, Chief of Staff to the Expedition, south to Abugessi near Korti (map B, p. 20). They took three months' rations but their role is not known. Possibly they were to form part of the reinforcements for Stewart's desert column but this is conjecture.

Wolseley, uncharacteristically, did not seem to have a firm grip on the way the campaign was developing. His troops were late in concentrating at Korti, and consequently the main desert column did not leave there until 8 January 1885. The story of the desert and river columns is well-known. Both met with disasters. Stewart was mortally wounded in the groin after the battle of Abu Klea (see map F, p. 59). Colonel Sir Charles Wilson, his deputy, doggedly reached the Nile and then, after a much criticised pause, made his dash by gunboat up the Nile to Khartoum only to find that he was too late and that Gordon's defences had been overrun two days before on 26 January. Hunter reported in his diary that he heard, while at Abugessi as Commandant there, of the exposure of Gordon's head in the market at Omdurman, before the news had been officially transmitted to Wolseley. As for the river column it had fought and won the battle of Kirkeban, but during it Earle had been killed when he had carelessly peered through the window of a hut occupied by the enemy. Both columns returned in poor condition to Korti. Wolseley's plans lay in ruins and he seems to have blamed everyone but himself.[8] The British government's policy too had failed, and they now prevaricated as to what action to take.

A period of stagnation and uncertainty ended with the announcement on 21 April by the government that the advance to Khartoum would not be continued and no more offensive action in the Sudan undertaken. Threats on the Afghanistan frontier provided a face-saving excuse for the government to wind up the expedition. The government ordered all forces to fall back on Wadi Halfa, and on 5 July 1885 the expedition's troops evacuated Dongola province. Shortly before, the Mahdi had died in Omdurman, probably of typhus. He was succeeded by his lieutenant, the Khalifa Abdullahi.

In 1885 and until towards the end of the year we obtain only tantalising glimpses of Hunter. It was an important year for him, for he was now on active service, learning the skills of his profession against worthy adversaries. He stayed with the 9th Sudanese at Abugessi until June.[9] Now

600-strong and at about full strength, the battalion was to act as a rearguard to the Gordon Relief expedition, soon to be disbanded, on its withdrawal north. Moving back down the Nile was a slow progress that took several months.

On one occasion Hunter was sent by boat to arrest a spy in a village north of Dongola. He had with him only a small escort, and when he caught his man, he found himself followed by an angry crowd of Dervish sympathisers who nearly rushed the boat. Hunter suddenly seized the prisoner and held him over the gunwale with a revolver in his hand. 'I'll blow his brains out if you don't stand back,' he shouted in Arabic to the crowd, and in this way made good his capture. On his way back, uncertain of the loyalties of the boat's captain, he sat by the wheel with revolver cocked, promising to dispose of the captain, should he touch the shore or sandbank.[10] This was the kind of spirit that was beginning to gain him a reputation for decisiveness and toughness.

By July Hunter and his men had fallen back to Akasha where he became Commandant, and Officer commanding the river patrol.[11] He took over the gunboat *Lotus* and other rivercraft from the navy. The Nile in spate could be dangerous; on one occasion he capsized and was nearly drowned, losing the bible given him by his mother. Also under his command were elements of the Camel Corps, for whom he developed a soft spot.

About now, in addition to his other duties, Hunter became Intelligence Officer of the rearguard force, and he spent much time examining refugees. This intelligence work, besides adding another string to his bow, he found to his liking. He thrived on his varied responsibilities and in August was promoted Kaimakam (Lieutenant-Colonel) in the Egyptian army.

From September the Dervishes were pushing northward with some vigour and making their presence felt, having suffered a temporary loss of morale following the death of the Mahdi. Naturally Hunter and his battalion were in the thick of it, skirmishing and hand-to-hand fighting becoming a daily occurrence in the semi-irregular warfare of the desert. Once in a letter to his brother Duncan, who was seeking his fortune in the United States, Hunter elatedly wrote that he had 'bagged' seven Dervishes with his Winchester repeater. But he then begged Duncan not to repeat this as it 'smacked of boasting and savagery'.[12] This approach to fighting the Dervishes was not uncommon among the officers of the Egyptian army.

Andrew Haggard, elder brother of the novelist Rider Haggard, and himself OC of the 1st Egyptian battalion, wrote admiringly of Hunter as a commanding officer, and Horace Smith-Dorrien who joined the Egyptian army with Hunter described him as 'always to the fore when there was a dangerous scrap'.[13] Once, when on picket duty, Hunter averted a night attack by the Dervishes when he received a coded message from an Arab agent warning him of enemy plans. He knew it was genuine because the agent produced a signet ring given him by a British officer.[14] It was all heady stuff and Hunter was enjoying it. He seemed the ideal man to be on the frontier.

A strong defensive position with a newly constructed fort had been established at Kosheh, just south of Akasha and about 100 miles from Wadi Halfa. This was held by a force which included the Cameron Highlanders as well as the 9th Sudanese battalion. The Dervishes, showing every sign of aggression, were deployed on both sides of the Nile at the village of Ginnis, just south of Kosheh (Map B, p. 20). One of their objectives was to destroy the railway line which had been extended south from Wadi Halfa. This necessitated lightning attacks by mounted men. More importantly the Dervish army entertained plans of invading Egypt[15] as part of the Mahdist plan of ultimately conquering the Middle East. By December Kosheh and its fort had become more or less invested by the Dervishes, now collecting in some strength. Extracts from Hunter's diary in the first fortnight of the month tell the story: 'threatened attack on Kosheh. Dervishes driven off . . .', 'sniping now regular . . .', 'heavy firing daily . . .', 'heavy attack on fort, gallant repulse . . .' and on 15 December 'prepare for sortie . . .'

The British at Wadi Halfa now decided to mount an attack in the last week of December, 1885 on the Dervish position at Ginnis which was being used as a forward base by the enemy. Two brigades of British infantry and supporting troops would be commanded by General Sir Frederick Stephenson, commander of the British troops of occupation in Egypt, with Major-General Sir Francis Grenfell, the new Sirdar, acting as his chief staff officer. British troops, who in the Gordon Relief Expedition had been clad predominantly in grey, were ordered to put on their red serge in order to appear more formidable to the enemy.[16] The Dervishes, in contrast, wore 'jibbas', short-sleeved smocks made of coarse cotton with a coloured patch sewn into the garb to denote their tribe. During the battle at Ginnis on 30 December there was much stubborn hand-to-hand fighting in the village, in which Egyptian army units did well. The Dervishes fell back with severe losses, and for some years military activity on the frontier was much reduced.

But what of Hunter at the battle of Ginnis? He missed it. During a sortie from the fort of Kosheh on 16 December there had been a skirmish. Hunter had fallen severely wounded, shot in the back of his left arm near the shoulder. His galloper, an orderly who carried messages, Lieutenant Cameron, was mortally wounded. According to G. W. Steevens, the *Daily Mail* war correspondent, Hunter was wounded 'when he lingered behind the retiring force during the sortie to pick off Dervishes with a rifle he was wont to carry on such occasions'. Lord Edward Cecil, son of the Prime Minister Lord Salisbury, in writing of the incident in his diary of 1896 during the Dongola expedition, referred to 'the black rock . . . where

Colonel Hunter killed six Dervishes with a Winchester at close quarters and was badly wounded himself.'[17] Smith-Dorrien said this black rock was conspicuous and only some 550 yards south of Kosheh; from it the enemy would snipe all day and it was here, he confirmed, that Hunter was wounded.[18]

At first Hunter's condition was considered too critical for him to be moved from Kosheh. But then on 27 December he was evacuated north under escort by boat to Akasha. Stephenson and Grenfell on their way up to the front went to see him in his hospital tent. They gave him a drink; oddly it was port, and, propped on a stretcher, he drew them a map of the enemy position at Ginnis, and in the ensuing discussion, made suggestions as to how the Dervishes might be attacked.[19] The strange little conference over, Hunter was taken by rail to Wadi Halfa, by steamer to Assouan and so on to hospital in Cairo.

For the action at Kosheh when he was wounded, Hunter was Mentioned in Despatches. A year later in recognition of his work on the frontier, he was awarded the DSO, a decoration only instituted in late 1886.

NOTES

1. SAD 110/11/1–89 hist IX Sud Bn.
2. Ibid.
3. Ternan *Some Experiences of an Old Bromsgrovian* 45–6; Wood 166.
4. Ternan 47.
5. Preston *In Relief of Gordon: Lord Wolseley's Campaign Journal* 31.
6. Maurice Collection 2/1/1 AH–Maurice, 4 Sep. 1885.
7. Maurice *Sir Frederick Maurice: A Record of Essays* 50.
8. Preston 112, 137 and 141.
9. SAD loc. cit.
10. Undated newscutting in 1896 from *Pall Mall Gazette*.
11. SAD loc. cit.
12. DHD 12; Keown-Boyd 119.
13. Smith-Dorrien *Memories of Forty-Eight Years Service* 58.
14. AHd 28/11/85.
15. Cromer II 30.
16. Barthorp, *The British Army on Campaign 4 1882–1902* 41.
17. Lord Edward Cecil's Diary 186.
18. Smith-Dorrien loc. cit.
19. AHd 27/12/85; DHD 10.

CHAPTER 4
On the Frontier

After being wounded at Kosheh, Hunter was lucky not to lose his arm and even his life. He was away from the Egyptian army for two years, not returning to duty until March 1888. From his hospital bed in Cairo he wrote to his brother Duncan describing his wound as 'very nasty' and saying his arm would be a 'useless member'. It would give him pain and discomfort for the rest of his life. According to the report of the surgeon in Cario, a bullet had entered at the inferior angle of the scapula and passing upwards had shattered the humerus before exiting in the upper arm. Fragments of the bullet were still in his arm when he was examined by doctors in Edinburgh in 1902.

As a result of his wound, Hunter developed bronchitis which turned to pleurisy. On admission to the Citadel hospital in Cario on 9 January 1886 he was suffering from high fever and in too weak a condition for an immediate operation. It was not until some ten days later that pieces of dead and splintered bone were removed from his arm under ether. Although his condition had slowly begun to improve it was decided to invalid him home. So in March he was put aboard *HMS Serapis* at Suez reaching Portsmouth in April. His mother met him in London, and he was at once admitted to Sir William MacCormac's private hospital in Manchester Square, where he was a patient for many months receiving the best available medical attention. MacCormac, of St Thomas's Hospital, was a leading authority on gunshot wounds and his works had been translated into many languages including Russian and Japanese.[2]

As predicted Hunter's recovery was slow. In Egypt notice was given in army orders that the command of the 9th Sudanese had been 'vacated' by Hunter. Then in the winter, just after he had arrived to convalesce in the south of France and enjoy a bit of gambling at Monte Carlo his arm began to trouble him again, and he had to hurry back to London. MacCormac told him another piece of bone had to come out and that yet another operation, his fourth, was necessary. Under the conditions of service for officers in the Egyptian army sick-leave could not exceed one year in three years' service. Hunter had already exceeded this allowance and he was obliged, therefore, to resign his appointment. It must have been a deep disappointment to him. He did, however, receive the thanks of the Khedive for the 'valuable services' he had rendered.[3]

Hunter now had to rejoin his old regiment, and he was posted in March

26

1887 to Buttevant north of Cork in Ireland. A Medical Board had concluded that the condition of his arm was 'nearly equivalent to the loss of a limb',[4] and he consequently received a wound pension of £200 a year. We have no information about how long he was in Ireland or what his job was, except that he was engaged on battalion duties. It is as if nearly a year of his life has been lost. At some stage, reasonably fit again, he either applied to rejoin the Egyptian army or was approached by the Sirdar. We do not know which. But on 29 February 1888 he received a letter ordering him to rejoin the Egyptian army. He moved fast and arrived in Cairo on 16 March. A week later, having lost £60 (about a month's pay) at baccarat in Cairo,[5] he left by stern-wheeler mail-boat for Korosko, a little way north of Wadi Halfa. He had been reappointed Officer Commanding his old battalion, the 9th Sudanese, taking over from Major Borrow, an old friend. He was not happy, however, at the circumstances of the posting. Apparently Borrow had been in violent conflict with his men. He had first struck an officer who had to go to hospital and then knocked a man senseless. So bitter had been the feelings against Borrow, that some men had deserted to the Dervishes with their equipment.[6] Hunter had therefore been put in to restore order. Tact, firmness and fair play could be expected from him and the men, apparently, were delighted that he was coming back.

It was a good omen. Hunter hoped that the authorities would not carry out their threat of withdrawing the battalion to Cairo. He much preferred the frontier, which was cheaper and above all offered the prospect of some fighting, though for some time military activity around Wadi Halfa had been only sporadic. In August he was writing jubilantly to Duncan, believing there was some real chance of a fight and confiding that he was a 'much bigger card out here now' than he was before.[7] At this moment his arm chose to trouble him yet again. By September the pain had increased and he developed a high fever from an abscess caused by movement of the bone. The army doctor advised immediate evacuation to Cairo, where it was decided that Hunter should return home by sea for an operation to remove the offending piece of bone. For a second time, therefore, he had to relinquish command of his battalion on grounds of sickness. Another irksome period in hospital in England followed, plus another long convalescence. Happily this period of enforced absence from duty lasted a mere six months or so. It was the last time that the arm would need such prolonged treatment.

That winter Hunter had some good news to distract him as he lay in his hospital bed, recovering from his operation. His brother George, no doubt encouraged by him, had decided to join the Egyptian army. He was posted that November to the 11th Sudanese battalion at Suakin, where Archie would spend some years in the early 1890s. The Dervishes under Osman Digna had entrenched themselves a mile from the town and were spoiling for a fight. George hoped that Archie might be fit enough to take part in the impending battle. So he telegraphed his brother telling him that the 9th Sudanese were coming to take part in the fray, as if this would be enough to bring Archie out to Egypt. In a letter to his brother Duncan, George said that Archie's battalion was reckoned 'about the best in the army' and that he, Archie, 'had more personal influence over Blacks than any other chap commanding them'. These men, moreover, 'will follow him to the Gates of Hell if needs be and if needs were, he would take them. Everybody is damned sorry he is not here'.[8]

The arm, though, was still troublesome, and with MacCormac keeping a close eye on him, there was no chance of Hunter returning to duty. After the battle of Gemaizah, just outside Suakin, when Osman Digna was defeated on 20 December 1888, Sir Francis Grenfell, the Sirdar, sent Hunter a telegram to say that George was all right – a nice gesture! In the event Hunter took longer to regain his fitness than expected and it was not until March 1889 that he was able to respond to the laconic telegram received at his London club, the Naval and Military, which read: 'Services wanted as soon as possible Sirdar'.

In the summer of 1889 the commander of the Frontier Field Force (as the Egyptian forces guarding the frontier were now known) at Wadi Halfa was Colonel Joscelin Wodehouse, an able and popular soldier. Hunter, on his return to duty, was appointed his second-in-command. The Dervishes were now beginning to gather for their long-expected advance north down the Nile. Hunter had been sent out in May to parry attacks which did not materialise. Wodehouse now decided that the Dervish outpost at the village of Matuka on the west bank of the river should be attacked. For this purpose he sent Hunter south on 4 June with 300 men of the 12th Sudanese, 100 cavalry and a company of the camel corps. Hunter elected first to take the high ground near the village. Next he cleared the houses in the village of Dervishes.[9] Many of the enemy took refuge on an island in the cataract already occupied by their forces. The Egyptian troops waded the river and rushed the Dervish positions. In hand-to-hand fighting, 18 Dervishes were killed and seven taken prisoner. A quantity of arms, ammunition and cattle were seized. This skirmish marked Hunter's first entirely independent command in battle with troops of all arms. Also it was his first action since being wounded.

The main Dervish force of some 12,000 fighting men and a huge number of camp-followers soon began to advance down the Nile under their leader Wad-el-Nejumi, a member of the Jaalik tribe and a considerable figure among Mahdists. Writing years later Baring (as Lord Cromer) thought that Nejumi embodied the 'true principles of militant Mahdism' and regarded him as the Prince Rupert of Dervish cavalry. It was he who had overthrown Hicks at Sheikan and later had led the assault on Khartoum. Some claimed that the Khalifa Abdullahi, the Mahdi's successor, had entrusted Nejumi with the invasion of Egypt to rid himself of a possible rival, for the invasion scheme was ill thought out.

Nejumi's plan was to ignore Wadi Halfa and proceed north on the west side of the Nile, parallel to, but a little away from, the river. Then, striking across the desert, he aimed to reach the Nile at Binban, north of Assouan (see map A, p. 16), where he optimistically hoped Egyptian rebels would flock to his standard.[10] During his march he would avoid, if possible, giving battle. For the moment, Wodehouse's men shadowed Nejumi and tried to prevent the enemy reaching the river to obtain supplies of much needed water. On the Nile Egyptian gunboats played a valuable defensive role.

By 2 July 1889 Nejumi had taken up a position in the desert close to Argin (see map C, p. 30), a village which lay on the west bank of the Nile, some $3\frac{1}{2}$ miles north of Wadi Halfa, and which was occupied by Wodehouse's troops. Now desperate for water, the Dervishes were forced to attack Argin, where Wodehouse's men were blocking Nejumi's access to the Nile. Hunter had been promoted to command a brigade of Egyptian army infantry composed of the 9th, 10th and 13th Sudanese battalions and played a prominent part in the battle. He was first sent by Wodehouse in mid-morning, with the 10th Sudanese, to the north of the village. As Dervish attacks there failed, he was then withdrawn with two companies of this battalion to reinforce the southern end of the village near the fort.[11] In the meantime a fierce enemy attack was developing at 1.30 p.m. in the centre of the village, where the Dervishes obtained a strong lodgement. It then fell to Hunter, joined in due course by Wodehouse himself, to counter-attack from the south with about 570 men from the 9th and 10th Sudanese and the camel corps. All through the afternoon and until the village was finally cleared at 6 p.m.[12], there was long drawn out house-to-house fighting. Many Dervishes perished when they were burnt out of the houses they were defending. On several occasions Dervish cavalry and spearmen charged gallantly from behind houses and dense screens of castor oil plants, but were always mown down by the steady fire of the Egyptian army.

At one time a threat emerged from some 2,000 Dervish troops gathering in the plain to the west of the village. Luckily the threat did not materialise. Had it done so, Hunter thought it might have been all up with his men, who could have been driven into the river. Hunter told Duncan that he fired all 50 cartridges he had with him and had his sword bent to boot. 'I think,' he wrote, 'we have taught them a lesson'.[13] Dervish losses had been severe: 900 men, including many Emirs, had been killed and 1,000 prisoners taken. The Egyptian army, whose losses in the battle had been 11 killed and 59 wounded, gained confidence from its success and this contributed significantly to its decisive victory at Toski the following month.

After the battle of Argin, Nejumi's second-in-command, Abdul Halim,

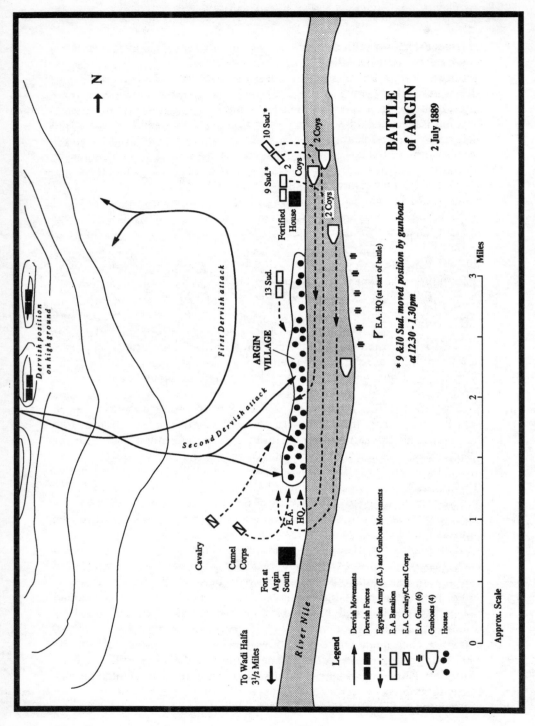

BATTLE
of ARGIN

2 July 1889

N

Dervish position on high ground

First Dervish attack

Second Dervish attack

ARGIN
VILLAGE

10 Sud.*

2 Coys

9 Sud.*

2
Coys

Fortified
House

2 Coys

13 Sud.

▼ E.A. HQ (at start of battle)

* 9 &10 Sud. moved position by gunboat
at 12.30 - 1.30pm

Cavalry

Camel
Corps

E.A.
HQ.

Fort at
Argin
South

To Wadi Halfa
3½ Miles

River Nile

Legend

Dervish Movements
Dervish Forces
Egyptian Army (E.A.) and Gunboat Movements
E.A. Battalion
E.A. Cavalry/Camel Corps
E.A. Guns (6)
Gunboats (4)
Houses

0   1   2   3
Miles

Approx. Scale

Map C

30

advised a retreat, or at least a postponement of invasion plans. But Nejumi was determined to continue his advance northwards with his unwieldy columns, despite losing men by desertion and being harried by Wode-house. In his diary entry for 2 July Hunter records that 'From now till the battle of Toski [on] 3 August we were fighting every day'. On 16 July Grenfell issued an ultimatum to Nejumi and his Emirs. He appealed to Nejumi to surrender and so avoid further bloodshed, pointing out the hopelessness of his task and the falseness of his leader, the Khalifa. The alternative was utter destruction.[14] Nejumi in robust and even heroic terms rejected the ultimatum and enjoined Grenfell at the same time to adopt the faith of Islam and be saved.

On 3 August near Toski, a village some 60 miles north of Wadi Halfa and not far from the great temple of Abu Simbel, Nejumi was brought to battle by the Egyptian army under Grenfell. At dawn that day Colonel Herbert Kitchener, in command of the mounted troops, was sent out to reconnoitre the Dervish position in the open desert and then, when they began to move, to head the enemy away from the river. Hunter, command-ing the 1st Brigade, was ordered at 8.30 a.m. to leave the village of Toski. Rather surprisingly, his troops had, before setting out, been on drill parade for two hours; this suggests that an immediate action against Nejumi was not anticipated. Hunter's brigade again consisting of the 9th, 10th and 13th Sudanese battalions – numbering some 1,450 men – was to take up a position under the cover of rising ground towards which Nejumi was advancing. The enemy's move northwards was thus intercepted and brought to a halt. The brigade soon came under heavy fire and, to dislodge the Dervishes, some high ground had to be won by the 9th Sudanese at the point of the bayonet. The 13th Sudanese, in the meantime, were coming under strong enfilading fire and suffering heavy casualties. Another charge had to be made to gain the top of the hills, this time by the 13th Sudanese together with the 1st Egyptians of the 2nd brigade who were acting in support of the 1st brigade. In the middle of the day at the hottest time of the year and led by Hunter, they stormed their way forward and the final Dervish position was ultimately carried, despite repeated counter-attacks. The enemy was now in full retreat and was pursued for some three miles until a halt was called at 2.30 p.m.[15] In the close-quarter fighting Hunter received a wound from a spearman in his right forearm, which had to be stitched. This was bound up in the field by Captain Ternan, Hunter's acting Brigade Major, whose horse in the ensuing advance up the hill was shot dead under him.

The Dervish defeat was complete. Nejumi himself was killed, together with 1,200 of his men. Beside the leader lay his five-year-old son also dead. Some 3,000 prisoners were taken, as well as many standards and a great quantity of spears, swords and rifles. In his diary, Hunter commented that all the prisoners were treated kindly, adding that after-

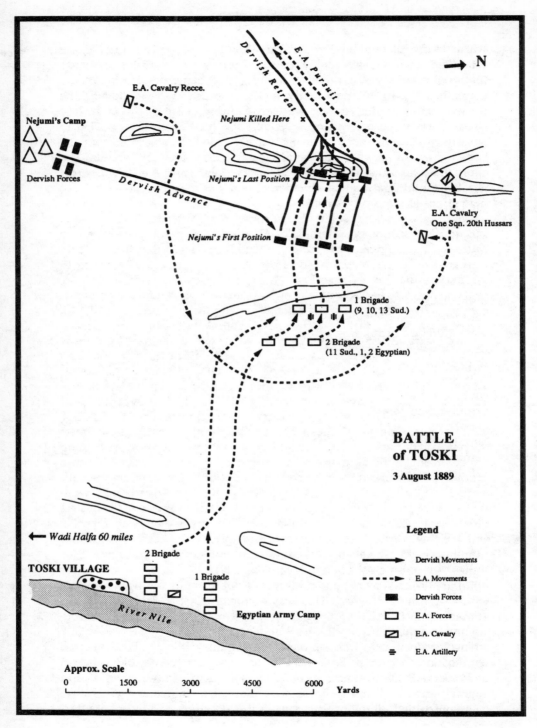

E.A. Cavalry Recce.

Nejumi's Camp

Dervish Forces

Dervish Advance

Nejumi Killed Here x

Nejumi's Last Position

Nejumi's First Position

Dervish Retreat

E.A. Pursuit

N

E.A. Cavalry
One Sqn. 20th Hussars

1 Brigade
(9, 10, 13 Sud.)

2 Brigade
(11 Sud., 1, 2 Egyptian)

**BATTLE
of TOSKI**

3 August 1889

← *Wadi Halfa 60 miles*

2 Brigade

1 Brigade

TOSKI VILLAGE

River Nile

Egyptian Army Camp

Legend

→ Dervish Movements

---▶ E.A. Movements

▰ Dervish Forces

▱ E.A. Forces

▨ E.A. Cavalry

≡ E.A. Artillery

Approx. Scale

0   1500   3000   4500   6000

Yards

Map D   32

wards many made good recruits. The Egyptian army lost 165 killed and wounded. In the desert 22,000 starving women and children were left scattered along the route followed by Nejumi. They had to be collected together and sent down to Egypt, where they were resettled. Toski was the first battle in which Kitchener and Hunter, whose fortunes were to be so closely linked seven years later, fought together. Their ages then were 39 and 32 respectively.

The outcome of the battle had far-reaching consequences. Baring considered it gave confidence to the Egyptian army and people, and also to the people of Europe. Certainly, with this defeat the aggressive power of the Dervishes collapsed and never again did they try to invade Egypt. In practical terms the country between Wadi Halfa and Assouan was made safe and was no longer subject to marauding Dervishes. So Thomas Cook was once again able to take parties of tourists up the Nile to Wadi Halfa.

The fighting of the past $2\frac{1}{2}$ months had put Hunter in a reflective mood. He wrote to Duncan about the horrors and cruelties of war and referred to the 'feast of blood' at Toski. While allowing that a charge of Dervishes could be 'the most glorious sight' he ever saw, he also recognised that war could be a brutalising experience. But at Toski the 'proudest moment of my life was when the men rallied round me and cheered in their wild impetuous way'.[16] Professionally Hunter must have satisfied his superiors with the handling of his brigade at the two battles, for next time large contingents of troops were used by the army on the Nile, in the Dongola expedition of 1896, Hunter would be in command of a division.

For over a year and a half after Toski, Hunter remained as Wodehouse's deputy. The frontier all this time remained quiet. Wadi Halfa was, in the summer, one of the hottest places on earth, temperatures reaching at times 122 deg F in the tents. Today it lies coolly under the waters of Lake Nubia. Then it was an unattractive military-cum-railway town, with barracks, offices, stores and workshops straggling along the river bank. The colour of its brown mud houses, which included a few Greek shops and some cafés, was relieved by a white mosque and the green of the palm trees. Training for the soldiers took place in the morning before the heat became unbearable. After lunch it was the practice for the British officers to change into pyjamas, and to sleep or read. Picquet and whist were played, and, curiously, there was a racquets court for the more energetic. A few sailing boats were available for recreation on the river in the cool of the evening.

Hunter, rarely idle, made reconnaissances by horse or camel deep into enemy territory. Returning from leading a six-man patrol he reported that the most northerly Dervish outpost was at Suarda, some 120 miles south of Wadi Halfa (see Map B, p. 20). Once he went south, surprised an enemy patrol, and took prisoners. On another occasion, in March 1890, he accompanied Wodehouse to Murat Wells. A small party of some eight officers and a few Arabs, they travelled fast, covering on the outward journey 101 miles in four days at the rate of between four and five miles an hour. Hunter was in his element, for he loved, as he confessed to Duncan, to be 'constantly on the move' or facing the 'excitement of being in danger'.

A few months after Toski he was promoted Lieutenant-Colonel in the British army. This was, as he described it to Duncan, the limit he had set to his 'fondest dreams and ambitions starting friendless in the Army'. But now he would aspire to greater advancement. He believed, for instance, that he ought to sit the Staff College exam and then with the qualification 'p.s.c.', he would be able to 'snap my fingers at most people'. He never mentions Staff College again, however, in any papers of his that have survived. The Egyptian army did not encourage its officers to go to Staff College, and it may well have been that Hunter did apply but could not be spared, or, perhaps, that with his great enjoyment of soldiering on the frontier, he never got round to applying.

Wodehouse was always generous in his praise of Hunter, and described him in the following terms in an Annual Confidential Report in 1891: 'an officer of exceptional ability and character . . . a strict disciplinarian and at the same time universally popular . . . a loyal zealous subordinate . . . gallant leader in action . . . has a great and salutary influence on his subordinates . . . a man of the world, generous to a fault'. This report was countersigned by the Sirdar, Grenfell.[17]

Somewhat to his regret, Hunter was appointed in April 1891 to a newly-established post – Governor commanding Tokar Sub-District in eastern Sudan. This was the country of the fierce 'Fuzzy-Wuzzy' warriors of the Haddendowa tribe immortalised by Rudyard Kipling, who had been for years a thorn in the flesh of the Egyptian government. Osman Digna, their wily commander, had for some years been unable to capture the enclave of Suakin which was protected by a ring of forts. Digna's influence was now in decline after his defeat at Arafit by Colonel Holled Smith, Governor of the Red Sea Littoral.

Hunter had liked his post at Wadi Halfa and rightly believed that it would be the place from which a future offensive against the Khalifa's empire would be launched. He did not want to miss the fun. Tokar and Suakin (see Map A, p. 16), on the other hand, were strategically speaking off the beaten track. At Tokar he would have many fewer troops under his command than at Wadi Halfa, and decisions would have to be referred to his local chief Holled Smith at Suakin. Admittedly his pay would go up to £1,000 a year but then the increase would be offset by the higher cost of living in remote Tokar.

Soon Hunter found himself at Suakin, which he described as 'a shamefully neglected dung-heap',[18] acting as Governor, while Holled Smith was on leave. As the *locum tenens*, he was not supposed to alter established procedures. This irked him. Holled Smith's performance as an administrator, military and civil, did not meet at all with Hunter's approval. He found so many 'glaring evils' that at first it was difficult to know what to do about them, without seeming disloyal to the absent Governor. Hunter, though, was a zealous man, always anxious to right wrongs, and to make reforms for the benefit of people. Many of the ills he brought to the notice of the Cairo authorities. Others he took upon himself to remedy, risking the consequences and showing himself to be a 'doer' and never afraid of taking responsibility. One problem he faced arose from slackness and bad discipline among the garrison. Thieves, he found, were stealing rifles from the armoury under the noses of men on guard; Hunter reacted decisively. Sentries were now obliged to patrol all night; officers and men had to leap out of bed at unheard-of hours to respond to alarm signals; and a system of rockets was introduced to test vigilance. Traps were set. These worked and two receivers were caught red-handed selling a stolen rifle. One was hanged and the other after being flogged was given a long prison sentence.[19] Sometimes Hunter was frustrated. For example, he soon became aware that in the mountains around Suakin there was a certain amount of violent robbery and brigandage. Typically enough, he offered to go out and put this down. His proposal was, however, turned down by higher authority.

When in July 1892 Hunter was appointed Governor of the Red Sea Littoral he took steps to increase the security of the area. On one trip into the hinterland he was accompanied by police and some local auxiliaries. During his journey he noted down in a log the name, length of service, appearance and capability of every man in his party. He clearly had taken great trouble with these details, which could only have been ascertained by talking individually with each man.[20] This kind of human approach explains why Hunter was so popular with those serving under him.

Since the military threat in the eastern Sudan had receded, Hunter was able to concentrate more of his time on civilian work. Administration appealed to him and he found himself engrossed by it. For instance he introduced new sanitary laws and improved the water supply at Suakin by laying new pipe-lines and installing modern pumping equipment from England.[21]

Hunter was in regular correspondence with Reginald Wingate, the young Director of Intelligence, in Cairo. Wingate, an intellectual and, like Hunter, a Lowland Scot, would succeed Kitchener as Sirdar in 1900 and have a distinguished career in the Sudan. He had an insatiable appetite for information. Once he told Hunter of his difficulties over intercepting letters, and asked him to find out who in Suakin was corresponding with the 'Palace' in Cairo. On another occasion Hunter was asked to look out for a mysterious one-eyed man carrying letters to the Sudan. Changes at the top of the army pending Grenfell's retirement as Sirdar in 1892 were

35

clearly of great interest to both men. A year earlier Hunter told his brother Duncan that 'if the Adjutant-General's billet becomes vacant I ought to get it'. He now assured Wingate that the post of 'A-G' had not been offered to him, and anyhow he did not want a post in Cairo.[22] As it was, Kitchener, to the surprise of many, became Sirdar, and Leslie Rundle, a Gunner, 'A-G'. The choice of Kitchener was not popular, for he was not regarded by his peers as a congenial man. Rundle was to have a distinguished career, becoming Governor of Malta, and he remained a life-long friend of Hunter.

Hunter was always conscientious about learning languages, and he improved his Arabic so that he could converse easily in the language. While on a visit to a Coptic monastery in Lower Egypt he was delighted to find that he could chatter away to the priests in Arabic. Though not a fluent linguist, he spoke some French, as well as a little German and Spanish. He was an avid reader and was always adding to his knowledge of military history; he claimed to have read every contemporary book on North and Central Africa.

For exercise and sport at Suakin there was plenty of rough shooting in the surrounding hills and bush. Hares, partridges, grouse, guinea fowl, quail and deer all fell to Hunter's gun. He was a fine shot and enjoyed the sport.

Hunter had a good constitution and despite the climate kept well. Hunter was an abstemious drinker. For instance, he restricted himself at Suakin to just two bottles of Pilsner beer, and two whisky and sodas a day. He thought this modest in view of how much a man sweated. There may have been a fatalistic element in Hunter's make-up. The sudden death at Suakin of an English sergeant prompted him to observe that 'My house is in order and so I don't care a snuff what happens'.[23] Some years later after the Dongola campaign he told Duncan that he could honestly say, 'I have never feared death'.

In April 1894 Hunter, now a Colonel, wrote to Wingate, who was to act as his *locum tenens* while he was on leave. He was full of friendly advice about accommodation, furnishings and servants. But he did not return to Suakin after his leave, having been transferred in July back to Wadi Halfa. He had been appointed Governor of the Nile Frontier, and Officer Commanding the Frontier Field Force.

NOTES

1. DHD 11. *Wellcome Institute for the History of Medicine WMS 6904 reports in 1886 and 1902.*
2. *Medical Directory 1887* 201.
3. SAD 110/11/1–89 hist IX Sud Bn.

4. Wellcome Institute for the History of Medicine, proceedings of Medical Board 18 Apr. 1887.
5. DHD 14.
6. Ibid. 13.
7. Ibid. 14.
8. Ibid. 15.
9. Wingate 397–400.
10. Milner 186.
11. NR AH report to DAAG Field Force 3 Jul. 1889.
12. SAD Staff Diary and Int Report DAAG Jul. 1889.
13. DHD 21.
14. NR Grenfell to Wad el Nejumi 16 Jul. 1889.
15. NR AH report to Senior Staff Officer GOC Nile Field Force 6 Aug. 1889.
16. DHD 21–22.
17. NR AH's Annual Confidential Report 1891. In his ACR for 1895, Kitchener, as 'Inspecting Officer', wrote that Hunter was a 'very able and careful administrator' and that he had given 'entire satisfaction'.
18. DHD 33.
19. Ibid. 35.
20. NR ms notes by AH covering period 14 to 21 Jul. 1892.
21. Sandes *The Royal Engineers in Egypt and the Sudan* 81.
22. SAD 257/1/299 AH–Wingate 4 Apr. 1892; 233/2/52 AH–Wingate 10 Apr. 1892; DHD 32.
23. DHD 41.

CHAPTER 5

Diversions

Back at Wadi Halfa Hunter found that the frontier was quiet, though there were occasional alarms and excursions as a result of minor Dervish activity, such as harrying villages and trying to cut the railway. Always eager to carry the fight to the enemy and ready, if so authorised, to invade and recapture Dongola Province, Hunter was disappointed to learn from his friend Wingate that there seemed in the winter of 1894 no chance of an offensive. With a lurid metaphor he complained that for years 'we haven't had a wet sword among us.'[1]

In March of the following year the routine was disturbed by an unusual event. The entry in Hunter's diary for 16 March 1895 reads: 'Slatin escaped from Omdurman 20 Feb, arrived at Assouan. I arrived by chance at Assouan the same day and a couple of hours after he did.'

This escape caused a great stir. Rudolf Slatin had been a prisoner of the Dervishes for eleven years before his dash for freedom by camel across hundreds of miles of desert. He had once served as a Lieutenant in a smart regiment of the Austrian army before joining Gordon in the Sudan and

37

becoming Governor of Darfur province in his twenties. In trying to keep his troops loyal to the Khedive in the Mahdi's rebellion, he turned Moslem. But he was forced to surrender and became a prisoner of the Dervishes, together with the small group of other Europeans who had survived the capture of Omdurman. In his book, *Fire and Sword in the Sudan* Slatin records the friendly welcome he received at Assouan from the officers of the Egyptian army, Hunter among them, who put their wardrobes at his disposal. Also Hunter gave him, he records, £10 – a large sum for those days – as a 'token of joy'.

With the absence of any serious fighting on the frontier, it was easier to obtain leave. British officers, most of them bachelors, sought their relaxation in cosmopolitan Cairo. A focal point was the famous Shepheard's Hotel, which was like an enormous club and where everyone gathered for gossip before dinner.

In his letters to Duncan, Hunter was never less than frank, whether he was writing of fighting or other matters. He confessed that, when in Cairo, he had been in the habit of 'hunting round town with other chaps' in search of fun, and 'always got the clap'. By 'clap' Hunter presumably meant gonorrhoea. For an ambitious soldier, anxious to keep himself as fit as possible, to consort with prostitutes in Cairo was obviously risky. But then Hunter was a red-blooded man, and he had become used to taking all kinds of risks. He might of course have contracted the more dangerous syphilis and this could have meant the end of his career. The treatment of venereal disease in those days was hazardous and of doubtful efficacy. Its side effects too could be unpleasant.

While at Suakin he told Duncan that he led 'a very steady life' and kept a 'very nice Abyssinian woman'. Abyssinian women he described as 'extremely pretty graceful creatures'.[2] Hunter was certainly not alone among British army officers in being attracted by young Abyssinian women. For instance, Andrew Haggard wrote about a visit he paid to a convent school at the French Mission near Senheit in northern Abyssinia. These Mission girls, he wrote, were of a light copper colour with straight hair and shapely figures. As teenagers, they were very attractive and all spoke French well. Coquettish, they ogled and laughed with the handsome Haggard, who took away the impression that all Abyssinian girls were dangerous flirts.[3]

Once, on a visit to Cairo from Suakin, Hunter had the temerity to take his Abyssinian mistress with him. His purpose, so he said, was to 'avoid unnecessary risks'. He described amusingly to Duncan what happened. They arrived at Suez docks whence their luggage had to be carted three miles to the station. They were both mounted on donkeys, but 'Madame's' baggage consisted of a lot of small bundles which kept falling off. They were late and missed the train.

'. . . so we went to the hotel of the place, full of P & O passengers who eyed me with curious glances . . . [Madame was] becomingly dressed in clouds of white muslin with bangles on arms and ankles. Her gold spangled slippers and her donkey, on which she sat straddle legged, with her embroidered drawers all showing, created quite a stir as we arrived . . . I could not help chuckling at the wonder and the looks of the elderly females'.[4]

In Cairo Madame stayed as a guest of a compatriot, who was a concubine too. The two women caused quite a commotion one day when, escorted by a manservant, they ventured to the polo ground where 'all the elite and fashion' were gathered. Hunter, not apparently a party to the excursion, had a good laugh over it all. He had a fine, dry sense of humour. As a contrast to his pretty Abyssinian mistress, Hunter was much enjoying the company of sophisticated women. He admitted that this had not always been so; once they had made him feel awkward. But not now. Older, more confident, a rising man in the army, he could hold his own with Cairo's leading ladies.

During one visit to Cairo, he had met an American couple. He found the wife 'a perfect angel, young and lovely'. They had apparently got on famously. Hunter had obviously monopolised her on the dance-floor to such an extent that her young husband, furiously jealous, had ordered her home as she was about to go into supper. There was a row between husband and Hunter, which Hunter apparently won because he took her into supper, and 'had a real good time. I was never sorry to leave Cairo before and just as well I did, for the spirit of the devil possessed me and I should only have made an ass of myself if my stay had been prolonged.'[5] This tale does not show Hunter off in a favourable light, but then he could be masterful and want his own way.

A woman whom Hunter admired, though perhaps at a distance, was Hylda Gorst. She was the daughter of Sir John Gorst, then a Minister in Lord Salisbury's government, and was staying with her brother, John Eldon Gorst, the adviser to the Ministry of Interior in Cairo. Hylda was in fact destined to marry Archie's brother, George. She was a very striking-looking woman and had also tremendous spirit and a sense of fun. Thus she once sat next to Cromer (as Evelyn Baring had become in 1892) at a great dinner, disguised and impersonating a visitor to Cairo. With the connivance of Lady Cromer, who could barely conceal her amusement, she proceeded to tease Cromer about all the things she knew he disliked. Cromer was at first taken in; afterwards he was not amused! Before Hylda married, Archie said of her, 'That is the girl I would marry if I could afford it. I think she is a ripper . . .'[6] After she was married, he would refer to his sister-in-law as 'very handsome'. But Hylda never cared much for Archie.

While Archie was busy making a name for himself in the Egyptian army his brother Duncan had met in Montana, and then married in 1893, a young American heiress, Abby Lippitt from Rhode Island. The Lippitts were a prominent family in Providence and owned cotton mills. Duncan had returned with his bride from the West, and settled down happily as a family man in Rhode Island. In March 1895 a school friend of Abby's, Daisy Low, with her sister Mabel Gordon, visited Egypt and went up the Nile. Daisy was married to an Englishman William Low, who moved in exalted social circles, but sadly the marriage was not a success. So Daisy, by way of recompense, used to travel with a woman companion to distant places. The two women, both attractive, reached Assouan, where they met Archie and George Hunter; the former's diary, probably significantly, noted the date as 25 March, but does not expand on it. The visitors must have been a popular pair because they were given a Gala evening by the Mess. As a compliment to the Americans, the band began to play 'Marching through Georgia'. Daisy and Mabel, loyal southerners both, with eyes blazing, rose to go and could only be persuaded to stay if the band played Dixie.[7] Their spirited behaviour struck a chord with Archie, who promptly took the sisters up to Wadi Halfa and then on to Sarras in the Sudan, the most southerly of the army's outposts. But early in the morning, even before breakfast, the visitors had to beat a hasty retreat to Wadi Halfa as information had come in that a party of Dervishes was trying to cut the railway.

Before Daisy and Mabel returned to Cairo and then went home, they had the thrill of going over the First Cataract of the Nile at low water by boat, part of an experiment apparently conducted by Hunter to find out how easily this could be done in view of the campaigning against the Dervishes, which clearly lay ahead. Both young Americans had begged to go in the boat and Hunter had yielded to their entreaties.[8] It looks as if Archie fell heavily for Daisy and in a biography written of her – she went on to found the American Girl Guides – the authors state that she received proposals of marriage from both Archie and George! Even if this story is not strictly true, it does tend to show again that the brothers were drawn to the same women. As a result of this visit Archie and Daisy began a friendship which lasted for many years. They corresponded regularly and sometimes saw each other. Most of Archie's letters were, sadly, destroyed by Daisy's brother Arthur, also her executor, because he considered they were not appropriate for posterity.[9]

Daisy and Mabel were by no means the only tourists coming up the Nile with whom Hunter hob-nobbed. He met at Wadi Halfa, and in Cairo as well, a surprising cross-section of people, many rich, and some titled and famous. He had no difficulty – he told Duncan – in getting on with those he described as blue-blooded. In a revealing comment he said 'in no way are they our superiors'. These visitors never overawed Hunter. When a French banker, a millionaire, was offensive Hunter reported him for disrespect! Almost tongue in cheek, he told Duncan that '. . . we are rather sticklers for our dignity when foreigners try and come it over us with a high hand'.[10]

In the autumn of 1895 the frontier was sufficiently quiet for Hunter to take his leave and to cross the Atlantic on a visit to Duncan and Abby and their young family in Rhode Island. This was the only time he ever visited the United States where he spent most of October. It was a joy for him, with his strong family ties, to see Duncan so well settled. A bonus was that he established a close rapport with his sister-in-law. After Duncan's tragic death at the age of 39 some years later, Archie took a close and very special interest in Abby and her four daughters, always the thoughtful and loving uncle.

It must have been a real surprise to the family to learn only just over two months after his visit to Duncan and Abby, that Archie had become engaged to a Scottish girl named Jemmie Douglas. It was all so sudden that it even astonished Archie himself. He had met Jemmie on board ship as she was going out to India via Egypt, presumably the same ship that carried Archie back to duty after his leave in Europe and in the United States. He had apparently quickly fallen for her and had, in the words of George writing to Duncan, 'carted her and her friends with whom she was travelling up to Halfa, instead of letting them go to India.'

It was a quick romance with, again, the masterful Colonel being as decisive in love as he was in battle. He described his fiancée as not beautiful but 'as good-looking as the majority of her neighbours'. She was also, he said, bonny and sweet [and] sensible'. He could not resist adding that he was not good enough for her. George had heard that she was not particularly clever and was inclined to be dull to outsiders. She had some money of her own. The opinion in the army was, so George said, that she was not good enough for Archie, as if anyone could be! Certainly she did not sound fun like, say, Hylda Gorst or Daisy Low. Later, Archie wrote to Duncan about his engagement, admitting he had 'rushed into this head-long'. Apparently he had had quite a lot on his mind at the time, including some disappointment at not going on the Ashanti expedition, and '. . . something else that I have got to forget and put behind me for the rest of my days'. This had made him 'first think seriously about Miss Douglas'.[11] It is hard to resist the conclusion that he was making an oblique reference to Daisy Low. If this was so, he was then in a sense on the rebound in getting engaged to Jemmie. Another factor that may have recommended the idea to him was the happy domestic state in which he had found Duncan. At this time marriage for officers in the Egyptian army was forbidden by the Sirdar, Herbert Kitchener; he believed, even though he had been engaged himself, that soldiers, at least on active service, had no time for wives. Hunter held somewhat similar views himself, and his engagement – was it cleared by Kitchener or was Hunter too senior for this? – consequently was to cause him much anguish in the coming months.

The Egyptian government, at the beginning of 1896, showed itself keen to use the services of the Hunter brothers in a civilian capacity. First, Archie was offered the post of Inspector-General of the Egyptian Coastguard Service at £1,000 a year. This Service was principally concerned with the prevention of smuggling, the maintenance of public security in the desert regions and the interception of Moslem pilgrims landing illegally on the coastline. He was interested in this proposition, perhaps because of his engagement, but he insisted on having £1,500, a house, and his brother, George, as his deputy.[12] In the bargaining that followed he was told he could not choose his deputy, and so in the end he lost interest in the post. Then George, planning to marry Hylda Gorst and attracted by the idea of a settled civilian life, was offered and accepted the job of Deputy Inspector-General of Coastguards.

NOTES

1. SAD 258/1 383 Wingate–AH 14 Dec. 1894; DHD 51.
2. DHD 40.
3. Haggard 238.
4. DHD loc. cit.
5. Ibid. 39.
6. Ibid. 30.
7. Schultz and Lawrence *Lady from Savannah* 208–9.
8. Ibid.
9. DHD 44.
10. Ibid. 28–9.
11. Ibid. 52.
12. Ibid. 48.

CHAPTER 6

The Dongola Campaign

The 1896 season in Cairo was in full swing. Every hotel was crowded with visitors, who had come to Egypt to see the sights, go up the Nile, gamble, enjoy the café society and sample the other attractions offered by this city, now so popular with West Europeans. Suddenly a rumour began to circulate that the Sirdar had received orders from the British government to advance up the Nile. It was true. Late in the evening on 12 March,

Kitchener had been handed a telegram, giving him instructions to advance to Dongola. For once the mask slipped and he had, in ecstasy and celebration, danced in his pyjamas a wild fandango round his hall.[1] Cairo became electric with excitement and military activity. Preparations for war began in earnest and very soon the workshops of the army began frenziedly to produce extra saddles, sword-belts, water-bottles and all the other vital pieces of equipment that would be needed for a desert campaign. On the frontier there was equal glee at the news. Hunter, an ardent supporter of the forward policy, had received the news by 14 March and wrote to Duncan:

'Hooray. We are going to advance. I believe I am to command the advance guard – Am pleased as Punch – It can make a man or mouse of me – Never was so pleased in my life. The men are all in grand fighting trim.'[2]

Hunter was ordered to take three battalions and seize the village of Akasha (see Map B, p. 20), 70 miles south of Wadi Halfa. He set out at dawn on 20 March through wild rocky country close to the Nile and two days later, without meeting any resistance from the Dervishes, he entered Akasha. He was eight days ahead of the date fixed for taking this first objective. So far so good.

The change of British policy which took even Cromer by surprise had come about through an Italian disaster. The Italians had on 1 March 1896 been severely defeated by the Abyssinians at Adowa, when some 7,000 Italian and Eritrean troops were killed. Cromer had always accepted that the Sudan would have to be reconquered at some time, but had placed two conditions on mounting an expedition. The first was that the new Egyptian army had to be efficient, and the second was that the Egyptian government had to be solvent and to have funds available. Both conditions, it could be said, had now been met. The army's performance was constantly improving and British officials had transformed the state of Egypt's finances.

The Italians, though, changed the outlook. Anxious to obtain colonies in Africa, they had, since Egypt's evacuation of Massawa in 1885, been busy in establishing themselves in Eritrea. In 1894 they had pushed forward and taken Kassala, then lightly defended by the Dervishes. But King Menelik II of Abyssinia was soon challenging Italian moves on his borders. The Italians decided to risk a confrontation and, as a consequence, suffered their disastrous defeat at Adowa, after which came news that the Dervishes under Osman Digna were concentrating behind Kassala. This brought matters to a head. The Italian ambassador in London urged the British government to make a diversion in the Sudan to relieve the pressure on the Italians at Kassala. Salisbury, returned to power in 1895 with a large majority, was decisive, and responded at once to his ally. In addition, he was, of course, anxious to prevent the Dervishes from achieving success. Accordingly, orders were given to retake Dongola province but to go no further, and Kitchener was named to lead the expedition.

As preparations for the campaign began, there was a moment of unease when Salisbury heard that the Sirdar was purchasing 5,000 camels. Visions were momentarily conjured up by Ministers of Kitchener meditating an invasion into the wilderness at the head of a string of camels! Cromer was able to reassure the Prime Minister that only 2,000 camels had been purchased.[3] To meet the cost of the expedition the British government agreed to provide a loan of £800,000 at $2\frac{3}{4}\%$ interest. In the event the campaign cost £E715,000. This bore testimony, Cromer thought, to Kitchener's well-known thrift.

This is a good moment to look at Khalifa Abdullahi, the Mahdist leader, and at the forces opposing each other. The Kahlifa was ignorant yet shrewd. He was usually depicted in his time as a cruel and bloody tyrant, who ruthlessly eliminated his opponents. Modern writers have tended to be more sympathetic and to emphasise his nationalism without denying he was a military dictator. For his troops the Khalifa had at his disposal a combination of regulars and auxiliaries. The regulars were composed of *jehadiya* and *mulazimin*. The *jehadiya* were riflemen and were armed mainly with the outdated Remingtons. The *mulazimin* were household troops of the Khalifa. The auxiliaries, either volunteers or pressed into service when required, were called *ansars* (helpers) and were armed only with swords and spears, with which they were expert. The fighting unit was known as the *rub* and might vary from hundreds to thousands, according to the status of the Emir or leader. To each *rub* was attached cavalry, usually Baggara tribesmen. The amount of artillery possessed by the Dervishes was negligible. Numbers of troops were difficult to calculate. In 1895 Slatin had estimated that the garrison of Omdurman amounted to a little over 53,000 men, including 32,300 *ansars*. Army training was thorough but limited. There was a shortage of ammunition and, therefore, a lack of practice; this resulted in low standards of marksmanship. Reliance was placed on officers' own powers of leadership and tactical sense. There were no NCOs as such.[4] One quality the Dervishes did not lack was courage. They fought with commitment and fearlessness. Twice they had, albeit momentarily, broken a British square; at Tamai near Suakin early in 1884 and at Abu Klea the following year. Their fighting, however, was instinctive and not calculated. Although he was not a military man, the Khalifa commanded his army, but he left the fighting, almost to the end, to his Emirs. Apart perhaps from Osman Digna and possibly Nejumi in his earlier days, none of them seemed in any way gifted as a general.

The Egyptian army at this time was composed of about 15,000 officers and men. This strength included 16 battalions of infantry, 8 squadrons of cavalry, 18 field guns in 4 batteries and 8 camel corps companies. In its 13 years of existence the new army had achieved some notable successes against the Dervishes, for instance, at Argin and Toski, though these admittedly had been essentially defensive actions. Many units, too, had been hardened by years on the frontier, involving much skirmishing with the enemy. Nevertheless, there were still some who doubted, like Wolseley, as to just how reliable – well led though it was – the new army would turn out to be in offensive operations. It had, therefore, something to prove.

Kitchener's first important objective was Firket, where the enemy was concentrating, 16 miles south of Akasha. All through April and May, men and supplies came up the Nile from Wadi Halfa to Sarras by the railway, which had been repaired after being damaged by the Dervishes. These lines of communication were vulnerable and there was the odd clash between patrols, though no attempt was made by the enemy to disrupt them.

Hunter was placed in command of the Egyptian division with its three brigades of infantry each in turn containing three battalions. In preparing for a military operation Hunter left as little to chance as possible. Throughout the forthcoming campaign in the Sudan he was tireless in his efforts personally to reconnoitre the enemy's position before battle, and consistently drew the correct conclusions from what he saw. On 1 June 1896, leaving Akasha at 2 a.m., Hunter and a small hand-picked party, all mounted, consisting of six British officers, one Egyptian cavalry officer and two orderlies, made a daring reconnaissance of the enemy position at Firket. At dawn they climbed a hill near the Dervish camp. Hunter wrote in his diary: 'we all in turn had a good look; I saw the Dervishes moving about, water[ing] their horses . . .' They returned to Akasha undetected, and Hunter drew up his plan of attack based on what he had seen on that reconnaissance.

In a long letter written in May to Abby, his American sister-in-law, Hunter explained the military position in outline. He told her that, for the forthcoming battle, he had worked out all the details for Kitchener. Without adopting in any way a bragging tone, he ventured that he hoped 'to be a General Officer out of this', would almost certainly become Governor of Dongola province, and 'if spared', might some day be a Governor of the Sudan.[5] He mentioned, *en passant*, the huge distances he had been riding each day and that he had visited all the posts and seen 'practically every man and animal' in the army. He was very fit but, at 39, getting 'distinctly grey'. He asked her to regard everything he wrote as 'quite Private and Confidential'.

The village of Firket was a confusion of mud houses nearly a mile long on the eastern bank of the Nile. A little over a mile to the north was the prominent hill known as Jebel Firket, while just to the east of the village

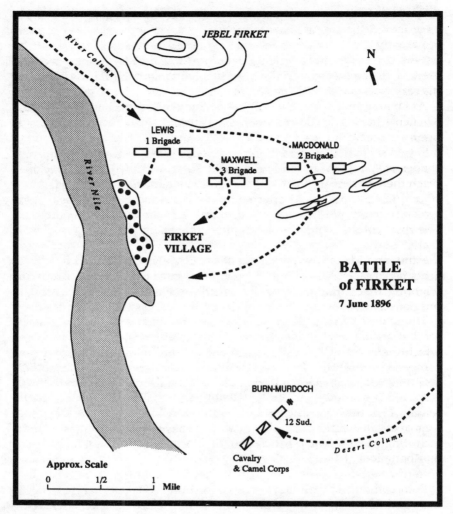

Map E

stood some low rocky hills. The Dervish forces numbered some 3,000 men consisting of *jehadiya*, Baggara cavalry and Jaalin tribesmen. They had just experienced a change of command. The Emir Hammuda had been considered by Wad Bishara, the Dervish Governor of Dongola, as slack and inept at hindering the advance of the Egyptian army. He had, therefore, just been replaced by a veteran of the frontier, Osman Azrak, a fanatical and loyal follower of the Khalifa. From captured documents and prisoners it was learned after the battle that the Dervishes were proposing

46

to adopt a much more aggressive posture in opposing the army's advance, once they realised that its real objective was Dongola. Also Bishara had apparently at one time suggested to Hammuda somewhat fancifully that he, the Governor, and Hunter should undergo a combat of arms in full view of both armies to decide the issue. Hunter, when this idea came to his ears, was half attracted by it.[6]

As far as numbers went the forces opposing each other were ill-matched, Kitchener having 10,000 men under his command. The battle plan worked out by Hunter and fully accepted by Kitchener was to divide the army into two separate columns, the 'river' column and the 'desert' column – shades of Wolseley in the Gordon Relief expedition! Both columns would reach their respective positions by night marches. The former was to take station to the north of the village, ready to assault it. The latter was to sweep round in a great arc and outflank the Mahdist forces in their rear. The river column consisted of Hunter's three brigades with Major D. F. 'Taffy' Lewis in command of the 1st brigade, Major Hector MacDonald the 2nd, and Major John Maxwell the 3rd. The last two named were both Scotsmen. MacDonald, three years Hunter's senior and already known as 'Fighting Mac', had a great reputation as a warrior, having been commissioned in the field from the ranks in the Afghan Wars.

The stiffest task had purposely been given by Hunter to Lewis' men, for they would have to make a frontal attack on the houses in the village, which the enemy were expected to defend stoutly. The 1st brigade was composed entirely of Egyptian battalions and this assault would certainly test their resolve. There was, Hunter acknowledged, some risk in this plan, but it needed to be taken. The desert column, 2,300 strong under Major J. F. Burn-Murdoch, were all mounted and consisted of seven squadrons of cavalry, eight camel corps companies and accompanying artillery, including Maxim machine-guns of the North Staffords. There was also one battalion of Sudanese infantry, the 12th, riding camels. Kitchener accompanied the river column.

Both columns started from Akasha on the afternoon of 6 June. Every man had 90 rounds of ammunition and carried two days' rations. The river column was personally led up to the start line by Hunter, who knew the way. The course of the river was followed south to a point one mile north of Firket. The desert column went first south-east away from the river, then due south, and finally west so that they were in a position to cut off the enemy's retreat. Both columns successfully carried out their night marches and were on the startline at 4.30 a.m. as planned. A neighing horse had caused Hunter, half-crouching in the dark under the shoulder of Jebel Firket, to mutter 'that's given the show away', but luckily all was well. Then a beating drum could be heard in the distance to the south. Was it a call to arms? No, it was only a call to morning prayer. Surprise, which had been demanded, had been achieved.

The attack by the infantry brigades went in with spirit. Lewis on the right headed for the village, while on the left MacDonald swept up through the low hills and then, rolling up the Dervish outposts, swung west for the river. Thus was created a gap between these two brigades and through it drove Maxwell with the 3rd brigade. Resistance for a time was fierce. A charge by the Baggara horse was repulsed. Eventually the Dervishes fell back on the village still fighting resolutely. Many defended the houses, often to the last man. But by 7 a.m. it was all over. Some survivors crossed the river and some fled southwards.

The desert column had been partially unsighted by the lie of the land and left unwatched a sandy track by the river.[7] This was used by Osman Azrak and some hundreds of Dervishes to make good their escape. The cavalry pursued the retreating forces, eventually as far as Suarda. The enemy left behind them 800 dead, 500 wounded and 600 prisoners. The Egyptian army's losses were light, 20 men killed and 83 wounded, including one British officer. Hunter, like some medieval knight, marked his position on the battlefield by having behind him a mounted standard-bearer carrying a red flag with a swallow-tail end. It helped staff officers carrying orders to and fro to find him. It helped the Dervishes too. They put three bullets into his flag and a horse next to him was killed.[8]

The battle of Firket proved to be decisive in the Dongola campaign. It marked a triumph for the Egyptian army, whose all-round superiority had been conclusive. Moreover, the conduct of the fellahin troops had been admirable. The approach marches and ensuing tactics had been well thought out, and the overall plan executed with dash and determination. The only real criticism was that the desert column had not properly cut off the retreat. Hunter wrote to his brother George about Firket and the army's performance, which he generally applauded. But the map produced by the Intelligence people was 'viciously misleading' and he paid no attention to it, preferring to rely on what he had seen on his reconnaissance.[9] The shooting by the army, the 3rd Egyptians apart, was bad. Also he wished that he had sent Lewis with the desert column.[10] Was this a veiled reference to what he perceived to be a failure of the 12th Sudanese, and the cavalry, to prevent the escape of Osman Azrak and other Dervishes with him? Certainly he had made the position clear to Kitchener when briefing him before the battle on 1 June, for he had told the Sirdar: 'You have them in the palm of your hand and if you send the mounted corps . . . to cut them off from Suarda not one man should escape'.[11] Yet on the other hand Kitchener, according to his biographer Philip Magnus, gave orders to the cavalry to pursue but not to intercept, as if he almost wished to leave an avenue of escape open for the enemy.

Some weeks after Firket, Hunter received a letter from his old friend, Frederick Maurice, now a General and Commandant at Woolwich, congratulating him heartily on the victory. Maurice had read between the lines in the reports coming in, and had concluded, correctly, that Hunter had had a major role in planning this success. Hunter wrote fully about the battle to him and to General Sir Frederick Stephenson, formerly the commander in Egypt. He told them that the Egyptian, with his splendid physique, was no longer to be despised as a fighting man, though he depended heavily on the leadership given by his British officers; under Egyptian officers he was infinitely less effective. The Sudanese, he believed, were now a reliable and disciplined force. Relations between British officers and their soldiers had been transformed over the years, because the British all spoke Arabic and could therefore communicate properly on all matters with their men.

Hunter told Maurice that he had 'written quite fearlessly to you what I think'. But he hated the idea of publicity and had never written a word for publication. He had a 'holy terror', as he described it, 'of self advertisement or any practice that might be reckoned to approach it', and asked Maurice to keep him out of print.[12]

Kitchener could now have pushed on to Dongola. But he was a cautious man, and with the example of the failure of the Gordon Relief Expedition to manage properly its transport and supply problems he wished to avoid all logistical errors. He, therefore, prepared to continue extending the railway south and to await the arrival of the gunboats, with which he hoped to smash the Dervish forts further up the Nile. Hunter, with his dash, was more inclined to go on to Dongola, where he was relishing a big fight, and not to worry overmuch at this stage about supplies, believing he could rely on dates and camel-meat to feed the troops.[13]

The gunboat fleet was formidable, being composed of four 90-foot vessels which had been in service some time and three new 140-foot vessels. The latter were 24 feet in breadth yet drew only 39 inches of water. Each gunboat was armed with five or six artillery pieces which included 12-pounders, 4-inch howitzers and Maxims. Their decks were protected by steel plates.

But sickness intervened. The camp site chosen by Kitchener at Firket was not to Hunter's liking. He called it a 'fetid filthy place', close to where the Dervish dead were buried and 'among the stinking carcasses' of dead animals. Charitably he put this mistake down to Kitchener's well-known poor eyesight. The site was shifted to a place near Kosheh earmarked previously, probably by Hunter, as the best spot. In the meantime, dysentery had broken out. Worse was to follow, for cholera, sweeping up the Nile, overtook the army. The epidemic accounted for some 280 soldiers in little over a month, more men than were killed in the whole long campaign to Omdurman. Hunter, no stranger to tropical disease, had not yet witnessed cholera. He described this strain as 'very violent and quick, no pain, intense thirst, collapse in three hours and death in under twelve'. He did not, though, let this perturb him. One of his officers, Major Martyr,

49

whom he described as a bit of a wag, calculated the risks for a British officer of sudden death in the Sudan as follows. The odds of being killed by a Dervish were about 1000 to 1, though it was only 100 to 1 against being hit by an enemy bullet. On the other hand, death from cholera, drink or the sun was each reckoned to be about 5 to 1![14]

Kitchener now had to consider how he was going to move his river craft, particularly his seven shallow-draft gunboats, up the Nile and over the Second Cataract (the Dal cataract would not be a problem). He decided simply to give the whole task to his trusty subordinate. Hunter regarded the job as something of a 'novelty', as he drily described it, and rose at once to its challenge. Although big boats had been dragged up the cataract before, no record existed on how this had been accomplished. Hunter remedied this for the future and wrote regular reports to the Chief of Staff, Rundle, about the work in hand and its progress.[15]

The main problems concerned the physical features of the Nile at the cataract and the size of the vessels to be dragged up it. The Second Cataract, just above Wadi Halfa, was about nine miles long with a total ascent of some 60 feet. The Nile over this distance flowed down, in the words of Winston Churchill, 'a rugged stairway formed by successive ledges of black granite'. The currents and swirling eddies along this length of rapids were strong and treacherous, especially when the river went through gorges. The most formidable place was Big Bab where the river narrowed to a mere 15 yards. The force of the water at this point was terrific. The work of passing large vessels up the cataract could only be done at high Nile, which normally occurred in July. As ill luck would have it, in 1896 this was late in coming, and Hunter and his special team of officers had to wait patiently until early August before starting their work, which then took three weeks. While marking time, Hunter played whist with Lieutenant Lord Athlumney, his staff officer, and the two naval officers allocated to help him, Captain Robertson and Lieutenant David Beatty, the latter to achieve fame in World War I as Commander-in-Chief of the Grand Fleet. But, above all, he wrote letters to friends and relatives. In one of them he confided to Duncan and Abby his worries about his engagement to Jemmie, rehearsing his old argument that a soldier had no right to marry. In the circumstances in which he found himself, he was beginning to regret his engagement.

A way was found to drag the gunboats up the cataract, using huge teams of men, combined with some technology. The trick was this. First, the gunboat was lightened by all possible means, such as dismounting its guns. Next, hawsers were attached to the sides and the bow. Those on the side were to steady the vessel as far as possible in midstream. The bow hawser was, of course, the instrument, by which the boat was heaved up over the rapids. Teams of men then pulled on the hawsers. Those on each side would consist of some 200 men, but the hawser in the bow would demand as many as 1,000 men, who would stand in a convenient flat place in the desert pulling, via steel blocks and tackle fixed on the banks, at right angles to the river. The whole exercise was put in overall charge of a British officer, who gave his commands by means of a bugler, the only way it was possible to make the teams hear the instructions against the roar of the water. The strain on the hands of those pulling on the wires and ropes was intense, and the work, therefore, had to be done in bursts. The men used were mainly Egyptian army troops but at one stage Hunter called for help from the North Staffords and, accordingly, 400 men reported for duty, hardly likely to be enthusiastic about what they were being ordered to do. After a toiling day in the sweltering heat, Hunter gave the men, out of his own pocket, a 'fiver' with which to buy beer. A welcome and thoughtful gesture. The vast teams of men striving ant-like at their work call to mind scenes from Pharaonic times, when the great monuments of Egypt were being constructed.

In the space of just over three weeks all seven gunboats were pulled up the Second Cataract and reached Kosheh, where there was clear water until the Third Cataract some way below Dongola. Some were damaged on the rocks but were quickly patched up by shipwrights. During this time some 70 gyassas (large sailing-boats) had also been safely passed up to Kosheh, though three others had been lost at Big Bab. The nuggars (barges), however, proved to be unstable in the water and the attempt to bring them up-river had to be eventually abandoned. There was risk involved in the work, both for those in the vessels and for those perilously directing operations, while standing astride the slippery rocks on the banks of the river. Once Hunter and Beatty were on a barge which got into difficulties and nearly capsized. Hunter was relieved to get the crew off safely. Inevitably there were serious accidents and three soldiers lost their lives. When this happened, Hunter, a stickler for proper procedures, at once ordered a board of inquiry.

There were times when Hunter fell behind with the tight timetable set for getting the gunboats to Kosheh. The next phase of Kitchener's advance largely depended on the success of the task at the cataract. Twice Hunter urged Kitchener to come and view the problems facing those at work on it. Both times he declined, saying he was too busy, and Hunter had to be content with just one meeting at Wadi Halfa. At the conclusion of the task set him, Hunter paid handsome tribute to all his cheerful helpers. In particular, he singled out the two naval officers. Without their expertise he considered the task would never have been so speedily accomplished. He was evidently proud of his achievement at the Second Cataract and, reminiscing as an old man about the Sudan campaign, he said that he regretted that Kitchener had never once thanked him for it.

As soon as the gunboats had reached Kosheh, Kitchener gave orders for his troops to march south, first to Absarat and then on to Kerma, which the Dervishes were holding. The river route was 127 miles. This distance could be reduced by some 40 miles by heading direct for Absarat across the desert, thereby cutting out Suarda, and also by avoiding the angle of the Nile from Fareeg to Kerma. MacDonald's 2nd brigade reached Absarat from Kosheh by the desert route on 23 August, and Lewis's 1st brigade, with Hunter accompanying it, was ordered on 26 August to the same destination by the same route. The distance was about 42 miles, and watering-places had been organised along the way.

The march began on 27 August and at once ran into tempestuous and unseasonal weather, which swept over the Nubian desert. The ordeal suffered by the brigade came to be dubbed by journalists the 'death march'. Hunter described the events, which followed in a report to the Chief of Staff dated 28 August.[16] No sooner had the column left Kosheh at 4.45 p.m., than it was enveloped in a violent and prolonged dust-storm, which caused great thirst. Happily the column found water during the first ten miles from mountain streams. A second dust-storm was met at 7 p.m. The troops struggled manfully on. Halts were called at 9 p.m. and then again at 20 minutes past midnight after 'we had been steadily advancing into a dense mass of dust cloud of immense extent moving towards us . . . nothing could be seen for dust . . . the roar of the wind made speech useless . . .'

By now many men had fallen out. Hunter gave orders that 50 camels should leave their loads so as to be able to carry those men in a state of collapse. Half the distance had now been covered and the march was resumed when the weather had cleared at 2.20 a.m. But the haze was still great and 'it was impossible to tell when men fell in their tracks. They were reeling like drunk men and falling helpless where they lay. The men were so weary, sleepy and thirsty that any further appeal to discipline was useless and we became a long straggling mass of weak humanity'.

The second watering place was reached at 6.15 a.m., and Hunter then had to decide whether to wait there all day, and then continue in the evening, or to water and then push on for their destination some 10 miles away. He decided on the latter course, and the head of the column reached Absarat at 1 p.m., the tail coming in $3\frac{1}{2}$ hours later. Hunter commented that the distress of the men was 'painful' and their 'collapse' complete, though help had arrived from Absarat in the shape of water and transport, MacDonald having correctly anticipated the column would be in distress. In his report Hunter tried to analyse what had gone wrong, after reminding Rundle that 'I was opposed *ab initio* on military grounds to this march'. He attributed the final break-down to the sultry, parching weather; the varied quality of the going; the poor condition of the men after an absence of training since Firket, and a period of sickness; the men, with 90 rounds of ammunition, being overladen; the lack of sufficient water on the way and finally a miscalculation of the distance which proved to be greater than estimated. He reported there were eight deaths on the march. 202 men had been unable to reach their destination unaided. With some feeling, he added, 'I have heard today from men at the point of death words attaching the blame of their agonies to me, which I had to pass by in silence'. Nowhere did he blame the men for what happened and none of them, he pointed out, had thrown away their arms or ammunition.

The real blame for this catastrophe lay, in Hunter's view, with Kitchener. On 31 August he wrote a personal letter to the Sirdar. Rarely can a subordinate officer have written so critically and frankly to his superior, but then Hunter was no ordinary subordinate. Hunter told Kitchener that he overheard during the march: '. . . muttered curses levelled against me for taking the men, heavily laden and ill-supplied with transport, into such a hell trap, and that out of consideration for you I did not report that the responsibility and blame lay with you'.[17] He would not question, he said, the Sirdar's orders but, on the other hand, he saw it as his duty to lay before the Sirdar matters concerning the well-being of the forces. He failed to see any advantage, he went on, to save one day's march of going by the desert route instead of by the river one, emphasising there was an 'absence of any urgent reason for haste'.[18] Further he, Kitchener, had provoked criticism 'by a rigid adherence to your own views'. He then, somewhat astonishingly, read Kitchener a lecture on the duties of a leader, who was required to provide for a soldier's wants and to guard against unnecessary danger and pain, these considerations 'not being beneath a man like Napoleon'. If men were to be expected to sacrifice themselves, when necessary, then their commander should know that they are not being exposed to needless risks and losses.

Finally he told Kitchener that the place chosen for a camp at Absarat was a bad one, for there was no shade, nothing to make shade with, the hills were stony, there was no soil to dig latrines in, no room to house men and animals and no place for drill! He proposed a move to nearby Delgo, which would be suitable. The troops duly moved to Delgo a few days later.

It is not known how Kitchener reacted to Hunter's outburst. It must have come at a patently bad moment, for he was busy having to deal with the damage caused by the torrential storms which had washed away 14 miles of newly-laid railway track. Hunter, always fearless, was sometimes rash in speaking out, a trait which would lead him into trouble later in his career. His exasperation with Kitchener is also forcefully illustrated by a letter he wrote to George at the time, when sending best wishes for his brother's forthcoming marriage to Hylda. After beginning by saying he was lucky that only 8 men died on the march he went on: '. . . I have plumbed to the bottom of Kitchener now – he is inhuman, heartless, with eccentric and freakish bursts of generosity specially when he is defeated:

53

he is a vain egotistical and self-confident mass of pride and ambition, expecting and usurping all and giving nothing: he is a mixture of the fox, Jew and snake and like all bullies is a dove when tackled.'[19]

A month later in a critical mood Hunter was writing to Kitchener about ensuring that the railway was not washed away again and decent wages being paid to railway staff; the design of steamers; the need to expand camel transport and provide medicines for the animals; the shortage of officers and clerks; and the urgent need to improve the ration scale, especially meat, for the troops. He pointed out that they were having to pay for extra food themselves. Also they had no tents. Finally he said there should be an increase in pay for those serving south of Wadi Halfa.

Many years later Lord Edward Cecil, son of Lord Salisbury and one of Kitchener's ADCs in the Sudan, wrote that the British officers of the Egyptian army were not a united body during the reconquest and that Kitchener needed to keep a firm hand to retain discipline, outspoken criticism of him being not uncommon. Interestingly, he also says that, among them, there was a 'frontier party, by far the largest, which believed in Hunter and did not like Kitchener' whose severity and economical ways were not popular.[20] This view seems to suggest that Hunter and Kitchener were virtually rivals. We shall consider the relationship between Kitchener and Hunter in more detail at the end of the Sudan campaign.

Just as Hunter had been busy criticising Kitchener both to his face and to George Hunter, so he in turn was being observed and criticised by Lord Edward Cecil whose diary on the Dongola expedition is revealing. He was inclined to find fault with his fellow officers. For instance, he thought Hunter 'pig-headed' in continuing the infamous march and believed he could have come back from the first watering place, or have waited for aid from MacDonald. Also, in his diary, he states that Hunter had written despatches after the march accusing Rundle and Kitchener of murder.[21]

Lord Edward had mixed views about Hunter, at one moment enjoying his congenial company and his yarns, and at another disliking strongly his outspoken opinions. Apparently Hunter had openly said that all enemy prisoners taken at Firket should have been shot and that it also deeply grieved him that 'none of us', that is the British officers, had been killed during the battle.[22] If Lord Edward correctly reported him it is difficult to know what Hunter meant. The available evidence does not show him to have been ill-disposed towards prisoners; indeed he often saw them as potential recruits for the Egyptian army. Nor did he wish to see unnecessary casualties taken on his own side. It is of course possible that an imp had sat on his shoulder and he had made these outrageous remarks to shock Lord Edward. At any rate, Hunter's behaviour led Lord Edward to describe him as 'a real live Cromwellian, brutal, cruel, licentious, religious, brave, able, blunt, cunning, all genuine too ...'.[23] Hunter may have appeared at times brutal; especially in his earlier days in the Sudan, he relished the fighting in which no quarter was asked for or given by either side. At the same time his tough, often uncompromising, approach to war may have been mistaken for brutality. He was certainly not cruel or licentious. In a letter to Duncan, written in only March 1896, he said: 'I have no religion'. In later years he described himself as Presbyterian, but never during his life did he show himself to be religious. Nor is 'cunning' the right adjective to use of Hunter. This word conveys a certain deviousness. Hunter, on the contrary, was a straightforward man. He was astute certainly, but never cunning.

The advance on Dongola had been delayed by the August storms. Kitchener had now amassed nearly 15,000 men for his final push, a larger force than any British general had had under his command since the Crimean War. Hunter had a fourth brigade added to his division, so that 15 out of the 19 Egyptian army infantry battalions were under his command. Of the British officers in the force, the only two who had been to Dongola before were Kitchener and Hunter in the 1884/85 Gordon Relief Expedition. The Dervish commander, Wad Bishara, had asked the Khalifa for reinforcements but only obtained a small number. He had some 5,600 men with him to defend Dongola so he was outnumbered by nearly three to one. When the Egyptian army reached Kerma on the east bank on 19 September, they found the place had been evacuated. Wad Bishara had cleverly withdrawn his forces in one night across the river to Hafir, where a strong defensive position had been established. Kitchener's artillery and gunboats were now brought into play and a bombardment of enemy positions began with the infantry in the role of spectators. The Dervishes took quite severe casualties losing some 200 men. Both Wad Bishara and Azrak were wounded. On the evening of 19 September, in order to find out what the Dervishes were up to, Hunter set out in a small boat to reconnoitre the opposite bank of the river. Before dawn he learnt that the Dervishes had evacuated their positions,[24] afraid of being cut off now that the gunboats were steaming upstream to Dongola. So the troops were ordered to be ferried across the Nile and Hafir was reoccupied peacefully. Although Hafir, for the Egyptian army, was a bloodless affair, nonetheless it counted as a battle and a special clasp for it was struck. The story is told that Rundle impatiently sent a message to Hunter demanding information about the progress of the crossing. Hunter replied laconically: 'See Hymn 221 [A&M] verse 3'. This reads: '. . . Part of the host have crossed the flood/And part are crossing now'.[25]

Once across the Nile the infantry division advanced south down the west bank, and early on 23 September was ready to attack Dongola. They were in for a disappointment. The campaign ended in anti-climax. Though a fortified town, Dongola was empty, except for 400 *jehadiya* who quickly surrendered to Hunter's Sudanese battalions. There was no fight. Bishara had wished to launch a suicidal attack but had been placed under arrest by his Emirs. The remnants of his army had then retreated across the Bayuda desert to Metemma, suffering hardship on the way. Further up the Nile, both Korti and Merowe fell to Kitchener's men. The campaign was at an end. Dongola province had been reconquered and at comparatively little cost in lives. In his report to the Chief of Staff on the work of the infantry division, Hunter as was his wont praised his officers and men. He wrote:

> 'discipline, morale and spirit had been excellent. For six months they had withstood the tests of hard and constant work ... of difficult marches over bad country, of great heat and severe storms, of a virulent attack of cholera. They had shown throughout a good and soldier-like spirit, a marvellous power of endurance and an undaunted determination from the outset to succeed in the work of the expedition.'[26]

NOTES

1. Royle *The Kitchener Enigma* 105.
2. DHD 53.
3. Magnus *Kitchener: Portrait of an Imperialist* 91.
4. Keown-Boyd 96.
5. DHD 63.
6. NR AH–family 10 Jul. 1896.
7. Churchill *The River War* 139–40.
8. DHD 81.
9. NR AH–unknown addressee 21 Jul. 1896.
10. DHD 65.
11. WO 175/428 note by AH on battle of Firket dated 29/4/1919. Hunter wrote this note to help Sir George Arthur who was writing his biography of Kitchener.
12. DHD 69.
13. Ibid. 89.
14. Ibid. 90.
15. NR reports and letters by AH to Kitchener, to the Chief of Staff, Col. Rundle, and to Major Martyr, the AAG, covering the period 29 Jul. 1896 to 24 Aug. 1896.
16. NR AH–COS 28 Aug. 1896.
17. NR AH–Kitchener 31 Aug. 1896.
18. Ibid.
19. NR AH–George Hunter 31 Aug. 1896.
20. Lord Edward Cecil *Leisure of an Egyptian Official* 181.
21. Lord Edward Cecil's Diary, p. 242.
22. Ibid. 185.
23. Ibid. 246.
24. DHD 97.
25. Sandes 170.
26. NR AH–Rundle 26 Sep. 1896.

CHAPTER 7

Lightning Advance

For their parts in the Dongola expedition, Hunter and Rundle were both promoted to Major-General. Hunter was also appointed Governor of Dongola province. Promotion came just two months after his 40th birthday. Not even Wolseley, Roberts of Kandahar fame, who became C-in-C in 1901, or indeed Kitchener, had attained that rank so young. Indeed he was said to be the youngest Major-General since Wellington. In a letter to John Troyte Acland, his old friend from Gibraltar days, he expressed surprise at his promotion, and thought at first it was a joke. In his view they had made two Major-Generals too many! 'I should have liked the CB and been allowed to go on in the even tenor of my ways instead of playing leapfrog . . .' To Duncan, in the same vein, he confided that there were drawbacks to being promoted over the heads of those more senior to him, for this would make him enemies. He did not see himself, he added with no hint of false modesty, as having conspicuous ability, though he did admit to his brother that he was a 'a favourite with soldiers . . . men have been willing to accept me as a leader on trying occasions.'[1]

With Dongola safely in his hands Kitchener hurried back to Cairo to ask Cromer to authorise a continued advance. Cromer had visualised a halt at Dongola for two or three years, but told Kitchener it was all a matter of finance. He would recommend an advance if the British government could provide £500,000. So Kitchener at once went to London to lobby for funds. He was successful and the Government authorised the money.

Kitchener now had to decide on his strategy for defeating the Khalifa. Two interrelated factors, critical to his success, had to be considered: what route to take to reach Khartoum and how to transport his men and supplies to the front. To help him make up his mind, he could draw on his own experience of Wolseley's unsuccessful bid to relieve Gordon twelve years before. There were several options available, including the Bayuda desert route, in respect of which there was, by mid-1897, a railway completed to Kerma, bypassing two cataracts. Kitchener's choice of route, however, was unexpected. Against all the technical advice received, he decided to build a new railway across the Nubian desert from Wadi Halfa to Abu Hamed, a distance of 230 miles, and so open up a line of advance to Khartoum via Berber, to which the railway could be extended. By this method he could avoid the difficulty of traversing the Bayuda desert, and

Khartoum would be brought to within some 200 miles of railhead. It was a bold choice. Work on the line began on 1 January 1897 and took ten months to reach Abu Hamed. In charge was an able young French Canadian Sapper, Lieutenant Percy Girouard.

In the meantime Hunter had been left on his own to administer his huge province. His impressions were that the Dervishes had not interfered unduly with the family life of local inhabitants, in contrast to the treatment they had meted out to Egyptian villagers over the years. On the other hand, the population of the province in terms of both people and cattle had fallen drastically. Dongola had once been a fertile province but agriculture had been badly neglected and trade was at a standstill. There was no civil government or police force, and no courts of law operated. The town of Dongola was found to be a heap of ruins.

Hunter set to work to remedy matters with his customary energy. He toured the whole province explaining, in his ever-improving Arabic, the requirements of government. He set up 11 administrative Districts, and arranged for the collection of information of every kind for the government. He re-established the courts and police force. At the same time, he took steps to revive agriculture and trade, and troops were used to rebuild Dongola. He found there was, inevitably, a shortage of money for development, and likened himself to a man with a 'new lease of a big farm on which all the buildings and plant are in ruins and without cattle, horses, ploughs, tools or anything to stock it, and no money or credit.'[2]

Hunter's directive to the Mamurs in charge of the 11 Districts in Dongola is quoted approvingly by J. S. R. Duncan, a former member of the Sudan Political Service.[3] In it Hunter stressed that the Mamurs should regard themselves as agents of a just and merciful government and do everything to gain the confidence and respect of the people. Crime must be put down and nothing taken from the people without payment. Cultivation of the land should be encouraged and women should not be molested. The Mamurs should hear grievances. Any indication that Mamurs or their employees were corrupt would make them liable to court-martial and dismissal. It was a model document.

During his time as Governor Hunter was judged by contemporaries to have brought order to the province and to have given the people good government by laws impartially administered.[4] The people came to like him and settled down happily under his rule. For his part he was never afraid to exercise administrative responsibility and made no bones about the enjoyment he found in doing this.

The news of the fall of Dongola caused consternation in Omdurman and it was some days before the Khalifa, who had retreated to his house, regained his nerve and was again seen in public. Fearing an immediate advance by Kitchener across the Bayuda desert, he ordered Bishara to occupy Metemma, the headquarters of the Jaalin tribe. He called up troops

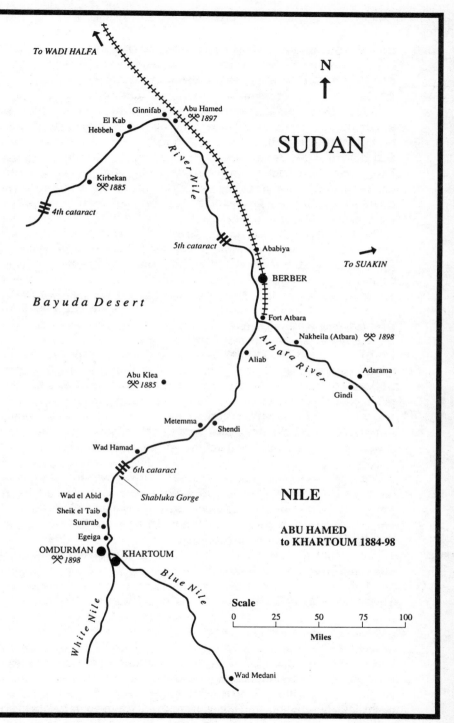

To WADI HALFA

N

Ginnifab
Abu Hamed
�֍ 1897

El Kab
Hebbeh

River Nile

SUDAN

Kirbekan
✖ 1885

4th cataract

5th cataract
Ababiya

To SUAKIN

BERBER

Bayuda Desert

Fort Atbara

Nakheila (Atbara) ✖ 1898

Aliab

Atbara River

Adarama

Abu Klea
✖ 1885

Gindi

Metemma
Shendi

Wad Hamad

6th cataract

Wad el Abid

Shabluka Gorge

NILE

Sheik el Taib
Sururab
Egeiga

ABU HAMED
to KHARTOUM 1884-98

OMDURMAN
✖ 1898

KHARTOUM

Blue Nile

Scale

0   25   50   75   100

Miles

White Nile

Wad Medani

Map F   59

from the distant parts of his empire to concentrate at Omdurman, including those under his young cousin, Mahmoud, who was commanding in Kordofan and Darfur. When an attack by Kitchener did not materialise, the Khalifa began to consider taking the offensive himself against the invaders. He determined therefore to send Mahmoud and his army to Metemma, where the riverain Jaalin tribe had become disenchanted with his rule. But the Jaalins objected strongly to what was being proposed, and defiantly decided to revolt and, furthermore, to join the Egyptians. The Khalifa responded angrily and speedily. On his orders Mahmoud hastened to Metemma. On 1 July 1897 with 10,000 men he stormed the town. No quarter was given and the garrison and many of the inhabitants were ruthlessly put to the sword.

Hunter did not let his duties as Governor distract him from considering what the next stage of the campaign should be. He took the view that the Egyptian army could not sit still in Dongola: it must either go forward or back. His plan, outlined to Duncan Hunter, was that the army should advance at least as far as Berber, open up the road to Suakin and join forces with the Italians at Kassala and along the Atbara river. To do this Abu Hamed would have to be taken and turned into an advance base served by the desert railway. If the Dervishes came up in strength to meet the invading troops, Hunter believed that the help of the British army would be necessary. Much of this he put to Kitchener in a paper marked 'strictly confidential'. At this time Hunter was again letting off steam privately to his brother George. He was confiding to him about the 'mean and dangerous economy' practised and indicated that, if things were not put right, he would denounce Kitchener 'to quarters where at least I should be listened to'. His chief, he added, did not care to be told these things.

Once the decision to build the desert railway and to pursue an axis of advance along it to Berber had been taken, Abu Hamed became an immediate target of the Egyptian army. Curiously, the Khalifa did not seem to realise this but still expected an advance through the Bayuda desert. The Khalifa, a shrewd enough ruler, was no military expert and appeared not to appreciate the importance of Abu Hamed and Berber. For some years he had regarded the open plains between the Kereri hills and Omdurman as the place where an invading army would be defeated. This may explain his somewhat passive attitude to the invasion of his country.

Besides these strategic, logistic and other matters, a more immediate question demanded a solution. At this time Dervish raiders, 1,000 strong, had been harrying Hunter's outposts and killing local people. He advocated an attack on them, but was told to his disgust to act strictly defensively. Next, certain wells, 80 miles into the Bayuda desert from Korti, were taken by the enemy, and he was refused leave to retake them. For a moment, he told George, he had thought of resigning. Instead, sensibly, he wired his misgivings about Headquarters' policy. As a result he was given by Kitchener the latitude to do as he wished;[5] the wells were, there- fore, reoccupied and MacDonald was ordered to attack forward Dervish positions.

As Hunter was expecting to be campaigning again soon, he packed up all his books, put some papers in stout envelopes and, together with some framed photographs, sent them all off to George in Lower Egypt to take care of. These items, he wrote, were 'of no value except as souvenirs and may serve in my old age and dotage, if I ever reach one to refresh my fading faculties and to pass a wet day . . .' Rather triumphantly, he told his brother that he was for the first time in his life out of debt. Nor did Hunter forget his sisters to whom he periodically wrote at length about his life and doings in the Sudan.

Hunter had also managed to get home for a few weeks' leave in the early summer. He saw Wolseley to sound out his prospects and was told that there would be further work for him for some years in the Sudan, once the country had been reconquered, though no hint was given what this work might be. He also saw his friend (now General) Frederick Maurice, who urged him to stay on in the Sudan to see the job through. The immediate question of his career had been exercising Hunter's mind because he had been pondering about his engagement to Jemmie. He saw her in Scotland and told her of 'the small chances there were of my being able to marry for 7 or 8 years to come' and that it was unfair to keep her waiting. He may have been taking an unduly pessimistic view of matters, but he was probably also half-wishing to escape from his entanglement. Jemmie's response to him was that she did not care how long she waited. In the end there was a compromise and they agreed to remain engaged for another year, after which they would review the question.[6]

On his way back to the Sudan Hunter enjoyed attending a parade of British troops in Cairo, at which Cromer took the salute. This stirring occasion prompted a patriotic outburst from Hunter. Always a convinced Imperialist he told his sister-in-law Abby: 'we are the greatest Nation the Universe ever saw . . . what we have got we can keep and what we want we take'. He then added by way of playing down what he had said '. . . we exercise our Might in the interests of Humanity, which no other power has succeeded in doing yet.' There were times when he engaged in flights of fancy – who wouldn't in the wide-open spaces of the desert – and dreamt of raising armies among the Shilluk and Dinka people that would conquer all Africa and 'settle the hash of meddling French and Belgians and Germans and Portuguese and Dutch et les autres.' He was especially enraged by what he had heard and read about the treatment of Africans in German East Africa and in the Congo Free State (the personal domain of King Leopold II of Belgium) under Wissman and Peters. He also considered the explorer Stanley a 'brute'. Dervish rule seemed to him to be quite mild in comparison to what was going on in other parts of Africa.

Progress with the desert railway had been remarkably swift and by July the track had reached a point some 120 miles from Wadi Halfa, just over half-way to Abu Hamed, and therefore within striking distance of Dervish raiders. So Kitchener decided after a discussion with Hunter on 14 July[7] that, to ensure the security of the railway workforce, the time had come to seize Abu Hamed. The appearance of Mahmoud's large force at Metemma and the uncertainty of its objective may also have been a factor which helped him reach this decision.

Kitchener therefore put Hunter in charge of a Flying Column of 3,600 troops, the cream of the army. Placed under his command was Mac-Donald's infantry brigade of four battalions, the 3rd Egyptians, the 9th, 10th and 11th Sudanese; No. 2 field battery of six Krupp 12-pounder guns, two Maxims, and two other machine-guns, one Gardner and one Nordenfeldt; a 30-strong troop of cavalry; a medical detachment and a transport echelon of 1,300 camels carrying 18 days' supply of food and ammunition. A Sapper officer, Lieutenant Manifold, would unwind the telegraph wire to keep in touch with Merowe. Hunter was given concise instructions by the Sirdar (see pages 00 and 00). He was told to surprise the enemy, occupy Abu Hamed and cut off the Dervishes' retreat to Berber; he was to construct a fort there for the garrison, but not to proceed further south.

According to the intelligence provided, the Dervishes had 600 men at Abu Hamed, including 200 riflemen and 200–300 mounted men, all under the command of Emir Mohamed el Zayn.[8] This was a slight underestimate for, in the event, the enemy's forces proved to number some 700 men, of whom 400 were ansars armed with swords and spears.

To achieve surprise, secrecy and speed were essential; if the enemy through its patrols became aware of the column's presence then the garrison at Abu Hamed might be reinforced. The distance to be covered from Kassinger was 132 miles. Because it was the hottest time of the year Hunter decided to do most of his marching at night, despite the difficulties. The force was to carry no tents, and with no trees, and so no shade on the route they were to follow, sleep would be hard to come by.

Kitchener inspected the force on 28 July, and the next day at 5.30 p.m. the column moved off. The terrain was difficult with much broken rocky ground. There were no tracks and the wilderness of the Monassir desert, an area without any vestige of vegetation beyond the Fourth Cataract, had to be traversed. The maps proved to be useless. There had been a good deal of drinking among the troops before the start, and so Hunter did not demand too much of his men to begin with, though on the first day he unavoidably had to cross a barren stretch of country in a march of $16\frac{1}{2}$ miles. As the men became fitter so the speed increased until 68 miles

62

Major General Hunter D.S.O.

1. A force as detailed in margin has been formed into a flying column under your command with the object of occupying Abu Hamed.

Cavalry. 30
Art. 2nd Field Batt.
3rd IX th X th XI th
Battalions.
Det. Medical Corps

Officer Commanding
Infantry Brigade.

El Miralai Macdonald
Bey C.B. D.S.O.

Staff Officers Infantry
Infantry Brigade.
El Bimbashi
Keith Falconer.
El Yuzbashi.
Baghat. Effendi

2. Should you find the enemy's force at Abu Hamed too strong to be attacked you will form an entrenched camp as near Abu Hamed as you may find suitable with a view to cover the railway — you will then report to me.

3. The most recent intelligence reports, state the Dervish force at Abu hamed to consist of 600 men with 200 rifles and one gun. Between 200 and 300 of this force are reported mounted

. . . .

Extract from Kitchener's Instructions to Hunter in July 1897

. . . .

10. You will, as far as possible keep me constantly informed of your movements

11. Your staff will consist of

El Kaimakam Kincaid Bey
    Asst Adjutant General

El Bimbashi Gorringe D.S.O
    Staff officer for Engineering duties

El. Bimbashi Hill-Smith.
    Senior Medical officer

Bimbashi Maxse.
   " Hnble. C. Walsh. } For Transport & general staff, duties.

Sagh. Mohammed Eff. Shafeek. Staff officer

Herbert Kitchener

Major General

Sirdar

Merowi
27. July 1897.

64

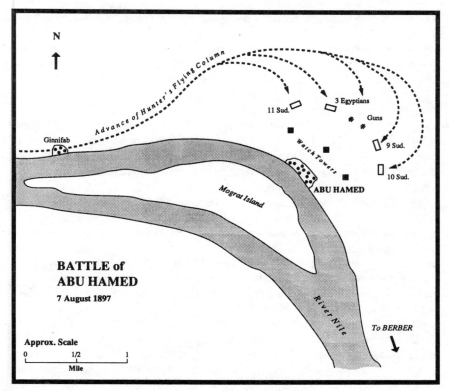

Map G

were covered in the last four days of the march. When the camels' loads of food and forage were consumed, Hunter had them sent back to Kassinger, whence they were turned round and despatched again with fresh loads for the Flying Column.

The column passed by two notable landmarks. The first, on the opposite bank of the Nile, was the site of the battle of Kirkeban in 1885 where General Earle was killed, and the second at Hebbeh was the place where Colonel J. D. Stewart, Gordon's deputy, had been decoyed to a house on the bank of the Nile and murdered in 1884 on his way back from Khartoum to Egypt. The column found portions of the boiler and hull from Stewart's shipwrecked steamer *Abbas*. At El Kab on 4 August a shot was fired at the column; they knew then that they had been spotted. The next day the column was joined, as planned, by 50 Ababdeh 'Friendlies', irregular forces from the pro-Egyptian Ababdeh tribe. The Friendlies asserted that reinforcements were on their way to the Dervishes. Not knowing whether the information was correct, Hunter kept up the pressure on the column. But the march had taken its toll. Five Egyptians had died of heat stroke and 50 more had collapsed. By 2 a.m. on 7 August, Ginnifab, just two miles short of Abu Hamed, was reached. The force had covered the 132 miles from Kassinger in a matter of nine days, averaging about 15 miles a day, a remarkable achievement in the extreme heat. There was now a two-hour delay while the camels were unloaded, a task which Hunter, always ready to recognise mistakes, admitted afterwards should have been done in daylight.[9] At dawn Major Kincaid was sent forward to reconnoitre, and was closely followed by Hunter and his staff. As they peered at the enemy positions, they were met by a furious volley of fire, which fortunately went too high.

Abu Hamed, a sizeable village, was about 600 yards long by 100 yards wide. It lay on the northern side of the river and was protected on its perimeter by three tall watch-towers built in Gordon's time. Inside the town there was a network of winding lanes and alleys. Mohamed el Zayn had had trenches dug round the town, and had fortified the houses in it. Nonetheless, as it turned out, the enemy were taken by surprise since they had not expected the Egyptian army without the gunboats, which they calculated could not arrive for another week.

Hunter now took his forces in a wide circuit to the left round the town. He then swung them to the right in an arc facing the Dervish position, his order of battle, from his left, being 10th and 9th Sudanese, 3rd Egyptian and 11th Sudanese, with his artillery in the centre. He was in position by 6 a.m. and wasted no time. After a bombardment by the artillery which lasted half an hour, the attack went in at once. The Dervish riflemen held their fire admirably, as Hunter, MacDonald and the other officers, all on horseback, led their troops towards the trenches and town. Then at a range of 100 yards the defenders fired a tremendous volley. The 10th Sudanese had been compelled to halt to avoid coming under the fire of the 11th Sudanese almost opposite to them. Two of their British officers, Major H. M. Sidney of the Duke of Cornwall's Light Infantry, and Lieutenant Edward Fitzclarence of the Dorsets, and 12 other soldiers, were killed under the hail of bullets and a further 50 men were wounded. But the attackers swept on over the trenches and into the town. Hunter described how '[We] went straight at it – house to house, up the street and round the corner, all of a hustle and a jostle . . . and blazing of roofs and climbing of walls and poking through doorways – they had shelter trenches in all kinds of places . . . they lay quite quiet in them till we were close up and then fired into our mass'.[10]

The Sudanese gloried in the use of the bayonet and were more than a match for the outnumbered defenders. By 7.30 a.m. it was all over. It had, though, been a stiff fight. Mohamed el Zayn had reportedly been found hiding under a bed and had been promised his life by the Egyptian officer to whom he had surrendered. Later, the Dervish leader was sent for by Hunter who questioned him:

Hunter: 'Why did you fight? Didn't you know it was useless?'
Mohamed el Zayn: 'I knew you had only three times as many men as I had and every one of my men is worth four of yours. You could not fire until you were quite close up and at that range our rifles were as good as yours and anyway I have killed a lot of your men'.
Hunter: 'What will Mahmoud do now? Will he stay looting and robbing at Metemma or will he come down here to attack me?'
Mohamed el Zayn: 'He will be down here in five days' time to wipe you out'.[11]

Some Dervish horsemen had escaped to the south, meeting during their flight reinforcements coming up from Berber. The latter were only 20 miles away to the south-east at the time of the battle so Hunter had reached his objective only just in time.

In his diary Hunter gave the Dervish casualties etc, out of their force of 700 as:

killed 450
prisoners 180
wounded 20
fled 50

The Egyptian army losses were 18 killed and 61 wounded. Major Sydney and Lieut Fitzclarence, a great-grandson of William IV, were buried side by side at sunset. Of them Hunter wrote, 'No more gallant soldiers or better men ever served the Queen'. They were, surprisingly, the only British officers of the Egyptian army to be killed during the whole campaign of reconquest. There was another moving moment for Hunter after the battle when the mortally wounded Private Hassan Ahmed, a veteran of the 10th Sudanese, asked that his medals be given to Hunter Pasha for long his comrade in arms.[12]

The public at home were always eager for news of the campaign in the Sudan, though for nearly a year there had been nothing to report. Now suddenly there was action and no correspondents at the front. The official telegram sent from Cairo by the GOC in Egypt to the Secretary of State for War, timed at 2.50 p.m. on 9 August 1897, was tantalisingly short; it ran to only seven lines. The news of the deaths of two British officers was, however, given separately. All this did not inhibit the *Daily Telegraph* war correspondent for making a full report in the paper on 10 August, which ran to no less than 19 column inches and which had to rely a good deal on the writer's imagination! In it he admiringly sang the praises of both Hunter and MacDonald for the 'brilliant march and capture of Abu Hamed'. The former was described as 'the best-liked man in Egypt and the Sudan . . . among natives and Europeans', who by his feat had 'added another laurel to his already splendid reputation as a soldier.'

Kitchener sent Hunter from his Headquarters at Merowe a letter of appreciation saying how well he had handled the expedition and how pleased Lord Salisbury, the Prime Minister, and Cromer were at his success.[13] Also Grenfell, the previous Sirdar, had written a few days after the battle, offering Hunter his congratulations. Kitchener tried to obtain a CB for Hunter for his victory, but he was unsuccessful.

The gunboats meanwhile had been despatched to support Hunter, and had begun their ascent of the Fourth Cataract above Kassinger. The *El Teb* unfortunately came to grief during its passage and capsized, Lieutenant Beatty and his crew being lucky to survive in the foaming waters of the rapids. But the other five vessels, *Tamai, Metemma, Fateh, Nasr* and the *Zafir* all arrived safely at Abu Hamed. On 22 August Hunter went off on the *Tamai* for a river patrol, which lasted for two days and took him 30 miles upstream.

Unexpectedly, events now began to move fast and Hunter found himself thrusting forward again. Zaki Osman, the Emir of Berber, had taken the sudden fall of Abu Hamed badly, and wishing to avoid the fate of Mohamed el Zayn and his men, withdrew his troops from Berber on 25 August, falling back to the Atbara river, 23 miles to the south. Hunter heard about this on 27 August[14], and therefore the next day sent the Ababdeh Friendlies, under Ahmed Bey Khalifa with 28 mounted men, down to Berber to investigate what was going on. The audacious Friendlies, as they rode up the right bank of the river, spread tales of the strength of the army following them. On 31 August Ahmed Bey reached Berber and reported back to Hunter that the town had been evacuated and that he was holding it in the name of the Egyptian government. In the meantime on 30 August Hunter himself had set off upstream with 150 men in the *Tamai* and the *Nasr* in the wake of the Friendlies. Unfortunately, the *Nasr* struck a sunken rock 42 miles into the journey south and was badly damaged. The force had therefore to return to Abu Hamed where a telegram from Kitchener was awaiting Hunter, ordering him to verify the evacuation of Berber; this was followed the next day by another telegram saying – incorrectly – that the information about Berber was untrue.[15]

So once again, Hunter left Abu Hamed, this time with 30 days' supply of food and with four gunboats, the *Tamai, Zafir, Fateh* and the *Nasr*, which had been brilliantly repaired by Lieutenant Gorringe, another of Kitchener's team of highly competent Sapper officers, of whom Hunter had a high opinion.[16] He took with him nine British officers and 350 men from the 9th Sudanese. They travelled upstream, made the passage of the long and rock-strewn Fifth Cataract and by nightfall on 5 September they were just seven miles north of Berber. At first there had been no sign of any inhabitants but as they approached their destination the place began to teem with people, cattle, goats and donkeys. Hunter and his men landed at Berber at 7.30 a.m. on 6 September. The attitude of the local people to the arrival of the flotilla was, in Hunter's words, 'quiet, cheerful and expectant, rather than jubilant and grateful',[17] but they responded unenthusiastically to requests for wood to fuel the hungry boilers of the gunboats.

Zaki Osman was not to be left in peace and Hunter ordered Major Kincaid to proceed south in the *Tamai* and *Nasr*, with Commander Colin Keppel and Lieutenant Hood and some 60 men on board, to the confluence of the Nile and Atbara rivers in pursuit of the Dervish Emir. A mounted patrol of Friendlies accompanied them along the river bank. Hunter had written to Zaki Osman, asking him to surrender and offering him, as he was authorised to do, generous treatment. Zaki Osman had with him a number of large sailing-boats containing grain and Hunter saw the advantage of possessing these. In the event Zaki Osman retreated but Kincaid intercepted the boats and captured their cargoes.

Berber was a large town with a population of about 12,000, sprawling for ten miles along the river though at a little distance from the right bank of the main channel. Hunter described the town as being mostly well-built with many houses standing in large courtyards. There were drains and ditches to carry off the rainwater and for a Sudanese town Hunter found it 'fairly clean.' Caravan traffic converged on Berber from different parts and many rich merchants lived there. But Hunter considered it to be unsuitable as a military post and difficult to defend because of the absence of a good field of fire. For a proper defensive position to be established, Hunter reckoned he would have to go inland, and then he would be separated from his gunboats. In due course this matter of defence was resolved when camps were set up along the Nile between Berber and the junction with the Atbara river, where a fort was established and a depot for gunboats set up.

Berber had been looted by the retreating enemy, and the bazaar and market were in ruins. But the grain supply was intact and might attract raiders. 'Any mischief might be brewing', Hunter reported back, 'without our knowing it.' As for the direction from which mischief might come, Hunter was paying particular attention to the reported movements of Osman Digna and his main force – said to be between 1,500 and 2,000 strong – away to the south east at Adarama (see map F, p. 59). No one knew Osman's intentions but his patrols were active on the Atbara river. Hunter was tempted to try and expel these forces from the area, but wisely, with his shortage of men and supplies, resisted the temptation for the time being. He recognised too the extreme vulnerability of his position at the end of a long line of communications, and later told his friend General Maurice that this had been a 'really anxious' time for him. He had known that certain merchants in Berber were in secret touch with the enemy, reporting on his weak position and urging the Dervish leaders to take the opportunity of cutting off the gunboats and capturing the town. But Hunter knew Kitchener's problems with his extended commitments and made no fuss.[18]

The day he arrived in Berber, Hunter lost no time in writing to the OC troops in Suakin. He wished to see the road to Suakin, some 220 miles away on the coast, opened up as soon as possible. In the letter he gave his view, restated to Duncan at about the same time, that the army had gone far enough this year, but that they should continue to harry the Dervishes by means of the gunboats operating up the Nile as far as Metemma. Keppel was soon given orders by Hunter to patrol with his vessels some 60 miles south of Berber, though he was told not to waste ammunition on 'long range' targets.[19] Once one of his patrols saw inland a force of some 1,500 men belonging to Mahmoud. At the sight of the gunboats, whose capabilities were, Hunter considered, overestimated at that time by the Dervishes, the force disappeared. Certainly these patrols were effective and contributed significantly to preventing serious raids by the Dervishes north towards Berber. Hunter was well served by the competent and daring naval officers with him. Beatty's future distinction has already been noted. Both Keppel and Hood were also to become Admirals.

In the middle of September Kitchener paid a visit to Berber to see at first hand the situation in which Hunter found himself. As a result of this, the rest of MacDonald's brigade was sent up to Berber during the second half of the month to reinforce the tiny garrison. In addition Hunter's position was consolidated by the arrival of two camel corps companies and some artillery, including the 2nd Field battery. No more troops could be spared, as Kitchener had to keep garrisons at Merowe and elsewhere in Dongola for fear the enemy would try to cross the Bayuda desert from Metemma, though Hunter did not consider this threat to be great. As it was, the Dervishes dithered, not knowing what action to take against the invaders, and in the event they did nothing.

All through September Hunter continued to send reports back to Abu Hamed for transmission to the Sirdar and his Chief of Staff, which included everything he could usefully learn about the Dervishes' dispositions and intentions. In a letter to the Sirdar dated 25 September, he gave his estimate of the forces currently at the disposal of the Khalifa as follows:

Rifles	Cavalry	Spears	Guns
10,600–12,000	5,800	21,000	62

To face about 40,000 men, the Sirdar would have, Hunter pointed out, some 16,000 men of the Egyptian army at the outside. How many more troops would be needed, he asked, 'to make a dead certainty of Khartoum? To make it less than a cert is pure madness.'[20] The implication was clear. The British army would have to help.

70

To obtain information Hunter did not neglect the use of agents, though it is not quite clear whether they were his or Wingate's. A report of his of 29 September ends with the almost biblical sentence, 'spies have gone out to Adarama and Metemma.' He obviously found it irksome not to have the financial authority to do certain simple things. For example, he asked Kitchener for approval to pay a boatbuilder the promised sum of E£10 for the completion of a half-built nuggar. In addition, he had to ask his chief how much should be paid to deserters who came over from the enemy with their arms, the previous going rate being a mere E£1 per head. To accommodate the army and provide them with barracks, certain towns-people in Berber had to be evicted and Hunter again had to ask for a scale for compensating evicted tenants. Such was the orderly way the invading army behaved! Kitchener continued to keep a tight rein on finances. Hunter really blamed Cromer, who had once been a Gunner, for the constant shortages of funds for the troops, and fulminated against him to Duncan, describing him as merely 'an inferior officer of the British Artillery'![21]

Hunter had for some time wanted to take a force up the little known Atbara river in search of Osman Digna, though by October it was reported that the Dervish leader had evacuated Adarama. The army's camel trans-port had hitherto been working supplies into Abu Hamed and there were no funds for expanding it.[22] This had precluded mounting the operation. At last the camels became available and Kitchener, confident that the Dervishes did not mean to attack Berber, authorised the expedition. So, to his evident delight, Hunter set off on 23 October 1897 for Adarama. He had with him 400 men from the 11th Sudanese, 100 camel corps, 2 guns and 60 irregulars. They had no idea of what to expect, but were ready for a fight in the rather unlikely eventuality of Osman Digna showing up.

On his return to Berber, Hunter wrote for the Chief of Staff an account of his long patrol,[23] in which he demonstrated a soldier's general eye for the country he was passing through, combined with unusual powers of observation, which would have done credit to an explorer reporting to the Royal Geographical Society. Indeed, with his stamina, sound sense and love of adventure, Hunter was made of the stuff of Victorian explorers, many of whom, like Burton, Speke and Grant, were army officers, and in later life he was elected FRGS.

The column had started by following a road beside the clear flowing waters of the Atbara river which teemed with crocodiles and fish. As usual, the maps were unreliable. In places along the way there were a few remains of the old telegraph line, but a combination of maurauding Arabs and the destructive powers of the white ant had caused the poles to vanish. Hunter was impressed, perhaps above all else, by the apparent potential for agriculture of the shallow Atbara valley with its rich alluvial soil, where in the past there had been much cultivation of grain and cotton.

Along the margins of the river the country was densely wooded with thorn and there were palms everywhere. Beyond, the grazing was 'a perfect paradise for animals.' He noted numerous gazelle, bustard, guinea fowl and wild asses. In places the column came across salt works, where deposits from the neighbouring desert had been worked and left piled in great heaps. Except for a small party of refugees heading for the Nile, no one was seen on the outward journey. 'The country', wrote Hunter, 'was swept clean as the palm of your hand, not a grain of food, not a goat.'

The distance to Adarama, reached in seven days, was more than anticipated, and turned out to be 107 miles. As expected the town, except for dogs and cats, was quite deserted. Its 6,000 inhabitants and all their cattle and belongings had been evacuated by Osman Digna to nearby Gindi. It may well have been with a pang that Hunter ordered the place to be burnt down, '. . . not a glorious proceeding', he wrote to General Maurice, 'merely to prove we had been there.'[24] Hunter with the camel corps had pushed on another 43 miles beyond Adarama, and while he was away, a small caravan from Sinkat, near Suakin, meant for Osman Digna, was intercepted by his column and its goods confiscated. These were later sold at Berber, most of the proceeds, amounting to £300, being given to a charity committee set up to help the starving and naked widows and orphans of the Jaalin people, survivors from Mahmoud's sack of Metemma, many of whom had fled to Berber. Hunter felt strongly that the government was not doing enough to help such people with food and clothing.[25]

When he returned to his base on 9 November, Hunter reckoned that he had travelled some 300 miles in 14 days. All the distances were carefully recorded by Hunter, always meticulous over detail. Curiously for a man who said he disliked press correspondents in the field, Hunter regretted that his patrol was not accompanied by a correspondent or artist, as there was plenty to write about and sketch.

Trade between Egypt and the Sudan had been forbidden by the Egyptian government for some time, though this did not of course put a stop to it. Hunter knew from his time at Suakin and Wadi Halfa all about the interception of contraband traffic on the borders of Egypt and the Sudan. At Berber, he discovered that the export of gum – a substance derived from acacia trees, widely used in the manufacture of perfume – was in the hands of a few men who were at the same time importing lead into the Sudan from Egypt.[26] Lead was an important commodity needed in Khartoum for the production of ammunition. Hunter recommended to the Sirdar that the gum, stored in certain identified houses in Berber, Suakin and elsewhere, should be seized. This, he argued, would be an act of confiscation against the Dervish government and not against individual gum owners. He was able to give the Sirdar the precise names of those involved in the gum and lead trades and had proposed in October that, where there was sufficient evidence, they should be prosecuted.

These entrepreneurs were of interest to Wingate, Director of Intelligence in Cairo, because they were also involved in the intelligence game. They now became the cause of a row between Hunter and Wingate. Up to now the two men had been friends. What happened was this. Wingate visited Berber, probably in November 1897, and apparently saw there a certain Medani Osman, one of his agents. The day after Wingate left the town, Hunter had this man put in prison, though only as a temporary measure. The reason for this was that Hunter had learnt that Medani Osman, a gum trader, was due to set off from Berber to Suakin on the same day as the Mamur (District Head) was travelling to the same destination on government business. Hunter believed that Medani Osman was intending to thwart the government's proposed action of seizing the gum held at Suakin. On the day the Mamur was calculated to reach Suakin, Hunter released the prisoner, arguing that Medani was no longer in a position to interfere with what was happening in Suakin. When he heard all about this, Wingate, who regarded Medani Osman as reliable, remonstrated with Hunter. In response, Hunter wrote to Wingate saying, 'I do not understand what purpose you hope to gain by trying to make me a party to a quarrel with you – you have allowed partiality to obscure your judgment . . .' Believing Medani to be a knave, he went on to say that his past services to Wingate and any promises made did not affect the question. One criminal, he argued, could not be pardoned while others were prosecuted for the same offence. He ended his letter rather testily by saying that he deprecated 'the waste of public money on lengthy telegrams and do not intend to be drawn into profitless argument.'[27] Wingate responded with spirit, 'making my reply as short as possible, as I have no wish to 'quarrel' with you as you put it.' He asserted that Hunter had no right to make deductions which were entirely incorrect, and pointed out that Medani had been a 'secret intelligence agent for many years' and had frequently conveyed money to European prisoners at Omdurman at great personal risk and had largely contributed to the eventual escape of Slatin and others. He, Wingate, had purposely made a fuss of him at Berber and had given him a pass to Suakin. He clearly rejected Hunter's opinion of his agent.[28] Wingate reported all this to Kitchener, who could not have been happy to hear that two of his most important subordinates had fallen out.

In the following March Hunter wrote to Wingate, due again at Berber, and asked him in a friendly manner to dine or to come for a meal. On the back of this letter Wingate had made an annotation addressed to 'K' which read: 'Hunter has been extraordinarily polite and evidently wishes to make up – whilst reciprocating his politeness, I am assuming the attitude of extreme deference but I cannot quite meet him on the former friendly terms – R[29]'. Hunter never mentioned this quarrel, if such it was, to any third party as far as is known and the two men seem to have composed their differences.

NOTES

1. Acland Papers AH–John Troyte Acland, 23 Nov. 1896; DHD 95.
2. DHD 99–100.
3. Duncan 64–66.
4. Alford and Sword *The Egyptian Soudan, its Loss and Recovery* 157–8.
5. DHD 102, 103 and 106.
6. Ibid. 112.
7. AHd 14/7/97.
8. NR Kitchener's written instructions to AH 27 Jul. 1897.
9. Maxse Papers 334, AH–Maxse 20 Aug. 1897.
10. DHD 122.
11. *Sudan Campaign 1896–99* by 'An Officer' at 111.
12. Keown-Boyd 183.
13. DHD 119.
14. AHd 27/8/97.
15. NR AH report to COS 3 Sep. 1897.
16. Ibid.; Sandes 196.
17. NR AH report to COS 6 Sep. 1897.
18. Maurice Collection 2/1/4 AH–Maurice 15 Feb. 1898.
19. NR AH's instructions to Commander Keppel 8 Sep. 1897.
20. NR AH–Kitchener 25 Sep. 1897.
21. DHD 125.
22. Maurice Collection 2/1/3 AH–Maurice 29 Nov. 1897.
23. DHD 128.
24. Maurice Collection loc. cit.
25. DHD 133.
26. NR AH–Kitchener 27 Sep. and 1 Oct. 1897.
27. SAD 267/1/83 AH–Wingate 27 Nov. 1897.
28. SAD 267/1/139 Wingate–AH 14 Dec. 1897.
29. SAD 267/1/288–9 AH–Wingate 6 Mar. 1898.

CHAPTER 8

The Battle of Atbara

Something of a stalemate developed on the Nile after the capture of Berber. Military activity was mainly confined in the last few months of 1897 to gunboat patrols and incursions down the undefended west bank of the Nile by Mahmoud's men, short of food, looking for grain in the villages. For their self-protection Hunter had issued the villagers with Remington rifles and these weapons were put to good use. The Egyptian army was fully stretched in holding territory recently won and could not consider further offensive operations. Rather, a period of consolidation was needed. For the next and perhaps final push to Khartoum reinforcements, including, it was generally accepted, British troops, would be required. Further adequate supply arrangements, so essential to this advance, awaited the completion of the railway to Fort Atbara. So it all looked as if the next offensive could not take place until the Nile flood in the summer of 1898.

Another matter much exercised Kitchener. On his left flank the Italians wished to leave Kassala (see map A, p. 16), which they now saw as an encumbrance. To ensure that the Dervishes did not move in, it was mutually agreed that the town should be occupied by an Egyptian reserve battalion, and this was done on Christmas Day. Thus, the army's left flank was secured.

During the last three months of the year rumours were rife about the intentions of the enemy and Hunter often speculated about them, exercising his mind by running over the options available to the Khalifa and Mahmoud. Nor did he fail to draw up contingency plans as to what he would do to meet any threat as it occurred. Some reports coming to Hunter suggested that Mahmoud, an aggressive leader, wished to march north to engage the Egyptian army, but this had been vetoed by the Khalifa, who continued to build defences around Omdurman, and wanted Mahmoud, at one time, to fall back on them. Then in December came rumours that the Khalifa was concentrating his troops outside Omdurman with a view to making a general offensive. Hunter, interestingly, in a letter written to Duncan on 22 December, did not give much credence to the rumours. Whatever their merits, and in the event nothing came of them, they provided the impetus for Kitchener to act. Urged on apparently by Wingate, he formally requested in a telegram sent to Cromer on 1 January 1898 the help of British troops on the basis that 'General Hunter reports confirming news of a Dervish advance.'[1] Hunter had presumably revised his earlier view of the rumours in the light of further information coming in from Omdurman.

The response to the request for reinforcements was swift. The first battalions of the Warwicks, the Lincolns and the Cameron Highlanders, all stationed in Egypt as part of the army of occupation, were ordered up the Nile. Supporting troops to accompany the infantry were to include artillery equipped with two 40-pounders, six 5-inch howitzers and six Maxim machine guns, and the Royal Engineers. Later, a reserve battalion of Seaforth Highlanders arrived in the Sudan from Malta. The British infantry was formed into a brigade, and placed under the command of a veteran from India, Major-General William Gatacre, a wiry 55-year-old martinet, who was brave but generally unpopular. At Cromer's insistence Kitchener continued to command the expedition. With these reinforcements the strength of the army was brought up to 14,000 men, plus 52 guns. Kitchener warned Cromer that for the final advance on Khartoum he would need a further British brigade with supporting cavalry and artillery.

With the prevailing uncertainty about the Dervish intentions, Hunter had to keep the Egyptian army at Berber on the alert, especially as the new British brigade was not due to arrive in the theatre for some time. Minor irritations were noted in his diary. For instance, presumably anticipating an eventual triumphant entry into Khartoum, he had sent to Cairo for his full dress uniform. A short entry reads: 'My medals stolen from Berber P.O. Though insured Sirdar refused to pay.'

Hunter was full of ideas of how the downfall of the Khalifa might be brought about. Today we would call this lateral thinking. Once he suggested to Kitchener that an attempt be made to treat with the Khalifa. This drew the response from Wingate: '. . . [Hunter] is a strange individual! As if the Khalifa would be likely to do such a thing . . .'[2]

As has been noticed before, there were sometimes differences between Headquarters and Hunter, the field commander, as the following extract from Wingate's diary dated 5 February 1898 shows:

'Numbers of refugees deserters and prisoners arrived this morning from Berber. Sirdar found them without food this led to a little squabble between us . . . explained to K [Kitchener] my reasons for non-interference with District Commanders and animadverted on the Berber question pointing out that the Intelligence Department under present system was powerless. K replied that we must do the best we could with what we have, that when Hunter deliberately disobeyed him it was little use attempting to interfere. The long and the short of it is that K is afraid of Hunter but I suppose the situation will last till Omdurman is taken – after that there must be many changes . . .'[3]

We do not know precisely what the 'Berber question' was, but it certainly looks from the extract as if Hunter was flouting Kitchener's orders about refugees and others by sending them north. Even more remarkable is Wingate's view that Kitchener was 'afraid of Hunter.' Was there anyone else of whom it could be said that Kitchener was ever afraid? To defeat the Dervishes Kitchener had to have success in the field. For this he was relying heavily on Hunter. Already, as we have seen, Hunter had taken Kitchener to task over the 'Death March'; there may well have been other occasions when he was equally outspoken. Consequently Kitchener could have become wary, even afraid, of how his subordinate might react to his proposals and even orders, or worse, rock the boat in Cairo and so frustrate his ambitions. Certainly there can be little doubt about the remarkable position of dominance Hunter had achieved in the Egyptian army.

Mahmoud could not stay indefinitely at Metemma. Suddenly on 15 February came the news everyone was waiting for. Mahmoud had begun to transfer troops across the Nile on to the right bank opposite to Metemma and to move them towards Shendi (see map F, p. 59). This indeed proved to be the start of the long-heralded Dervish advance, though it took Mahmoud some time to make any noticeable progress. Thus Commander Keppel reported to Hunter that Mahmoud himself was still in Shendi on 5 March. But a week later he was marching north fast with an estimated 15,000 men, including a large force of cavalry.

While this was happening further up the Nile, Hunter was ensuring that his defences were ready for an imminent attack. At this time MacDonald's Sudanese brigade was stationed on the fringes of Berber in houses deserted by the Dervishes; in all, five battalions were guarding the town and its various facilities including the hospital and the Headquarters. A few miles up the Nile another battalion protected the commissariat. Finally at Fort Atbara, where Lewis was in charge, a defensive complex had been established by Hunter. The principal feature was a large fortified camp sited on the eastern bank of the Nile just below the Atbara river. It was enclosed in classic fortification style by a six-foot-high dry mud wall and protected by a wide trench. Inside were gun platforms for the artillery, blockhouses and look-out towers. New mud barracks and tents housed the three battalions of infantry and two squadrons of cavalry stationed there. Enterprising Greek traders had opened a café in the compound and some shops were beginning to take shape on the foreshore. Among the craft on the river there would normally be one off-duty gunboat out of the three on station; the other two would be tirelessly patrolling up as far as Shendi 100 miles away.

On the opposite bank of the Nile, another but smaller post was garrisoned by a further battalion, which had good views up and down the river, while in the fork of the acute angle made by the two rivers there was also a fortified post. The ground had been cleared in every direction around these fortifications to give a field of fire and stakes had been placed at regular intervals into the distance marked from 100 to 500 yards to assist marksmen. To safeguard communications with Berber, telegraph lines were laid along both banks of the Nile. Hunter had planned his position with great skill. Having inspected everything on 4 March he commented in his diary that the defences were 'very strong', and that the density of the bush inland from the Atbara river was bad for 'fire development, good for savage warfare.'

The British brigade started to approach Berber early in March, having marched continuously some 70 miles or so from the railhead. Hunter thought they looked 'dead beat. They have overdone it and are not fit for much fighting in present condition.'[4] He did not mention anything about the poor quality of their boots which rasped the skin and crumpled like cardboard under pressure. They marched through Berber on 3 March and deployed in camp sites south of the town at Darmali (see map H, inset,

p. 84) and elsewhere. The British officers were given a cordial reception and entertained by their brother officers in the Egyptian army.

The conditions they found themselves in were primitive. War on the Indian frontier was apparently luxury compared to campaigning in the Sudan. Lieutenant William Stewart of the Cameron Highlanders, like other British officers, came with little personal kit. All he had, he wrote in April, was 'one small towel, one rug, one piece of soap, one toothbrush, one filter, one tin cocoa and one Bovril to be kept for emergencies. No washing of any kind is allowed for fear of polluting the water here. We look more like coalheavers than officers. All our clothes are in rags from mimosa thorn.'[5] Hunter himself cared little for the comforts of life while in the desert, and could manage on the bare necessities. But he was no ascetic, and when not on active service, enjoyed the good things of life as much as any man.

Hunter noted in his diary certain arrivals. One of them was Douglas Haig of the 7th Hussars recently seconded to the Egyptian cavalry, who, in turn, noted that he received 'kindly consideration from Hunter', and concluded after a brief acquaintance that he was a 'first rate fellow.'[6] In early March one of Hunter's guests at dinner was his friend Father Robert Brindle, the ubiquitous Roman Catholic chaplain, a veteran of the Gordon Relief expedition and holder of the DSO; later he would become Bishop of Nottingham. Another dinner guest was Wingate, to whom Hunter had held out an olive branch, after the disagreement between them. While conditions in the desert were uncomfortable, there were compensations and Steevens reports that at the Egyptian army mess there was a good supply of champagne, claret, hock, whisky and so on. From the shops in Berber it was possible to buy delicacies such as oysters and asparagus brought in by caravans from Suakin. But how the oysters travelled and remained fresh is not revealed!

The pace of events was now quickening. Kitchener had already arrived in Berber and in early March closed the Berber–Suakin road, no doubt to the fury of the traders and mess managers. A system of cavalry patrols under Lt.-Col. Broadwood was organised to go 25 miles from Fort Atbara. Hunter, though apparently scoffed at by MacDonald and others, ordered a camp-site to be prepared, protected by a zariba – that is a fence of rough thorn – at Upper Hudi some 15 miles up the Atbara; some instinct seemed to be telling him that the army was destined to go that way to do battle with the Dervishes. On 11 March Kitchener and Hunter saw the local sheikhs and told them, if raids occurred, to take their families and cattle across to the west bank of the Nile, and also 'to arrest strangers.'

Entries in Hunter's diary, concise and staccato as they are, help to tell the story as the tension rises and the two armies converge:

'13 March Mahmoud marched north of Shendi yesterday at dawn . . . moving fast on Taboora. 1,000 cavalry 7 guns ?15,000 men.

14 March Sirdar and my Headquarters to Kunur. No scoffing now.

15 March Kunur 9 am. Beatty's reports show [Mahdist] army marching north fast and strong . . . concentration [of Anglo-Eygptian force] ordered at Kunur tomorrow. Seaforths to be hurried up quick.

16 March MacDonald, Maxwell and British brigade concentrated at Kunur. Sirdar sees Brigadiers and OC Battalions explains situation.

17 March Mahmoud said moving Nile to Atbara. Orders sent to Lewis re his action Atbara Camp . . . orders sent re defence of Berber if we are crushed by Mahmoud . . . rode out to study ground.

18 March deserter reports Mahmoud leaves Aliab today for Upper Atbara.'

Beyond the general objective of taking Berber the Dervishes had no definitive plans when they began their advance, for their two principal commanders were divided. Mahmoud, spoiling for a fight, was all for advancing straight down the Nile from Aliab to Fort Atbara and engaging his opponents there. The experienced Osman Digna considered they should move east to the Atbara, obviously believing an outflanking movement was more likely to succeed than a head-on clash. The Khalifa, to whom an appeal was made, came down on Osman Digna's side.[7] On reaching the Atbara, the two men disagreed again. Osman Digna wished to go south-east away from the Anglo-Egyptian force while Mahmoud wished to go in the opposite direction towards it. Now without any more prevarication, Mahmoud, who was the overall commander, took his men north-west and set up camp at Nakheila on the north bank of the Atbara river, which was drying up into a series of great pools, some 35 miles south-east of Fort Atbara. Hunter's diary continues:

'20 March [force marched from] Kunur to Lower Hudi.

21 March [force marched from] Lower Hudi to Upper Hudi. Cavalry in touch with enemy. Lose eight killed seven wounded. Enemy eight killed, wounded unknown. Locate enemy's camp at Nakheila, 20 miles from Upper Hudi . . .

22 March 13 battalion and 6 squadron to Abadar to observe. report strong force foot and horse advancing. 6 squadron got into infantry square. 13 [battalion] fired volleys, killed some at long range. cavalry and artillery drive enemy back. whole force parades in case enemy come on. Excellent practice. Force looked splendid . . . Lewis' brigade ordered to us at 4 am tomorrow.

23 March [at Fort Atbara] I wrote Hickman his instructions to go to Shendi and attack it. Detail steamers for Hickman. camp fires locate Mahmoud's position.

The Anglo-Egyptian army now stayed somewhat immobile for some 14 days, except for patrolling and the raid on Shendi. The troops had to be patient under the merciless sun. Luckily, the nights were cool. Kitchener was suffering from a bout of indecision, which continued until at last he gave battle on 8 April. Hunter's diary throws no light on the reasons for such long inactivity, nor whether it was his idea to send Hickman with an Egyptian battalion up the Nile with three gunboats under Keppel to raid Shendi, Mahmoud's rear depot. The object of this operation was to destroy the town, to hamper Mahmoud's eventual retreat and to demoralise his forces by taking away his women and belongings. The troops landed as planned on 26 March and created mayhem. They returned to base unscathed with a 'great haul of stuff and 600 souls.'[8] It was a highly successful raid and must have unnerved Mahmoud's men encamped on the Atbara, for after it there was an increase in the numbers of deserters.

Agents and deserters continued to bring in reports about Mahmoud and his plans. They were often contradictory and must have been hard to assess. Thus on 27 March Hunter noted that a 'secret agent' reported that Mahmoud had received a letter from the Khalifa, who had agreed to a withdrawal 'if the enemy were too strong . . .' The next day it was reported that the Khalifa had written to Mahmoud 'come back if you are afraid.'[9] But other reports showed that Mahmoud fully intended to fight and believed his was the stronger army.

The exact location of Mahmoud's zariba with details of its layout had not yet, surprisingly perhaps, been established. On 30 March Kitchener sent Hunter out on a reconnaissance up the Atbara to find Mahmoud's camp and report on its defences. The party consisted of all eight squadrons of cavalry under the highly professional Broadwood, a horse battery and four Maxims. Captain H. G. Fitton of the Intelligence staff and Captain J. K. Watson, Kitchener's ADC, went too. After passing Abadar, the site of an old fort, the party went into the desert and after 10 miles turned back towards the river where, sure enough, signs of movement and dust betrayed the site of the Dervish camp. It was 8.30 a.m. Hunter at once shelled the camp and drove back some emerging Dervish cavalry with the Maxims. The party then proceeded to observe the Dervish position. Hunter and Watson rode up to within 300 yards of the perimeter, trying unsuccessfully to provoke the defenders to fire so that the line of their trenches could be judged. By the dust, Hunter reckoned the camp to be about 1,200 yards long and 1,000 yards deep. It was stockaded at intervals and covered in front with a strong zariba hedge. The interior of the camp was thickly grown with bush and a belt of palms prevented any sight or estimation of the rear defences. In Hunter's view the position looked to be a strong one.[10]

The next day there was a conference between Kitchener, Gatacre and Hunter to discuss the next move in the light of the reconnaissance. Gatacre favoured an attack, while Hunter, rather out of character but showing his native streak of caution, thought they should wait. He may also have wondered if Mahmoud might not be tempted, through his impetuosity, to leave his zariba and thus play into their hands by himself attacking. This divided opinion put Kitchener in a quandary. He resolved his difficulty by the somewhat unusual expedient for a General in the field of referring back on 1 April to his civilian chief, Cromer, in Cairo for advice, explaining the conflicting views of his two Generals. Cromer, for his part, turned to Grenfell, now commanding British troops in Egypt, for an opinion. The latter in turn telegraphed the War Office. The Commander-in-Chief, Wolseley, was indignant that the Sirdar as the man on the spot could not make up his own mind on the matter and felt he had to consult a man nearly 1,000 miles from the Atbara river.[11]

What struck Cromer most about Kitchener's messages was that Hunter, known to be a fighting General, doubted the wisdom of attacking. He thought it likely that Hunter had taken this view because he was uncertain of the outcome of a hand-to-hand encounter with the Dervishes in the heavy bush within the camp. Cromer telegraphed back to Kitchener on 2 April summarising what he and Grenfell saw as being the arguments for and against an attack, and placing special emphasis on the weight to be given to Hunter's opinion as a man experienced, unlike Gatacre, in local conditions. Cromer ended by saying he thought that Kitchener 'had better not attack for the present . . .' But before this telegram had reached Kitchener, Cromer received another telegram on 3 April from the Sirdar. This stated that 'Generals Hunter and Gatacre and myself now think an attack on Mahmoud's position advisable . . .'. It is not known what prompted the change in Hunter's stance. But when Cromer heard of this change, all his hesitation about attacking disappeared and he telegraphed again to Kitchener, saying the situation was now 'materially altered', though the decision had to be left to Kitchener.[12] Thus ended the flurry of telegrams, which had arisen because of Hunter's unease about an immediate attack and Kitchener's continuing lack of confidence, not helped by his subordinates' initial disagreement.

Although the die now seemed to be cast, there was still some niggling doubt in the Sirdar's mind and he decided to send Hunter out on 5 April on one final reconnaissance. That Hunter was irritated by this is shown in a letter to Duncan:

'This 5th April business was within an ace at one time of being disastrous. There was no purpose to be gained by sending me a second time to reconnoitre. It was a certainty I could learn no more than I had already discovered ... The Sirdar wanted to know if the enemy were still *in situ*. I could have told him that by not going nearer than two miles off, by the dust. But he also wanted to know where their left flank was. I could not establish that fact by a reconnaissance of the strength he sent me with.'[13]

The Anglo-Egyptian force had by 4 April moved to Abadar, five miles nearer the enemy, and it was from this place that the second reconnaissance party set off. As before it was composed of Broadwood's cavalry with the same artillery and Maxims; Hunter also took with him Colonel Maxwell, Colonel Long who was in command of the artillery, Major W. S. Kincaid and Captain Sir Henry Rawlinson, one of Kitchener's staff officers. Rawlinson, son of a distinguished diplomat and Assyriologist, was an observant diarist. A successful soldier, he became C-in-C India in 1920.

When the party approached Mahmoud's zariba, as on the previous occasion, a large number of Baggara horsemen, some 700 of them, emerged upstream of the zariba, only to be forced back by the Maxims. Then at 9.20 a.m. another force of Dervish cavalry, about 500-strong, approached from the downstream side of the camp. They looked as if they meant business but halted within 300 yards of the reconnaissance party. At this moment the upstream force of Baggara chose to advance again. As this was happening a force of at least 1,500 infantry emerged from the face of the camp. Then at 600 yards they halted and opened fire. In the meantime the two cavalry forces, with a pincer movement, proceeded to try and surround the reconnaissance force. While the enemy's upstream force was held in check by Maxim and artillery fire, Broadwood decided to charge the downstream cavalry and, in doing so, forced them back. Hunter had never ridden in a cavalry charge and in his own words, 'I rode in this to see what it was like.'[14]

The position was critical and in the circumstances Hunter decided it was time to leave. The reconnaissance party extricated itself with some difficulty and the officers had to use their revolvers and swords. In the action 10 men were killed and 16 wounded. Hunter believed the Dervish cavalry missed a great chance. If they had not been so reluctant to close, his force would have been 'smashed'. The Maxims, and to an extent the cavalry charge, he thought, saved the day. But there can be little doubt that Hunter's own quick thinking and skill in battlefield tactics were important factors in avoiding a serious reverse. He paid at this time a handsome tribute to the Dervish cavalry asserting that 'man for man they are better than we are ... better individual men at arms ... at hand to hand fighting the Arab is the better man.' This called to his mind, even if the analogy was not strictly appropriate, Napoleon's dictum in comparing French and Bedouin cavalry, that is: one Bedouin equals three Frenchmen;

20 Bedouin equals 20 Frenchmen; 100 Frenchmen equals 200 Bedouin. But, Hunter said, 'our superior discipline and training tells.'[15]

On 6 April the Sirdar moved his force to the deserted village of Umdabia some 8 miles from Nakheila. He sent Hunter in the afternoon to select a resting and watering place, from which a night march up to the enemy's camp could be made. Hunter chose Mutrus, another deserted village, about $4\frac{1}{2}$ miles from Mahmoud's camp. Everything was fixed except the day of the battle. Kitchener wanted to fight on Thursday, 7 April while Hunter, wishing to give the men a day's rest, preferred Friday, 8 April, which was Good Friday. Although he was supposed to have been superstitious about Fridays, Kitchener yielded and Hunter wrote the orders for the night march and the attack.[16] For the night march there was to be silence, no fires, no cooking. Rawlinson has Hunter saying that anyone shooting off firearms should be seized and beaten over his head with his gun![17]

The combined Anglo-Egyptian force, less the cavalry who came on later, set out from their camp at Umdabia at 6 p.m. on 7 April, the British brigade leading. Each man had a full water bottle and carried one day's biscuit ration and 110 rounds of ammunition. Each gun had 100 rounds and each Maxim 5,500 rounds. Hickman was left behind to guard the camp and to light fires to give the impression it was still fully occupied by the army. At Mutrus they halted, rested and watered until 1 a.m. Then the final curving march of about six miles began in bright moonlight, led by Captain Fitton, a man always highly regarded by Hunter. They moved at about 3,000 yards an hour and had periodic stops. At 4.30 a.m. now close to the Dervishes, they deployed into attack formation, and as dawn was breaking, moved to within 600 yards of their position. The zariba was circular in shape and lay in a slight depression. To the east and west the ground was thick with scrub, giving good cover. In front, to the north, it was open, and it was from this side and the higher ground that the attack was to be launched.

Kitchener's army was drawn up in an arc extending for about 1,500 yards. Gatacre's brigade was on the left. The Camerons were in front, for it was their task to find a way through the zariba. Behind them came the Warwicks, Seaforths and Lincolns. In the centre was MacDonald's brigade, composed of the 11th, 10th and 9th Sudanese with the 2nd Egyptian in the rear, and on the right was Maxwell with the 14th, 12th, 13th Sudanese, with the 8th Egyptian to the rear. Lewis's brigade was held in reserve in the rear, together with all the animals carrying water and reserve ammunition. The Maxims were placed on the far left, and the field batteries, in pairs, were in the centre and on the right. On the extreme right was a naval rocket detachment under the redoubtable Beatty. Broadwood's eight squadrons of cavalry were in the rear, ready to move to either flank. The

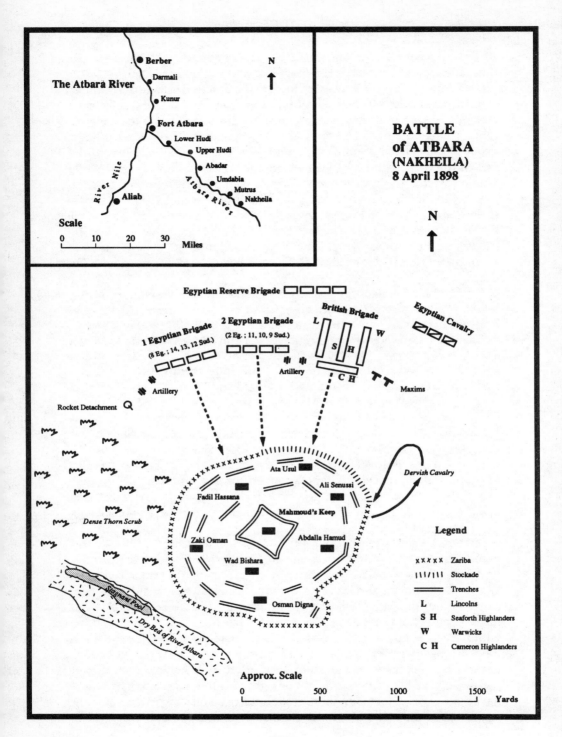

The Atbara River

Berber
Darmali
Kunur
Fort Atbara
Lower Hudi
Upper Hudi
Abadar
Umdabia
Mutrus
Nakheila
Aliab

River Nile
Atbara River

N

Scale

0   10   20   30   Miles

BATTLE
of ATBARA
(NAKHEILA)
8 April 1898

N

Egyptian Reserve Brigade

1 Egyptian Brigade
(8 Eg.; 14, 13, 12 Sud.)

2 Egyptian Brigade
(2 Eg.; 11, 10, 9 Sud.)

British Brigade

L   W
S H
C H

Egyptian Cavalry

Artillery

Artillery

Maxims

Rocket Detachment

Dense Thorn Scrub

Ata Usul

Fadil Hassana

Ali Senussi

Mahmoud's Keep

Dervish Cavalry

Zaki Osman

Abdalla Hamud

Wad Bishara

Osman Digna

Stagnant Pool

Dry Bed of River Atbara

Legend

x x x x x   Zariba
|||/||| Stockade
=======   Trenches
L   Lincolns
S H   Seaforth Highlanders
W   Warwicks
C H   Cameron Highlanders

Approx. Scale

0   500   1000   1500   Yards

Sirdar's total force numbered about 14,000, while Mahmoud had some 16,000 men under him, of whom 4,000 were cavalry; however, Osman Digna's men, positioned appropriately at the rear of Mahmoud's zariba, removed themselves from the scene of the battle early on in the proceedings.

The battle plan was simple enough. The artillery was to bombard. The infantry was to deploy under the cover of the guns, advance frontally to the enemy's position, tear the zariba to pieces, assault the trenches and clear the enclosure with bayonet and rifle fire. Cavalry was to deal with cavalry. These were all traditional tactics.

The course of the battle followed the preconceived plan with the bombardment starting at 6.15 a.m. The camp enclosed within its two-mile perimeter fence was observed to be strangely bereft of movement. There was no sign of man or beast except for the silhouette of a tethered camel. For well over an hour shell, shrapnel and rocket rained down on the hapless defenders. It must have been a terrifying experience, few of them having been subjected to this kind of ordeal before. Hunter said afterwards that the effect of the bombardment must have been 'murderous'.[18] At one stage, early on, the enemy's cavalry emerged upstream of the zariba but was quickly driven back by Maxim fire.

At 7.40 a.m., after the guns stopped firing, Kitchener sounded the general advance, and the massed contingents of infantry set out with their pipes and bands playing, and their drums beating. Shouts of 'Remember Gordon' were heard. Hunter, MacDonald and Maxwell elected, as was their wont, to ride into battle on their horses in front of their troops, the only mounted men among the infantry. Gatacre, too, led his men from the front with drawn sword, and was accompanied by his chief clerk carrying a huge Union Jack. These senior commanders must have certainly presented the Dervishes with conspicuous targets but they all came through unscathed.

As the infantry reached a point some 300 yards from the Dervish position, they met what Hunter described as a 'very hot and fairly well directed fire . . .' from the trenches behind the zariba and stockade. Steadily, however, they continued on, attracting praise from Hunter for their splendid spirit. Their general line, as if on parade, was apparently 'fairly well dressed', though Gatacre's brigade had fallen slightly behind the Egyptian Division, which was led by Hunter 'waving his sword and helmet'. There had been worries beforehand about the difficulties of overcoming the obstacle posed by the zariba, and sappers had contrived explosive and grappling devices.[19] But the thorn fence did not prove to be in practice the serious impediment expected. The men threw blankets over the thorns to protect their hands, and pulled the branches aside.

In his account of the battle given to Duncan, Hunter said that once the main line of trenches had been reached, he sounded, as agreed, the second 'advance'. On this signal the line pushed on through the zariba, which was found in Hunter's words to be 'a maze of trenches, pits, thorn fences, bush, straw huts with heaps of dead and dying, men and animals.' Churchill in his description of the battle – in which he did not take part – refers to women and children being found among the dead in the enclosure. Also, E. W. C. Sandes in his account of the fight, quoting Lieutenant Manifold, who did take part in it, refers to 'the dead and wounded women, often naked' found in the zariba. Hunter may have omitted mention of the women and children to spare the feelings of his sister-in-law. In the middle of the zariba was an inner compound stubbornly defended by Mahmoud's bodyguard. The 10th Sudanese overran this last position and in it captured Mahmoud himself. In the meantime resistance in the rest of the great enclosure, except that offered opposite the 11th Sudanese, was diminishing and the troops reached the river bed at 8.35 a.m., when the cease fire was sounded. It had been a comparatively short fight but a decisive one. Dervishes had escaped to the south across the river and into the dense bush, in which it was impossible for the cavalry to pursue them. The official figures for the Dervish casualties was 3,000 killed, including 40 Emirs in and around the zariba. Hunter gave the number of prisoners taken as 2,000. In the British brigade 3 officers and 22 NCOs and men were killed, and 92 wounded. In the Egyptian army 57 NCOs and men were killed, and 386 wounded,[20] the 11th Sudanese taking the highest casualties. The British brigade fired 56,000 rounds of ammunition, while the Egyptian Division used 193,000 rounds.

Financial stringency had tempted Kitchener to economise on medical services. So it is not surprising that the arrangements made for collecting and looking after the wounded have been criticised. Rawlinson contrasted the British medical services unfavourably with the Egyptian but blamed the Senior Medical Officer of the British brigade. After the battle, the Egyptian division built hospital huts for the wounded and Hickman arrived at 3 p.m. from camp with rations and transport for the wounded. The main force of troops left the scene of the battle in the cool of the evening and arrived back at Umdabia at midnight. Hunter stayed on with Lewis's brigade, two other Egyptian battalions and the Camel Corps to carry back the wounded, reaching camp at 3 a.m. The 7th battalion was detailed to stay on the ground to search for wounded refugees. Years later, King George V was told by one of Hunter's admirers that the General had spent 'the weary night searching for the dead, the dying and the wounded.'[21] The stench from the battlefield must have been foul and Rawlinson said he was 'thankful to get away without being sick.'[22]

There seems little doubt that Kitchener left the direction of the fight, as he had done at Firket, to Hunter, not that a divisional, or even brigade, commander could give much direction in the general *mêlée* obtaining, once the zariba had been reached. Kitchener's main role, as he himself saw it, was to bring his troops in good shape up to the Atbara – a remarkable logistical achievement in itself. When appealed to for orders he said: 'I have been for three years bringing you face to face with these fellows, now go in and fight it out', and throughout the battle he never gave a single order leaving it to Hunter to direct the fight.[23] The tactics employed by Kitchener, or rather it must be said those proposed and carried out by Hunter and Gatacre, have been criticised by some commentators and historians as being unimaginative, though the newspapers of the day were full of praise for the victory achieved. Also Hunter is considered to have overestimated the strength of the enemy's defences. There is perhaps some truth in these criticisms, and it can well be asked – as for instance Douglas Haig asked – why the frontal assault was favoured when dense bush on the flanks offered good cover for attacking infantry. In Hunter's defence it can be argued that the kind of simple tactics employed, including the physical risks run, were those clearly understood and accepted at the time by the troops and were ones for which they had trained. Men fought in close formation, as if on the barrack square, and orders could be comparatively easily given by junior commanders and responded to. Using unfamiliar ground like dense bush might lead to disaster, or so it could have seemed to Hunter. As it was, attacking over open ground had succeeded at Firket and Abu Hamed, and the casualties taken against poorly equipped adversaries, a key consideration in assessing all the factors, had not been unduly high.

After the battle, in a letter he wrote to General Sir William Cameron, at the time Colonel of the King's Own Regiment, Hunter criticised Gatacre saying: 'his formation for attack was as bad as bad can be. Ours was the correct one.' Further, Gatacre's advance was 'slow as a funeral . . . and everybody got jumbled together.' Typically Hunter, a magnanimous man, continued, 'criticisms perhaps sound unfair and undeserved and spiteful so I shall not continue them.'[24] One might have expected an element of competition between Hunter and Gatacre, for the former must have been keen that his Egyptian troops, once despised, showed up well alongside their British comrades. But the discerning Repington, who was on Kitchener's staff at Atbara and was *The Times* defence correspondent in World War I said that the rivalry between the two men, whom he described as 'great Paladins', was only one of gallantry.[25]

After his defeat, Mahmoud was brought before Kitchener with Hunter present. His jibba (smock) was heavily stained with blood from a bayonet wound in the leg and he was limping. He was sullen but showed no fear. 'This is his Excellency, the Sirdar', said Hunter. Mahmoud did not deign to reply, and Kitchener then demanded to know of Mahmoud why he had come to the Sudan to burn and kill, presumably referring to the carnage at Metemma. In answer Mahmoud said with some dignity: 'As a soldier I have to obey the Khalifa's orders as you must the Khedive – I am not a woman to run away.'[26]

On the day after the fighting, Owen Watkins, a Methodist chaplain with the army, accepted Hunter's invitation to dinner and wrote an eye-witness account of the occasion. The meal proved to be interminable, for Hunter was keeping 'open table . . . in the open air'. Officers kept coming and going. They were in their torn and soiled uniforms. They were seated, some with their arms in slings and some with their heads bandaged, at a rough table. His smiling host, wrote Watkins, exchanged jest for jest with those about him. He wondered if he could be the same General, who only a few hours before, rode at the head of his division 'thro a hail of lead, over pits and trenches from which blazed innumerable rifles?'.[27] On the subject of leading from the front, Hunter's sister-in-law, Abby, later chided him for being reckless at Atbara. He stoutly defended himself, saying: 'the country was very thick and rough. From behind I could see nothing. There were two untried regiments . . . one was half composed of men at Dongola, who had been in the ranks of the enemy – it was essential to see how they behaved and to know at once if they wanted support.'

On 14 April just after sunrise, the Sirdar rode in a kind of Roman triumph through an arch into Berber to be received by a guard of honour of the 1st Egyptians. At his side were Hunter and his staff, followed by Lewis and then an escort of cavalry. A little way behind on his own walked Mahmoud with his hands tied behind his back. One account of this procession has Mahmoud with chains round his ankles and a halter about his neck driven forward by guards, who lashed at him with whips.[28] The town was decorated with bunting and coloured paper. The towns-people pressed forward and, according to Steevens of the *Daily Mail*, who described the scene as 'barbaric', the women shrieked their delight in a chant of 'Lu-u-u, lu-u-u . . .' The Egyptian government was not disposed to be lenient to Dervish leaders whom they saw as rebels against their rule in the Sudan. Mahmoud was consequently sentenced to a harsh term of imprisonment at Rosetta in lower Egypt, and died in 1906 not yet 40.

The press, a mixed crowd, had arrived at Berber in some strength before the battle of Atbara. Hunter disliked journalists, but being a considerate man he treated them politely. In a letter to General Maurice he complained about their conduct and why he objected to having them at the front. They drank, he said, quarrelled in their cups and pestered him for news, thus interfering with his work. He also regarded them as ill-qualified 'to criticise military operations or to pose as instructors of public opinion.' He clearly, however, had a realistic understanding of the power of the press. Thus, he wrote 'People judge nowadays a good deal by the number of times one's name appears in the papers and that of course depends on one's accessibility by correspondents and sometimes on one's treatment of them.'[29] Usually, during his campaigns, he had a good press. History does not relate what he thought of the highly flattering portrait painted of him by Steevens. After reminding his readers that Hunter, whom he dubbed the 'sword-arm' of the Egyptian army, had for 14 years been in the front of all the fighting on the southern border of Egypt, Steevens went on:

'In all he is and does he is the true knight-errant – a paladin drifted into the wrong century. He is one of those happy men whom nature has made all in one piece – consistent, simple, unvarying . . . He is short and thick-set; but that, instead of making him unromantic, only draws your eye to his long sword. From the feather in his helmet to the spurs on his heels, he is all energy and dancing triumph; every moment is vivacious, and he walks with his keen conquering hazel eye looking out and upward, like an eagle's. Sometimes you will see on his face a look of strain and tension, which tells of the wound he always carries with him. Then you will see him lolling under a palm-tree, while his staff are sitting on chairs; light-brown hair rumpled over his bare head, like a happy schoolboy. When I first saw him thus, being blind, I conceived him a subaltern, and offered opinions with indecorous freedom: he left the error to rebuke itself.

Reconnoitring almost alone up to the muzzles of the enemy's rifles, charging bare-headed and leading on his blacks, going without his rest to watch over the comfort of the wounded, he is always the same – always the same impossible hero of a book of chivalry. He is renowned as a brave man even among British officers . . . he is one of the finest leaders of troops in the army. Report has it that the Sirdar, knowing his worth, leaves the handling of the actual fighting largely to Hunter, and he never fails to plan and execute a masterly victory. A sound and brilliant general, you would say his one fault was his reckless daring.'[30]

Another correspondent soon to be on the scene as a soldier journalist was Winston Churchill, then just 24 years old. In *The River War*, his highly readable account of the Sudan campaign, he described Hunter as the most imposing figure in the Egyptian Army '. . . always distinguished for valour and conduct, Hunter won the admiration of his comrades and superiors. During the River War he became, in spite of his hard severity, the darling of the Egyptian Army.' The personal popularity which great success might have brought to the Sirdar, he went on, was focussed on his daring and good-humoured subordinate.[31]

The troops now went into their summer quarters on the Nile between Berber and Fort Atbara to face a long hot spell of military inactivity. The main enemies were disease and boredom. For the British in particular it was a trying time. There was some training of course and then there was swimming and football. The ever ingenious Tommies and Jocks found some unusual forms of regimental competition. Thus the Warwicks matched their huge tarantula spider against the Cameronians' scorpion. Apparently, the Cameronians' scorpion, known as 'slogger', became champion![32] For the officers there was polo and duck-shooting and some were lucky enough to be allowed leave.

Hunter himself went home on leave for some weeks in the summer. According to Wingate he had to be sent home by Kitchener for a break.[33] There was one important development in his private life. His engagement to Jemmie came to an end, probably broken off by letter and not as a result of a meeting at home. Jemmie now leaves the story for ever. All the evidence we have – it is not very great – suggests that Archie's engagement to her was something he had entered into impulsively, and quite quickly came to regret. He must have regarded the whole business as a transitory episode. George Hunter was glad the match was off and opined that she would not have 'held him a week'. He went on, presciently, to say that 'he should only marry someone with a good deal of money to enable him to do himself justice professionally.'[34] But we have to wait over ten years before Archie Hunter finally took the plunge into holy matrimony.

NOTES

1. SAD 102/1/1–119 Wingate Diary 31/12/1897; Cromer II 96.
2. SAD loc. cit. 15/1/1898.
3. Ibid. 5/2/1898.
4. AHd 1/3/98.
5. Stewart *A Subaltern in the Sudan 1898 (The Stewart Society Journal)*, 1987.
6. Haig Papers Acc 3155, no. 1K Sudan Diary 1 Apr. 1898; Terraine *Douglas Haig: The Educated Soldier* 18.
7. Keown-Boyd 192.
8. DHD 154.
9. AHd 28/3/98.
10. DHD loc. cit; Cromer II 99.
11. Sandes 213.
12. Cromer II 101–2.
13. DHD 160.
14. Ibid. 155–161.
15. Ibid. 161.
16. Ibid. 157.
17. Rawlinson Collection Journal of Egypt and Sudan 1898 5201–33–4.
18. DHD 158.
19. DHD loc. cit.; Alford and Sword 222; Keown-Boyd 199.
20. *London Gazette* 24 May 1898 3232–5; AHd 8/4/98.
21. RA G V L521/1; DHD 159.
22. Maurice, *The Life of General Rawlinson of Trent* 38.
23. RA W 38/110.
24. DHD 163.
25. Repington 162.
26. Sandes 219.
27. Watkins *With Kitchener's Army* 36.

28. Magnus 122.
29. Maurice Collection 2/1/4 AH–Maurice, 15 Feb. 1898.
30. Steevens *With Kitchener to Khartoum* 76–7.
31. Churchill 192.
32. Ziegler *Omdurman* 49.
33. SAD loc. cit. 22 May 1898.
34. DHD 165.

CHAPTER 9

Omdurman

On his return to Berber in late July 1898 Hunter found preparations in an advanced state for the next phase of the campaign. A second British infantry brigade of four battalions had arrived under Brigadier-General Neville Lyttleton, a man destined to become the Chief of the General Staff in 1904. A fourth brigade under Lieutenant-Colonel J. B. Collinson was added to Hunter's division. Other arms were reinforced too, notably the cavalry with four squadrons of the 21st Lancers, a ninth squadron for Broadwood and two more companies for Tudway's Camel Corps. The artillery, under Long, now consisted of 44 field guns and 20 Maxims. Altogether there were 8,200 British and 17,600 Egyptian troops in Kitchener's force, not to mention the huge retinue of transport animals required. Also Keppel's flotilla had been augmented by three new gunboats, all carried in sections upcountry by rail. Hunter fully appreciated the part played by the Sudan military railway, extended to its terminus at Fort Atbara on 3 July in the build-up. In a tribute to Kitchener he described this railway as 'a monument to the skill and resources of the Sirdar. It was his idea and his only . . . the railway is the all important factor of this expedition . . .'[1]

In August the expeditionary force, together with all its equipment and supplies, began to move up the Nile by steamer, gyassa and nuggar to a forward base being prepared at Wad Hamad (see map F, p. 59), just below the Sixth Cataract and some 60 miles from Omdurman. Hunter left the Atbara River on 2 August with the advance party, travelling in a steamer with double-decked barges attached and full of troops. It was Hunter's original idea to give these barges the second deck. There was a risk that they would become top-heavy but this was accepted.[2] In the event there were, happily, no accidents.

What, though, was the Khalifa doing in the meantime to impede Kitchener's steamroller? For a time it had looked as if he meant to make a determined stand at the Shabluka gorge on the Sixth Cataract. Here, on the advice of Osman Digna, he had seven forts constructed to command the river and any craft trying to make a passage upstream. These and the rocky hills on either side of the Nile in the area of the cataract seemed as if they would form a defensive line, which would hinder the progress of the invading force. But early in July for no obvious good reason work on the forts was abandoned. There were plans, too, for a great chain, linked by a series of buoys, to be placed across the Nile, and for mining the river by using old boilers stuffed with explosive. But these ideas were perhaps too ambitious for the Mahdists and were not carried through. At Omdurman and its approaches the Khalifa had also been busy building forts, no less than 22 of them springing up in the area. A plea by Zaki Osman to withdraw to Kordofan and Dafur in the far west of the Sudan was rejected by the Khalifa. It therefore began to look as if, with some 50,000 fighting men amassed near Omdurman, a final battle was going to be fought either in the plains north of the town, or in its houses and streets.

Hunter just had time in a short letter to Duncan dated 22 August to say the fight would soon take place and that he was confident of victory, but what, he asked, would be its price. Besides commanding the Egyptian division Hunter was now second in command of the expeditionary force. Already the army had found the villages to be deserted and Metemma a ghost town, the bleached skeletons and bones of thousands of animals bearing witness to the ravages it had suffered over the past year. On the east bank a motley force of Friendlies, mainly composed of the Jaalin tribe out for revenge and loot would take care of any opposition encountered. The main force, marching up the west bank in stages from Wad Hamad, began to concentrate on 29 August at Wad el Abid, having found the defences at Shabluka, as expected, unmanned. On 30 August Kitchener wrote a letter to the Khalifa, telling him to remove to safety all innocent people, old men, women and children. If he and his Emirs surrendered, however, they would be justly treated. But surrender was not in Khalifa's mind.

That same day the army, marching in fighting formation, the British division on its left by the river because they drank the most water, and Hunter's Egyptian division on the right, reached Sheik el Taib. The gunboats, nine in number (the *Zafir* had sprung a leak and sank on 28 August), steamed slowly up the Nile alongside the troops. Hunter was held responsible by Kitchener for the daily march and for the protection of the camp site chosen at night.[3] The rains had broken and on the night of 31 August there was a tremendous storm, which soaked the troops as they tried to sleep in their camp at Sururab. The next day the march began at 5.45 a.m. Hunter's diary for 1 September was short. It read: 'Reach Kereri [hills]. Entrench the Egyptian Army. A memorable day and night.' The army crossed the Kereri hills at about 9 a.m and came to the village of Egeiga on the Nile, some seven miles or so from the Mahdi's tomb in Omdurman. The gunboats were sent up the river to bombard Omdurman, and some howitzers were landed for a similar purpose opposite the town on the east bank of the Nile, now cleared of the enemy by the Friendlies after a small-scale but fierce battle.

Scouts had been sent out in front of the main force and had seen from high ground enemy troops streaming north out of Omdurman. At noon Kitchener himself had climbed up the slopes of Jebel Surgham, a prominent hill some two miles south-west of Egeiga. Hunter, in the meantime, had been busy organising the camp site. As he finished this he received a message from Kitchener asking him to come to Jebel Surgham. Hunter galloped off and met Kitchener, who was half-way down the hill, and who looked apparently, as Hunter wrote in a long letter to General Maurice after the battle, 'as if he had seen a ghost and no wonder for he said the enemy were only 5 miles beyond the hill advancing 50,000 strong against us.' As if to reassure his chief Hunter said: 'Come back and we'll get into fighting formation and fill all tanks and water-bottles before dark and entrench ourselves and it will be all right.'[4] So they returned to camp and speedily prepared for an attack. The Egyptian Division on Hunter's orders dug shallow shelter trenches, giving them low parapets. Gatacre, however, only ordered his men to prepare a thorn zariba. It was always Hunter's conviction that if the Dervishes had attacked in the dark before dawn with the same bravery that they displayed a 'few hours later in daylight then we should have been pierced, divided, broken and rolled into the river.' Graphically he described what happened when an enemy penetrated an army encampment. 'Friend kills friend, contrary orders are given, bugles are sounded to everyone's confusion. All is dark and dust, and roar of animals and shrieks of dying and wounded, and clamour of natives, and shrill yells of enemy, and curses and prayers and a babel of confusion and horror.'[5]

Up to 1 September there had been little evidence of the enemy on the west bank. This prompted Major M. G. Talbot, a sapper on Hunter's staff, to go so far as to say to Hunter that he had never yet seen a Dervish soldier. As the Dervish host had just been sighted by the Sirdar from Jebel Surgham, Hunter at once composed a limerick. It read:

> 'At Kereri said Major Talbot
> No Dervish I've seen yet at all, but
> There appeared there and then
> Two thousand times ten
> which quite satisfied Major Talbot.'[6]

This is not perhaps the most brilliant of limericks but at least it shows the composer to be a cool customer, ready on the eve of a great battle, and despite the weight of responsibility on his shoulders, to knock off a short verse for a little light-hearted fun.

That night the enemy never came, and a great chance, Hunter thought, had been missed by the Khalifa. Everyone took it in turns to keep watch and Hunter was never so glad in all his days to see the sun rise.

The battle of Omdurman is usually divided into three phases. The first one is straightforward enough involving the post-dawn attack by the Dervishes on the perimeter of the Anglo-Egyptian camp. The second phase, at times confused, begins after Kitchener's men have left their camp to continue their advance. During this phase, the critical one, two succeeding attacks directed on MacDonald's 1st Egyptian brigade have to be beaten off. Once these attacks are repulsed, the third phase begins and covers the more or less uninterrupted progress of the army into Omdurman.

Dawn broke on 2 September, again it was a Friday, at about 5.45 a.m. Cavalry patrols were already out, and soon reported the enemy host preparing to advance from behind Jebel Surgham. The Lancers returned to camp but Broadwood remained with his nine Egyptian squadrons, eight companies of the camel corps and a horse artillery battery on the Kereri hills to guard the outer right flank. The defending force had been drawn up in a great arc, the troops facing west with their backs to the Nile, as follows: on the left was the British division composed of Lyttleton's brigade and that of Brig.-Gen. Wauchope, both equipped with the new and deadly magazine-loading Lee Metford .303 rifle. The 21st Lancers were to their left by the Nile. In the centre and on the right was the Egyptian division. First, next to Wauchope, came Maxwell's 2nd brigade. On his right was MacDonald's 1st brigade, and finally, between him and the Nile Lewis's 3rd brigade. Collinson's 4th brigade was held in reserve and was close to the transport and hospital area. The field guns and Maxims were placed between the front-line brigades, while the gunboats were on station to protect the flanks of the position.

There are differing views as to precisely when the army, encamped at Egeiga, saw the first flags and spears of the Mahdists bearing down on them. According to Kitchener's official despatch the shouts of the Dervish army became audible at 6.40 a.m., just a few minutes before their flags appeared. Hunter states in his report to the Chief of Staff, Rundle, after the battle that the enemy advanced at 6.50 a.m. in two large bodies on either side of Jebel Surgham.[7] In fact the larger body consisted of Osman Azrak and his 8,000 men, who, emerging from round the western shoulder of Jebel Surgham, swung east and headed for Maxwell's brigade. He was supported by the Emir Ibrahim Khalil's army of 4,000, who came on his right over the eastern part of Jebel Surgham and made for the British division. The Khalifa's men surged across the plain, brandishing their swords and spears in their uniforms of the patched jibba. Some, incredibly, were dressed in medieval chain mail. They carried on banners texts from the Koran and chanted their prayers begging for victory.

The appearance of this mighty and fearsome host brought the gunners

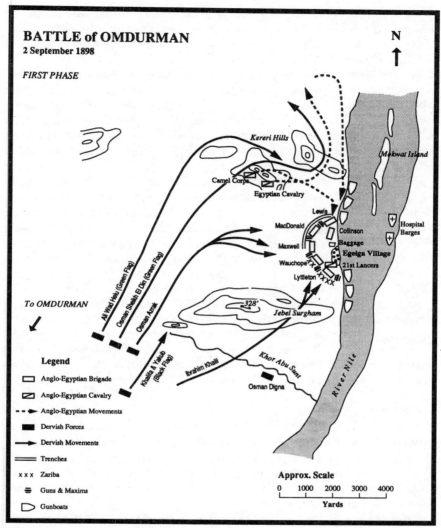

BATTLE of OMDURMAN
2 September 1898

N ↑

FIRST PHASE

Kereri Hills

Mekwat Island

Camel Corps

Egyptian Cavalry

Lewis

MacDonald

Collinson

Hospital Barges

Maxwell

Baggage

Egeiga Village

Wauchope

21st Lancers

Lyttleton

Jebel Surgham

-328'

To OMDURMAN

Khor Abu Sunt

River Nile

Osman Digna

Ibrahim Khalil

Ali Wad Helu (Green Flag)

Osman Sheikh El Din (Green Flag)

Osman Azrak

Khalifa & Yakub (Black Flag)

Legend

☐ Anglo-Egyptian Brigade

▨ Anglo-Egyptian Cavalry

- - - ▶ Anglo-Egyptian Movements

▆ Dervish Forces

→ Dervish Movements

═══ Trenches

x x x Zariba

⬗ Guns & Maxims

▷ Gunboats

Approx. Scale

0 1000 2000 3000 4000

Yards

Map I

into action at 2,800 yards range,[8] followed by the infantry at 2,000 yards or less. The Dervishes, holding their fire until 1,500 yards, came on with conspicuous bravery, but they were unable to reach the Anglo-Egyptian perimeter. As Hunter wrote, 'The lead belched forth was like a deluge of rain. They [the enemy] faced it like men and died shouting their Belief, not one whit intimidated by our weapons, marksmanship and discipline.'[9] It has been estimated that 200,000 rounds of small arms fire were directed against the Dervishes in this phase. The result was carnage. By 8 a.m. the attack was beaten off and the enemy force retired behind Jebel Surgham, leaving heaps of dead and wounded. Both leaders, Osman Azrak and Ibrahim Khalil, were killed.

As this attack drew to a close, a huge force of Dervishes was seen moving across the army's front from left to right. Hunter described it as a 'demonstration'. The force passed behind the Kereri hills after being bombarded by the artillery and gunboats. It was in fact composed of the *rubs* of Ali Wad Helu and the *mulazamin* of Sheikh el Din, its combined strength being estimated at 14,000 men.[10] This force is sometimes called by commentators Green Flag. It is worth making the point at this stage that some students of the battle consider that the Khalifa may have been for some reason mistaken about the exact location of the Sirdar's army, believing the main body to be behind the Kereri hills, and so sent Green Flag off in that direction. Certainly, the Khalifa can have been left in no doubt about Kitchener's position after the battering Osman Azrak received. It might also be supposed that the position of the gunboats on the river at Egeiga on 1 September would have given the game away to Dervish observers on high ground.

As Green Flag advanced into the Kereri hills, Broadwood, who had only a comparatively small force, had to respond rapidly to the overwhelming numbers approaching him and to avoid being cut off from his base. The camel corps was ordered back to the camp and, hard-pressed by the enemy, it reached the zariba in the nick of time with the help of covering fire from the gunboats on the right. Broadwood himself, with his main cavalry force, cleverly drew the Dervishes northwards and away from the army before he managed eventually to slip back to the zariba along the river bank, again protected by the gunboats' fire. This manoeuvre was to prove invaluable since it delayed Green Flag in delivering its attack on the Egyptian division. Up to now the casualties in the Anglo-Egyptian army had been comparatively light. The British had, it may be assumed, suffered more casualties than the Egyptians who were afforded cover by their shelter trenches.

Once the attack by Osman Azrak had been smashed, Kitchener was anxious to resume his advance on Omdurman. Above all he wished to gain the town before the surviving Dervish forces returned to it, so as to avoid fighting in the streets and houses. The 21st Lancers were, therefore, sent out at about 8 a.m. to reconnoitre on the left and to harass the remnants of the beaten enemy. This led the over-eager Lancers to fall into a trap laid for them by Osman Digna, concealed in a gully behind Jebel Surgham. The Lancers did not see the size of Osman's force until too late, and there followed their epic, but militarily pointless, charge so vividly described by its most illustrious participant, Winston Churchill. Despite this heroic episode, during which three of five VCs given in the battle were won, the

Lancers failed in the mission entrusted to them, for they had to return to camp after their charge without learning, for instance, the whereabouts of the prestigious soldiers of the Khalifa's own Black Flag, still uncommitted to the battle and then lurking behind Surgham.

At about 8.35 a.m. and before the return of the 21st Lancers, Kitchener ordered his troops to advance in echelon out of the zariba. As they made towards the ridge connecting Jebel Surgham with the river, the two British brigades, keen to be first into Omdurman, raced ahead. Maxwell, following on behind and to the right, was slightly delayed and so outpaced by the British. He had had to deal with Dervishes who, shamming dead (their well-known tactic), suddenly jumped up in front of his brigade. Hunter, uneasy about the reliability of Lewis's 3rd brigade, had decided to switch it with MacDonald's 1st brigade[11] so that the trusty Sudanese battalions were on the exposed outer flank; he was soon to be proved right in making this decision.

The order of march was thus: Lyttleton – Wauchope – Maxwell – Lewis – MacDonald. Collinson's 4th brigade was still for the moment in camp. Hunter must have seen from his position with the Egyptian division that there was a certain disarray about the advance. He now sent one of his Orderly officers, Lieutenant Manifold, forward to Kitchener, who was riding with the British division, with a request to allow him time for the switched brigades to reach their proper positions. He also reminded Kitchener of the Dervishes behind the hills,[12] by which he was presumably referring to Green Flag. Hunter seems to have been worried, understandably enough, that Kitchener in his haste had overlooked the large Dervish forces still in the field.

At 9.15 a.m. Hunter ordered two companies of the 13th Sudanese Battalion of Maxwell's brigade to clear Jebel Surgham, the summit of which lay in the path of Maxwell's advance. They showed spirit in doing this and at the same time surprised a large body of the enemy coming up the other side of the hill to support those on top.[13] According to Churchill, it was Kitchener who ordered this assault though at a slightly later stage in the battle; the taking of the hill does not, however, feature in Kitchener's official despatch.

In the rear, the advance had not been going too smoothly. For one thing the Egyptian brigades had further to go than the British to reach their correct position in the line. For another it had taken time to switch the 3rd and 1st Egyptian brigades, with MacDonald having to wait for Lewis to pass him. The result of the 'hurry and skurry', as Hunter put it, was that these brigades were not in the places they should have been and a gap had opened up between them, MacDonald finding himself nearly a mile from Lewis.

According to Sandes's detailed account of the battle, MacDonald from his position on the right had seen what seemed like a body of the enemy

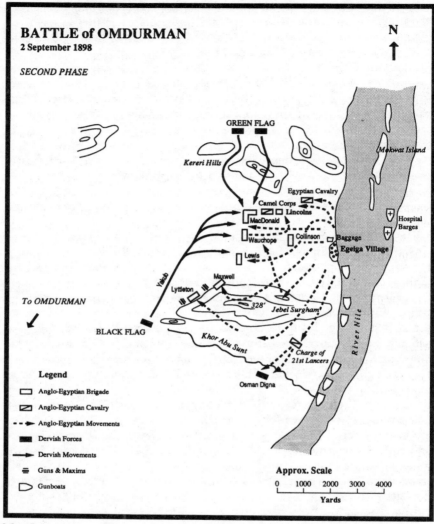

BATTLE of OMDURMAN
2 September 1898

SECOND PHASE

N

GREEN FLAG

Mekwat Island

Kereri Hills

Egyptian Cavalry

Camel Corps
Lincolns

MacDonald

Hospital
Barges

Wauchope
Collinson

Baggage
Egeiga Village

Lewis

Yakub

Maxwell

Lyttleton

To OMDURMAN

328'
Jebel Surgham

BLACK FLAG

Khor Abu Sunt

River Nile

*Charge of
21st Lancers*

Osman Digna

Legend

☐ Anglo-Egyptian Brigade

▱ Anglo-Egyptian Cavalry

- - ➤ Anglo-Egyptian Movements

▰ Dervish Forces

➤ Dervish Movements

≡ Guns & Maxims

▷ Gunboats

Approx. Scale

0   1000   2000   3000   4000

Yards

Map J

in front of him. He therefore asked Lewis to co-operate in safeguarding his right flank. Unfortunately Lewis had just received orders (not from Hunter) to catch up with Maxwell and so he ignored MacDonald's request. MacDonald then sent a galloper, Pritchard, to the Sirdar, asking whether he should attack the Dervishes. Kitchener told Pritchard: 'Can not he see that we are marching on Omdurman? Tell him to follow on.' It was about now – Hunter puts the time as being 9.30 a.m.[14] – that the Khalifa chose to launch his attack on MacDonald's now isolated brigade with his own Black Flag troops, 12,000 strong and commanded by his brother Emir Yakub, who had been waiting behind the western slopes of Jebel Surgham.

As the attack developed Kitchener's leading brigades were halted and Lewis was ordered – it is not clear whether this was by Kitchener or Hunter – to change front and to enfilade Black Flag. During the second phase of the battle there is some confusion about the messages and orders which flew around the battlefield. Kitchener has been accused by a number of commentators of bypassing his two divisional commanders and giving orders directly to his brigade and even battalion commanders.[15] So it is sometimes difficult, to say the least, to know when and from whom orders originated. At some stage Hunter sent a message to Kitchener requesting the help of a British brigade.[16] It is not precisely known when this request was made or where it was received but the probability is that Hunter sent his message to the Sirdar just before the attack by Black Flag or as it was developing. This would be consistent with what Kitchener wrote in his official despatch about hearing from Hunter that MacDonald's brigade 'might require support.' It seems, therefore, that Hunter's message prompted Kitchener to halt the advance and to despatch Wauchope's brigade to the assistance of MacDonald, some 3,000 yards away to the north-west.

A nasty moment now occurred when Lewis's 7th Egyptian battalion faltered when ordered into the firing line. Hunter happily was on the spot. His instinct and experience often told him where there might be a weakness among the troops and he at once ordered up two reserve companies of the 15th Egyptians, with fixed bayonets,[17] under the seasoned Major Hickman. This did the trick. Morale was restored and all was well. As expected, MacDonald's men dealt with the assault with great steadiness and repulsed the attack inflicting heavy casualties on the enemy side. No sooner had Black Flag begun to retreat when at 9.40 a.m., according to Hunter's report, another attack, again against MacDonald, was on its way but from a different direction, this time from the north. It was now the turn of the forces of Green Flag who, cheering and firing, came suddenly pouring down from the crests and gullies of the Kereri hills. Rapidly and skilfully Macdonald changed front by withdrawing troops from his left to form a new line at right angles to his former position and prepared to receive the fresh attack.

Having heard that Kitchener was sending Wauchope, Hunter then sent a message by Manifold to MacDonald to say that the British brigade was coming to his support. By the same messenger MacDonald replied that he was 'quite able to withstand this attack.'[18] Some accounts of the battle have MacDonald being rather testy with his superiors, during the heat of his fight with the Dervishes, and this may possibly have been the moment. According to Sandes, Hunter sent Manifold to ask Wauchope to hurry up, and then in the absence of Kitchener, gave orders that the British brigade should fill the gap on MacDonald's left.[19] In the event the Lincolns, famed for their musketry standards, were detached from Wauchope's brigade and went into the line on the right, together with Horse Artillery and the faithful Camel Corps, the rest of Wauchope's men remaining in support. Just how useful the reinforcements proved to be is difficult to gauge. Hunter later said that MacDonald 'beat [the Dervishes] off alone . . . did not require the Lincolns.'[20] Modern weapons had again that day proved their complete superiority over the various but poorly armed Dervishes. Green Flag was decimated and withdrew in groups, pursued by the Egyptian cavalry. The front was clear, Hunter reported, at about 10.10 a.m. Thus ended the second phase. The gap that had opened up between Lewis and MacDonald obviously offered the Khalifa an opportunity in the field which he failed to exploit. Had the Khalifa coordinated properly the attacks by Black Flag and Green Flag so they occurred simultaneously, then MacDonald's 1st brigade, together with the untried 4th brigade and the supply echelon in the rear, might have been in serious difficulties. As it was, MacDonald was able to parry first one assault and then, separately, the next.

The main blame for the opening up of the gap lay in the first place with Kitchener, for as the overall commander he should have ensured that the line of advance was ordered satisfactorily, especially when there were so many Dervish soldiers still in the field and about whom he had been warned by Hunter. Douglas Haig later criticised Kitchener for mishandling the battle of Omdurman. For instance, he considered that Kitchener should have thrown his left flank forward to Jebel Surgham and drawn in his right, which should not have been left so dangerously exposed.[21]

Hunter, as divisional commander, was not, it can be argued, entirely free from blame for the gap. On the other hand, we do not know to what extent the rather impatient Kitchener consulted him about the 'break-out' from the perimeter, and certainly he had requested Kitchener to give him more time to sort out the repositioning of the brigades which had been switched. The evidence suggests Hunter was not happy about the way the advance was being conducted, but was not of course in a position to restrain the leading brigades.

The last phase of the battle consists of the advance into Omdurman of Kitchener's forces. It can be said to begin when Kitchener, from his eminence on Jebel Surgham where he had been watching the final attack by Green Flag, snapped shut his glasses and made his famous comment about the enemy having had 'a good dusting'! He then moved down westwards with Lyttleton's and Maxwell's brigades and set off toward Khor Shambat, a water course just north of Omdurman, which he reached at 12.30 p.m. and where they rested and watered. Little resistance was encountered on

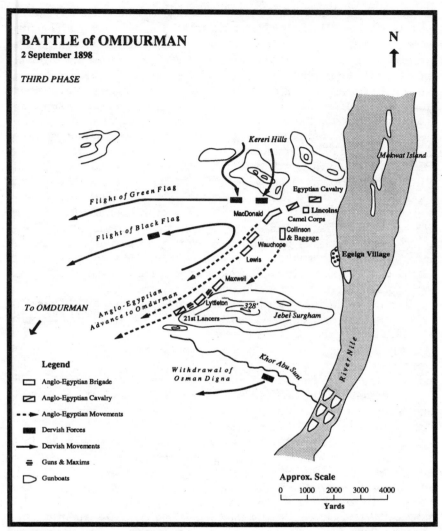

BATTLE of OMDURMAN
2 September 1898

THIRD PHASE

N ↑

Kereri Hills

Mekwat Island

Flight of Green Flag

Egyptian Cavalry

MacDonald

☐ Lincolns
Camel Corps

Flight of Black Flag

Collinson
& Baggage

Wauchope

Egeiga Village

Lewis

Maxwell

Anglo-Egyptian Advance to Omdurman

To OMDURMAN

Lyttleton

328'

21st Lancers

Jebel Surgham

River Nile

Khor Abu Sunt

Withdrawal of
Osman Digna

Legend

☐ Anglo-Egyptian Brigade

▨ Anglo-Egyptian Cavalry

- - ▶ Anglo-Egyptian Movements

▬ Dervish Forces

→ Dervish Movements

≡ Guns & Maxims

▷ Gunboats

Approx. Scale

0   1000   2000   3000   4000

Yards

Map K

the way, and the remnants of the enemy's troops had been seen fleeing in a disorganised mass towards the hills beyond Omdurman.

The brigades that had been closely engaged with the men of Green Flag now reformed about a mile south of the battle area and, under Hunter, a search began at about 11 a.m. for those killed and wounded. Hunter left the battlefield with the last brigade at about 2 p.m. An hour later MacDonald's and Lewis's brigades were at Khor Shambat. Kitchener had

101

already moved on towards Omdurman taking with him Maxwell's troops and the 32nd Field battery. Hunter, content that all was well with his men, rode after him, giving orders that his brigades should follow on after watering. He caught up with Kitchener eventually near the Khalifa's enclosure in the middle of the town. In his exhilaration Hunter told his Chief that he was 'Lord of Khartoum if he cared to be', and that he 'hoped the government would give him a big sum down' now that the campaign was over.[22] Not long after this the two men had a narrow escape from death. A shell landed near them, fired by men of the 37th battery on the east bank of the Nile. Oblivious of Kitchener's presence in the middle of Omdurman, they were still pounding away at the Mahdi's tomb. Both Kitchener and Hunter escaped injury but the Hon. Hubert Howard, a war reporter for *The Times* and *The New York Herald*, was killed instantly by a splinter. Hunter now left Kitchener, who went to liberate the prisoners. Hunter thought them, dismissively, to be mostly 'rogues and vagabonds.'

Organised resistance in Omdurman had by now come to an end but individual Dervish soldiers were still being hunted down as Hunter reported to Maurice: '. . . we did have an afternoon, poking into houses, in and out of narrow alleys, kicking down doors, forcing gateways, chasing devils all over the place, most surrendered, but we had to kill some 300 or 400.' Some of the Sudanese, Hunter admitted, did nothing but loot the 'prettiest slave girls and best trophies.'[23]

But what of the Khalifa? After the rout of his army, he had returned to Omdurman. When it became clear to him that there was to be no last stand in the town, he decided to escape to the west. So, together with part of his entourage, he headed off towards El Obeid. When this was discovered, the cavalry under Broadwood gave pursuit, but returned in due course exhausted and unsuccessful.

On the night after the battle it was 1 a.m. before Hunter was able to go to bed. He and Wingate sat up writing telegrams and reports for despatch by steamer at daybreak.[24] Hunter's transport was elsewhere and so he was without his kit. But Smith-Dorrien, OC of the 13th Sudanese, gave him 'a mug of soup and a mug of the best champagne and both were delicious.' He was lent a blanket and a bed and 'slept till dawn like a top after one of the best days I ever passed.'[25] He could rest in the knowledge that he had himself made a signal contribution to the fall of the Khalifa's empire, marked by the destruction of his army at Omdurman.

As he grew more senior and therefore responsible as a General for the lives of thousands of men on the battlefield, Hunter became more concerned about casualties. He was greatly thankful that the loss of life in the Anglo-Egyptian army had been so small at Omdurman. Two British and two Egyptian officers, one war correspondent, and 47 other ranks, 29 of them British, had been killed. A total of 382 of all ranks had been wounded. This contrasted with the terrible toll on the Dervish side. On 4 September

10,800 dead were counted. The numbers of wounded were impossible to compute but might have been twice that number. During the whole campaign fewer than 60 British officers and men were killed in action, while the total for the Egyptian army was 150 killed. The figures for those wounded are more difficult to arrive at, as are the numbers of those who died of disease.

In his report to the Chief of Staff Hunter was lavish in his praise of the infantry division of the Egyptian army, except he had a scathing comment on the 'bad example' of the 7th Egyptians, whose behaviour 'left much to be desired.' Some 70 British officers and NCOs serving with the Egyptian army were mentioned by Hunter by name, as were no less than 173 officers, NCOs and men of the Egyptian army. Sergeant J. Scott Barbour of the Gordon Highlanders attached to the 11th Sudanese was specially recommended for a commission. Hunter praised his three staff officers, Kincaid, Fitton and Talbot, his two gallopers, Captain R. H. Penton (the Senior Medical Officer) and Captain F. J. Howard, and his two Orderly officers Captain N. M. Smyth, who was awarded the VC, and Lieutenant M. G. Manifold.

He singled out three special points about the action that day. First, the steadiness of the troops during the attack on the entrenched camp, the valuable cooperation of the gunboats and horse artillery 'and the total absence of any flurry or alarm even among the servants and other undisciplined persons' (here he was referring to the non-fighting elements of the army). Second, the gallantry of Captains Capper and Whigham and of the 13th Sudanese in capturing the summit of Surgham hill. Third, and above all, the repulse of the enemy by the skilful MacDonald and his brigade. In this part of the battle the 9th Sudanese battalion who had suffered most heavily, and the gratifying conduct of the 2nd Egyptian battalion under Major Pink, were specially mentioned. Hunter added that 'the superiority of our modern guns and breech loading rifles' was most pronounced. A chivalrous man, Hunter had the last word for the Dervish enemy: 'one is compelled to offer a tribute of admiration to the desperate gallantry of the foe.'

The day after the battle Hunter set about finding a decent clean place in which the army could camp, and so the victorious troops moved out of Omdurman and its suburbs to Khor Shambat. Omdurman was in a dreadful state, its alleys and roads filled with putrid rubbish and dead donkeys. Many of the Dervishes wounded in the battle had somehow managed to drag themselves back to the town to die, while many of the dead on the battlefield were carried in by night by the women and buried under the flooring of their houses and huts. On Kitchener's orders the shell-damaged Mahdi's tomb, built in red brick and the only notable building in Omdurman, was demolished. Hunter, like most of his peers no doubt, thoroughly agreed with this decision, seeing the tomb as a monument celebrating the victory of Mahdism. By its destruction the disgrace suffered by Britain in 1885 could now, in Hunter's view, be forgotten and atoned for.[26] Khartoum, undefended, was quickly occupied and a memorial served for Gordon was held in the ruins of his palace.

NOTES

1. DHD 152.
2. WO 175/428 note by AH on Omdurman 29/4/1919.
3. Ibid.
4. Ibid.; NR AH to various addressees, including Maurice, 14 Oct. 1898.
5. Ibid. (NR).
6. Sandes 447.
7. NR AH–COS 7/9/98.
8. *Daily Telegraph* 1 Oct. 1898 (despatch by Kitchener 16 Sep. 1898).
9. NR AH letter loc. cit.
10. The numbers have been estimated variously. Churchill gave them as nearly 15,000 and Hunter as fully 10,000. Other writers have put the numbers at 14,000 (Keown-Boyd) and over 20,000 (Ziegler).
11. NR AH–COS loc. cit.
12. NR AH letter loc. cit.; Sandes 267.
13. NR AH–COS loc. cit.
14. Ibid.
15. Keown-Boyd 32.
16. NR AH–COS loc. cit.
17. Churchill 295.
18. NR AH–COS loc. cit.
19. Sandes 269.
20. NR AH letter loc. cit.
21. Ziegler 163.
22. NR AH letter loc. cit.
23. Ibid.
24. WO loc. cit.
25. NR AH letter loc. cit.
26. Ibid.

CHAPTER 10

The Blue Nile

There was to be no respite for Kitchener or Hunter. The former had carried up the Nile sealed instructions from the Foreign Office dated 2 August, to be opened only after the capture of Khartoum[1]. The British government were concerned about French ambitions in the Upper Nile valley and considered that no European power, other than Britain, had a claim to occupy any part of that valley. These instructions did not envisage further large-scale military operations after the occupation of Khartoum; but they authorised the Sirdar to send two flotillas, one up the White Nile as far as Fashoda (see map A, p. 16) under his personal command, and the other up the Blue Nile, which rose in Lake Tana in the Abyssinian highlands, to Rosaires.

Information reached Kitchener after the battle that a French military force under Captain Jean-Baptiste Marchand was established at Fashoda. So on 10 September he set out for the south taking with him five gunboats, troops and artillery. He reached Fashoda on 26 September and, under the wide discretionary powers he had been given, set about with some panache to defuse the tricky situation. Marchand had been given the task of trying to grab the regions of the upper Nile valley for France. At one time the French planned to send two other expeditions from Abyssinia, with the approval and support of Emperor Menelik, to Fashoda to join hands with Marchand.[2] In all this the intentions of the Abyssinians, from the British point of view, were unclear.

Kitchener entrusted the mission up the Blue Nile to Hunter, who was authorised to go as far as the foot of the cataract believed to start at Rosaires but was not to land troops or march them beyond the navigable point in the river. If he were to encounter any Abyssinian outposts, he was to report back and await further instructions. For his enterprise Hunter was ordered to take three gunboats, one battalion and two Maxims, and to use his discretion as to where he should hoist flags and leave garrisons. He should offer peaceful greetings to local chiefs and sheikhs, the principal ones being required to attend at Khartoum. If he met Ahmed Fadel, one of the Khalifa's most zealous lieutenants, still at large with a sizeable force in the south-east of the Sudan, he was to offer him terms of surrender. If these were refused, Hunter was given discretion to deal with Fadel as he thought fit.[3] The expedition encountered no opposition in its progress, Hunter describing his reception up the Nile as being cordial everywhere. The people, who had long resented the rule of the Khalifa, seemed genuinely pleased there was to be a change of government. After stops on the way Hunter finally reached his destination, Rosaires, late on 29 September. Here, some 425 miles south of Omdurman by river, he issued a proclamation, and raised the flags of Britain and Egypt as an indication that these countries had taken the district under their protection. There was no sign of Ahmed Fadel or of Abyssinian outposts, though some weeks before Hunter's arrival, three emissaries from Menelik had visited Rosaires and left a flag behind.

The next day Hunter left Rosaires, having posted a small garrison there, and began a rapid journey downstream. After establishing other garrisons at Karkoj, Sennar and Wad Medani Hunter continued downstream to Omdurman, arriving there on 2 October, having completed the journey from Rosaires in 50 hours. He immediately filed a report to the Chief of Staff about his expedition. At the same time he offered to provide full details later about 'boats, and boat-building, river currents . . ., clothing, crops, cattle and flocks, the mosque at Sennar, market days, prices of wood, corrections to intelligence handbook, principal sheikhs, routes adopted by Abyssinian messengers to Khalifa, trade, taxes in former days, salt.'[4] There seemed no limit to the matters that caught his attention!

We do not know the reason for Hunter's hurried journey down the Nile from Rosaires, but he may well have wished to reach Omdurman in time to report to Kitchener before the Sirdar left for Cairo on 3 October. Hunter was not, however, destined to be in charge at Omdurman for long for he fell ill. He went down with fever and more seriously, developed an abscess in his rectum. He was at once sent down to Cairo where he underwent a succession of operations. Hunter was visited by Cromer while in hospital, and wrote in his diary on 1 November: 'Ld. Cromer offered me Sirdar when vacant. I declined: preferred India.' We must infer from this that the gift of this post lay with Cromer and not with the government at home. Wingate wrote sympathetically to Hunter[5] ten days or so later, referring to 'the long and severe illness you have had', and saying that the change home, which the doctors were recommending, would set him up 'for the more important duties which will no doubt devolve upon you when the Sirdar goes.' Wingate did not expect Kitchener to stay much longer in the Sudan, and clearly thought Hunter would succeed him. Kitchener, too, considered Hunter his logical successor.[6]

By late November he was well on the way to a good recovery. During his stay in hospital he had ample time to reflect on his 14 year's service with the Egyptian army. For him it had all begun with the 9th Sudanese battalion, which he considered taught the Egyptian army to fight, and were worth two of any other battalions. 'My greatest pride' he wrote, 'is that they never refused me anything.'[7] His record over the last ten years spoke for itself. Of the six major battles in which he had taken part (Hafir can be excluded), he had commanded a brigade in two (Argin and Toski), and a division in three (Firket, Atbara and Omdurman), all during the reconquest, while in the sixth (Abu Hamed) he was in sole command. On the long campaign just concluded there had been difficult moments such as dragging the gunboats up the Second Cataract, the so-called 'death march', the lightning strike at Abu Hamed, his vulnerable position at Berber, the second reconnaissance at Atbara when his force was virtually surrounded and finally the fierce attacks on his first brigade at Omdurman. Usually the actual battles against the Dervishes were relatively straightforward. Once the forces had been lined up against each other, the commander could not exert a lot of tactical influence on the course of the fighting. Discipline, the bringing to bear of superior fire power and, above all, courage, were the ingredients necessary to achieve success. Leadership during the fighting tended to be exercised by example, as has been seen, and this was one of the areas in which Hunter excelled.

But at Omdurman, a more complex battle, at least in its second phase, than the earlier battles in the reconquest campaign, things had gone wrong, happily not fatally, when there arose a need for urgent battlefield decisions by the commander. There has in the past been speculation about the exact role played by Kitchener at Omdurman. For instance, Hunter was asked more than 20 years after the battle (when Sir George Arthur was preparing his biography of Kitchener) whether Kitchener issued the tactical orders off his own bat or whether Hunter suggested them to him. Hunter's answer is interesting as far as it goes. He said: '. . . it was practically as in the old sailing days. The Admiral said to the Sailing Master or Mate, "Lay me alongside such a ship".'[8] The trouble at Omdurman was that in his haste to reach the town, Kitchener had failed to consider properly the battlefield role of his divisional commanders and how he should respond tactically to any further attacks which the Dervishes might make. Furthermore, as far as the chain of command went, there was an absence of clarity as to how the orders given by the overall commander should be conveyed to the troops. This was the one battle where there seems to have been a lack of planning or liaison between Kitchener and Hunter. Whose was the fault? It is impossible to give a fair answer, but the strong suspicion is that it lay mainly with Kitchener.

The working relationship between Kitchener and Hunter was critical to the success of both the Dongola campaign in 1896 and the succeeding reconquest of the Sudan in 1897–98. It was an unusual one, not easy to untangle and one that has not, as far as is known, been evaluated by historians. Writers, with some notable exceptions, have tended to give most of the credit for the defeat of the Dervishes to Kitchener, and have often failed to give Hunter his due.

The starting point is that the two men have to be seen, even after Kitchener was made Sirdar, as being almost rivals, though Hunter did not have Kitchener's inordinate ambition. Eventually, by the time of the battle of Omdurman, Hunter had become the loyal subordinate, but along the way he was fiercely critical of his chief, whom he sometimes saw as a mean bully and deficient in certain military qualities which he perceived as essential in a senior commander. For one thing, Hunter considered, justifiably, that Kitchener had no real concern for his troops and their welfare. For another, he lacked a professional knowledge of military tactics and had no real eye for country. At one stage, after the 'death march', Hunter felt so strongly that there must have been a danger that Kitchener would lose his support. No one who saw himself other than a virtual equal could have written to his chief in such blunt terms as Hunter wrote to Kitchener in August 1896. The crisis began to pass when virtually independent commands were given to Hunter as Governor of Dongola and during the advance to Berber, although there was still conflict between the two men over the economies insisted on by the Sirdar.

Hunter knew well enough that Kitchener looked to him to plan the battles and then to do the fighting. This made Hunter's position as the tough yet popular commander in the field practically unassailable, and consequently enabled him sometimes to take liberties with his chief. Thus, as we have seen earlier on at least one occasion, Hunter calmly disobeyed Kitchener's orders. This was the act of a man both independently-minded and supremely confident in his own ability and judgement. At this stage in his career Hunter, the happy warrior, had less need of Kitchener than his chief had of him.

For his part, Kitchener, always ready to use people to further his career, clearly saw Hunter as his indispensable 'sword-arm'. At the same time he had been on the receiving end of Hunter's outspokenness, and may well have been afraid that Hunter, unless carefully handled, would undermine his position in Cairo by exposing his deficiencies as a commander. With Hunter, he could not play the part of the overbearing C-in-C of popular repute. With commendable realism he allowed Hunter his head and this contributed in no small way to the successful outcome of the reconquest campaign.

There were times when Kitchener showed himself to be indecisive and to lack confidence in his own judgement. This indecision was most noticeable on the Atbara before battle was joined with Mahmoud. There is also a suggestion of some loss of confidence the day before the battle of Omdurman when he saw the Dervish hordes and seemed to require bolstering by Hunter.

In the course of the campaign Hunter came to respect his chief's organisational and logistical feat of bringing the railway, the men and their supplies up to the Atbara for the final advance to Omdurman. He acknowledged too that it was Kitchener who bore the overall burden and responsibility for the expedition. Undoubtedly the combination of Kitchener and Hunter proved highly effective in defeating the Khalifa. This was because the two men, both formidable in their different ways, complemented each other. Further, they had been able to work out a satisfactory *modus operandi* by which each was able to utilise his special talents.

After the victory of Omdurman Hunter was generous in the praise he gave his chief both to his face and in the letters he wrote home. Henceforth we are not aware in our story of any further criticism by Hunter of Kitchener. On the contrary at home Hunter defended his chief in public against attacks on him by the press for his alleged ill-treatment of the Dervish wounded. Personal relations between the two men always remained good though not close. In 1910 Kitchener was best man at Hunter's wedding.

The rewards for the Nile expedition were not long in coming through, and were announced in the *London Gazette* on 15 November. Hunter was made a KCB. He was also raised by the Khedive, Abbas Hilmi II (who had succeeded his father Tewfik in 1892) to the Second class of the Turkish Order of Osmanieh. Unlike Kitchener he always had good relations with Abbas Hilmi and found him to be the 'essence of courtesy and earnest in seeking opportunities to assure me that he appreciates the work I have done for him and his people.'[9]

The doctors having pronounced Hunter well enough to travel home to England and face the receptions awaiting a hero's return, he left Cairo on 21 December for the sea journey which took him to Plymouth via Marseilles. He reached the French port on Christmas Day at the precise moment that Ahmed Fadel was attempting to cross the Blue Nile to join the Khalifa in Kordofan. But by now he had mixed feelings over what part, if any, he should be playing in the process of tracking down the diminishing bands of Dervishes. On the one hand his fighting instincts urged him to help finish off the Dervishes once and for all. On the other, after over 14 years' service in Egypt and the Sudan, he was looking for fresh fields to conquer.

NOTES

1. Magnus 138.
2. Pakenham *The Scramble for Africa* 527–31 and 533.
3. NR Kitchener's written instructions to AH 10/9/98.
4. NR AH–COS 2/10/98.
5. SAD 267/1/437 Wingate–AH 12/11/1898.
6. Keown-Boyd 258.
7. SAD 110/11/1–89 hist IX Sud Bn.
8. WO 175/428 note by AH 29/4/1919.
9. DHD 179.

CHAPTER 11

Between Wars

Back in London with his career in the forefront of his mind, Hunter lost no time in calling on the Commander-in-Chief, Lord Wolseley, whom he saw on 4 January 1899. He was offered command, as he noted in his diary, of a 'First Class District' in India. But this offer presented Hunter with difficulties which he could not immediately resolve. The Sudan had just been divided by Kitchener, the newly appointed Governor-General, into four Districts, and Hunter had been appointed Governor of Omdurman, the most important of these. In a few weeks time he was writing to Duncan from the Naval and Military Club, his London headquarters, saying that his future was still undecided. There had been fresh developments. Apparently no fewer than four tempting offers had now been made to him: 1. to stay in the Sudan and become, when Kitchener left, Sirdar; 2. to go to South Africa where serious difficulties had begun to arise with the Boers in the Transvaal; 3. to go to China; 4. to take command on the North-West Frontier of India where there had been a Russian threat to Afghanistan and so to India for decades. As he commented, it was 'very difficult for a greedy person like me to settle where to fight next.' The fourth proposition appealed to him most, given there was a proviso that he would have the right to go back to Africa if anything happened there.[1] It seems remarkable that a junior Major-General should be given these choices of posting. As remarkable perhaps was the outcome. For he obtained in due course his posting to India, but only to be lent a few months later to the British expeditionary force in South Africa. But Hunter had become to an extent a protégé of Wolseley, though not perhaps quite a member of his so-called 'ring'.

In the meantime, as one of the heroes of the Sudan, he was in great demand. A genuinely modest man who shunned publicity, Hunter was determined to avoid being excessively lionised. But first of all the Queen summoned him to Osborne in the Isle of Wight. He arrived on the evening of Monday 9 January and was invested before dinner with the KCB. He and Rundle, the chief of staff in the Sudan, who had also just been knighted, then dined alone with the Queen and her eldest daughter Victoria, widow of the late German Emperor and the mother of the reigning Kaiser Wilhelm II. The Queen wrote in her diary that she had a good deal of conversation with the two Generals. She noted what Hunter had to say about the battle of Omdurman, and the heavy losses they would have suffered had the enemy attacked earlier.[2] The Queen liked to have photographs of her leading Generals and some six months later Hunter had a letter from Sir Arthur Bigge, the Queen's Private Secretary, to say Her Majesty would like a photograph of him in Egyptian Army uniform![3] While at Osborne Hunter wrote an enthusiastic letter to Duncan about his visit to Osborne that began: 'It is a proud man I am to write to you from the Queen's home . . .' and ended: 'She is a marvellous Lady and no wonder that her subjects are willing to die for her.'[4]

After Osborne Hunter's regiment was quick to honour him, when Lt.-Col. Crofton and the Officers of the 2nd battalion of the King's Own Regiment entertained him lavishly at Whittingham barracks, Lichfield.

Next it was the turn of his native heath in Scotland, and on 21 January 1899 Hunter with his proud mother travelled to West Kilbride. An open carriage drawn by four greys preceded by the pipes took him through the gaily decorated streets to the School House where he was presented with a magnificent illuminated Address. He was deeply touched by this local show of affection and pride in his achievement, and in his diary he wrote: 'Great Day.'

Lancaster, the home of Hunter's regiment, was not to be outdone by Scotland, and on 30 January he arrived there to be made a Freeman of the ancient borough. First he was entertained at a banquet by the officers of the regiment. The next day he drove through densely-packed streets to the Town Hall, accompanied by Colonel Fitzherbert, an eminent officer in the King's Own Regiment. In his reply to the Mayor's speech he referred in particular to the constructive side of the campaigns in which he had fought. No one who heard Hunter speak that day could have doubted that his was the authentic voice of the Victorian soldier-administrator, confident in his belief that Britain had a civilising mission in which the preservation of law and order was paramount.

There were other formal engagements in Scotland. He received at Ayr from the Provost a finely-wrought Sword of Honour, and then on a very special occasion he was made a Freeman of the Royal Burgh of Irvine and presented with a handsome silver casket. At Irvine he was following in the footsteps of his soldier uncle Nicol Grahame a hero of the Crimean war and Indian mutiny. Grahame had been made a Freeman at the tender age of 27. He had been a leader of the storming party on the assault on the Redan fortress at Sebastopol. Then a year after Hunter's birth he had been killed at the relief of Lucknow. Lord Wolseley, once a brother officer, had years later described Grahame as 'the bravest of the brave'.

Back in London Hunter enjoyed a busy social life. On one occasion he addressed the audience of the Ambassador Theatre from the stage in aid of the new college at Khartoum which had been founded in memory of Gordon. He was invited to the Hunterian Oration at the Royal College of Surgeons, Lincoln's Inn Fields, delivered by Sir William MacCormac, the President and the surgeon who had saved Hunter's arm years before. Another guest was the Prince of Wales, who arrived for the Oration and stayed for dinner. Hunter noted in his diary 'HRH Prince of Wales sent for me after dinner and kept me by his side all night.'

Quite suddenly he was summoned back to Egypt. A crisis had apparently arisen in the Sudan, with reports of renewed military activity by the Khalifa.

The journey to Cairo, which he reached on 1 March, ended in anti-climax. On arrival he at once reported by telegram to the Sirdar who was, of course, in the Sudan. Back came an answer from Kitchener the next day just saying with no apparent reference to Hunter's presence being

111

needed in the Sudan: 'Better take India.' Hunter called on Cromer, saw the Khedive, lunched with Wingate and dined with Eldon Gorst, now the Financial Adviser. He hurried off to stay a night at Sidi Gaber outside Alexandria with George and Hylda Hunter, and then returned home, having decided to accept the Quetta command. A few days later he told Duncan and Abby that if an army corps had been vacant in India Kitchener would have taken it, and so made way for Hunter to become Sirdar. Wolseley's advice had been to accept Quetta and take the job of Sirdar later, if worth having.[5] This apparently coincided with Hunter's own thinking. If he did well in India, he confided to Duncan, the next step would be an army corps, equivalent to one of the four great Commands in India. After that he foresaw a spell at army headquarters in London. He would then know the army 'in all its phases.' Hunter in his own way had become highly ambitious.

The summoning of Hunter by Kitchener 2,000 miles only to tell him to accept the Quetta post is perhaps, on the face of it, bizarre. In the light of patchy intelligence available, Kitchener may have had one of his fits of indecision, this time about how finally to put down the Khalifa. At first he must have thought that Hunter was needed for the task, and then simply changed his mind, considering it could be safely left to others. The account of how the Khalifa and his hard core of supporters were brought to battle by Wingate and how they all perished at Um Dibaykarat (see Map A, p. 16) in November 1899 is, however, beyond the scope of this story. Hunter was elsewhere and not involved.

Hunter may well have been relieved when the various presentations made to him ended and he was no longer required to make speeches. While not being specially gifted or witty as a speaker, he spoke from the heart and what he said was simply expressed and easily understood. His voice was pleasant, and the warmth and strength of his personality would undoubtedly have reached his audience. Certainly he needed all his common sense to remain with his feet on the ground after he had listened to so many eulogies about himself.[6] He had also received the thanks of both Houses of Parliament for his services in the Sudan. But he seems to have survived it all without becoming big-headed and a year later Jimmy Grierson, his old schoolfriend and now a rising soldier himself, said when he met Hunter after a long gap that he was 'just the same old man not a bit puffed up' with all his advancement and success.[7]

Confirmation of Hunter's appointment at Quetta came through from the Indian government and his last few weeks at home were a hectic round of official visits (they would be called 'briefings' today), lunches, dinner parties and theatres. He lunched with Lord Roberts, who would have told him all there was to know about the North-West Frontier, and saw Sir Evelyn Wood, now the Adjutant-General, who had recruited him to the Egyptian army.

On 28 April Hunter left London. He travelled via Brindisi and Egypt, reaching Bombay a fortnight later. Eleven days after he had first set foot in India he arrived at his destination, Quetta, nearly 400 miles upcountry from Karachi. This famous army post, situated in Baluchistan, lay 5,700 feet up, surrounded by snow-capped peaks. The Afghan frontier was at its nearest point some 40 miles to the west. Hunter in his District had to guard 800 miles of frontier, almost all of it in wild and rugged country bordering Afghanistan and Persia. The region was sparsely populated by fierce Pathans. But the frontier was quiet, and during his short time in Quetta it gave Hunter – perhaps to his disappointment – no trouble.

He lost no time in going off for a three-week tour of his District. The long days in the saddle, the tough physical conditions, the new scenes and people would have been meat and drink to him. But in a different continent the war clouds were gathering, as a crisis began to loom in South Africa between Britain and the Boer republic of the Transvaal. Soon after his return to Quetta Hunter learnt that he had been designated Chief of Staff to Sir Redvers Buller in case of war in South Africa. In his diary he commented: 'Thank God and Wolseley!' Buller, commanding an army corps at Aldershot and one of the leading members of Wolseley's 'ring', had apparently specially requested Hunter for the job.[8] It was at first sight an odd appointment for Hunter who was above all a front-line soldier and a fighting General. He had little staff experience and had been away, effectively, from the British army and its methods for 15 years. On the credit side he had much experience of campaigning and what was needed in war, and he was regarded as a good administrator. He, himself, no doubt would have preferred a division.

Preparations for war in South Africa were now speeding up. The British cabinet had at length decided to send reinforcements there, and the Indian authorities offered 5,500 seasoned British soldiers stationed in India. Hunter was now urgently wanted in South Africa. On 2 September he left Quetta for Simla where he had discussions with Sir William Lockhart, the Commander-in-Chief, India, and met the Viceroy, Lord Curzon. He found everyone in Simla from Viceroy and Vicereine downwards 'the essence of kindness' and enjoyed his short time there. On 21 September Hunter embarked at Bombay on the *SS City of London* with a contingent of soldiers bound for Durban nearly 4,000 miles away, the first troops having sailed four days before. The whole exercise of making the troops in India ready for service in Africa was performed with efficiency and speed. Within 48 hours of receiving embarkation orders the men were on the quayside at Bombay and Calcutta waiting to board their transports.[9]

The British and Boers had long had an uneasy relationship in South Africa. To avoid what they saw as the heavy hand of British rule the Boers founded two distant independent republics, the Orange Free State and the Transvaal, which by 1854 had been recognised by Britain. But then in 1877 the British changed their policy and somewhat unexpectedly annexed the two republics. As a result there followed the First Boer war in 1881 when the British were defeated at Majuba Hill (see map M, p. 119). Under the ensuing conventions the two republics again became independent, though Britain reserved a measure of control over them in some matters including foreign affairs, not a recipe for accord. The discovery of gold on the Rand in 1886 transformed the Transvaal, almost overnight, from a poor country into a rich one. There was soon the inevitable influx of people from all over the world. These foreigners – or Uitlanders – came to out-number the Boer population. It was not long before they were demanding equal rights with the Boers, especially over the franchise. These were emphatically denied by the conservative President, Paul Kruger.

Frustrations had built up among the Uitlanders and this led to a clumsy attempt at a *coup d'état* planned by Cecil Rhodes, Prime Minister of the Cape. It misfired and the small invading force led by Dr Jameson was ignominiously rounded up. Rhodes was disgraced and Jameson went to prison, while Joseph Chamberlain, the British Colonial Secretary, was suspected of complicity. A new High Commissioner, Alfred Milner, was sent out to mend fences. But he was as convinced an Imperialist as Chamberlain and decided that the Transvaal must reform itself in accord-ance with British wishes, or there would be war. Kruger determined to resist British pressure, and drew on the wealth of the Transvaal to re-equip its citizen army. President Steyn of the Orange Free State, a conciliatory man, took the initiative in arranging discussions between Kruger and Milner at Bloemfontein. Unhappily these lengthy negotiations finally ended in June 1899 with nothing achieved.

At this point Milner began to worry about the small number of British troops in South Africa, 10,000 men under General Sir William Butler, who were facing a potential force of over 50,000 men from the two republics combined.[10] Both Milner and Wolseley began to agitate with Lord Lansdowne, the Secretary of State for War, for reinforcements to be sent to South Africa. Wolseley considered 10,000 men were needed. He also wanted an army corps and a cavalry division mobilised as a show of force; this request was at once turned down. Butler in South Africa sympathised with the Boers and said that reinforcements were not needed. Lansdowne moved slowly over all this but in the second week of June he told Sir Redvers Buller, Commander of the first army corps at Aldershot, that in the event of war he would command in South Africa. Surprisingly Buller, a man with a formidable reputation as a soldier, had never had an independ-ent command. His response to Lansdowne's news was not enthusiastic.

In July Lansdowne appointed Major-General Sir Penn Symons, a friend of his with an Indian Army background, as General Officer Commanding Natal and the next month sent him 2,000 troops as reinforcements. Milner

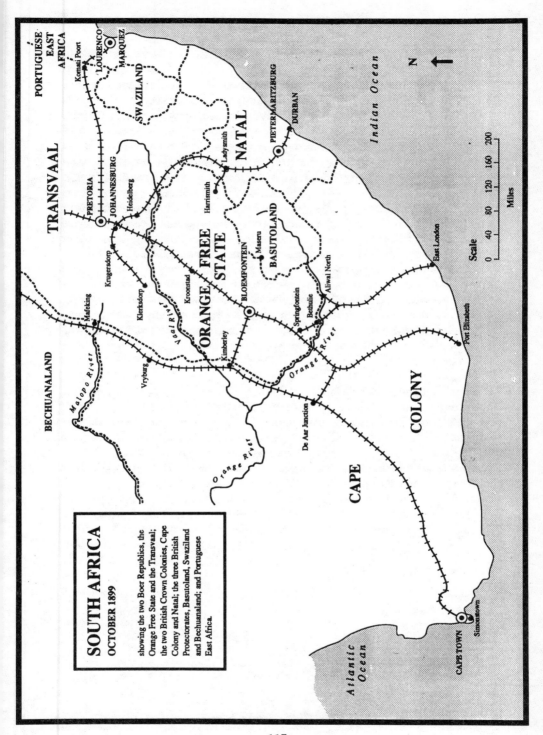

SOUTH AFRICA
OCTOBER 1899

showing the two Boer Republics, the
Orange Free State and the Transvaal;
the two British Crown Colonies, Cape
Colony and Natal; the three British
Protectorates, Basutoland, Swaziland
and Bechuanaland; and Portuguese
East Africa.

PORTUGUESE EAST AFRICA

Komati Poort

LOURENCO MARQUEZ

SWAZILAND

TRANSVAAL

PRETORIA

JOHANNESBURG

Heidelberg

Krugersdorp

Klerksdorp

Vaal River

Kroonstad

ORANGE FREE STATE

Vryburg

Kimberley

BLOEMFONTEIN

Maseru

BASUTOLAND

Harrismith

Ladysmith

PIETERMARITZBURG

DURBAN

NATAL

Indian Ocean

N

BECHUANALAND

Mafeking

Malopo River

Orange River

De Aar Junction

Springfontein
Bethulie

Aliwal North

Orange River

East London

Port Elizabeth

CAPE COLONY

Atlantic Ocean

CAPE TOWN

Simonstown

Scale

0 40 80 120 160 200

Miles

Map L

115

had been canvassing to have Butler dismissed and in August the latter duly resigned but was not at once replaced.

On 8 September the Cabinet agreed to proposals put up by Chamberlain for 8,000 more troops to be sent to Natal which was seen as the place most vulnerable to a Boer attack. Many of these troops came from India. Wolseley had wanted someone other than Penn Symons, who lacked African experience, to command these men and so it was decided, as something of a compromise, that the Quartermaster-General Sir George White VC, a former C-in-C India, would go out from Britain as GOC Natal with Symons coming under him. He sailed on 16 September with the two staff officers he had chosen, Colonel Ian Hamilton, of whom we shall hear much more, and Colonel Sir Henry Rawlinson who has already entered our story. White had been given no detailed instruction by the War Office on what course he should pursue when he reached Natal. But then in those days there was no staff to prepare plans and Generals were usually given wide discretion in their overseas military commands.

On 23 September, when Hunter was already at sea, the Cabinet agreed at last to send the army corps, which Wolseley had been saying since June was needed, to South Africa. A few days later the Transvaal mobilised and her sister republic, the Orange Free State, followed in her wake. War was now inevitable.

Hunter's journey from Bombay to Durban lasted 15 days. In a letter to Duncan written while at sea, ever cautious in this sort of matter, he offered no view about how long the impending conflict might last. He hoped the 'stigma' of Majuba Hill – which he compared to the disgrace of not relieving Gordon at Khartoum – would be erased. Musingly, as he gazed at the ocean, he wondered what the outcome would be of the America's Cup yacht race, then taking place at Newport, Rhode Island, a stone's throw from Duncan and his family. Finally looking ahead and no doubt considering the qualities and mettle of his new foes he warned his brother that there would be little time for him to indulge in letter-writing.[11]

NOTES

1. DHD 185–6.
2. RA QVJ 9 Jan. 1899.
3. AHd 18/7/1899.
4. DHD 182.
5. Ibid. 187.
6. The various presentations made to Hunter and the speeches he made at them were widely reported. See for instance *Lancaster Guardian* 4 Feb 1899; *Ardrossan and Saltcoats Herald* 10 Feb. 1899 and *Glasgow Herald* 3 Apr 1899.
7. Macdiarmid *The Life of Lieutenant-General Sir J. H. Grierson* 163.
8. Pemberton *Battles of the Boer War* 35.

9. TH II 106.
10. Conan Doyle *The Great Boer War* 57.
11. DHD 191.

CHAPTER 12

Natal Invaded

When the *City of London* docked at Durban on 5 October 1899 Hunter found that no state of war as yet existed between Transvaal and Britain. War in fact was just six days away. Sir Redvers Buller, the C-in-C, had still not left London and would not set foot in Cape Town until 31 October, while Sir George White, the new commander in Natal, had not yet arrived in Durban though he was due very shortly.

Even if the two senior commanders were not yet present in the country which was about to be attacked – of that there could be little doubt – at least the army in Natal had been reinforced by seasoned and well-equipped troops. These were being sent rapidly by train north to Ladysmith and beyond, though not up to the frontier. The military position insofar as numbers of troops went was not, therefore, quite as precarious as it had been, and Sir Penn Symons, still GOC Natal, now had about 12,000 men under him mainly split between Ladysmith and the area of Glencoe and Dundee. Nonetheless the arrangements by the British to defend their colony against a threat that had been growing steadily over the last four months had been made hurriedly, and, as would soon be discovered, insufficient thought had been given as to where precisely the defences should be concentrated against an invading army. In particular, there appeared to be no local plan for the defence of Ladysmith[1], the main army centre in the colony.

The Boers were, in contrast, much better prepared for war. Mobilisation was swift and there was an ambitious invasion plan. The two Boer republics were acting as one, and their Presidents had sent 21,000 men to the frontiers of Natal[2] to invade the British colony at various points. Working on interior lines of communication the troops assembled quickly, but, fortunately for the British, the Boer leaders had not launched, as Wolseley feared at one time they might, a pre-emptive attack directed at capturing Durban before reinforcements arrived. The armies of both republics were mainly composed of part-time soldiers. Every burgher between the age of 16 and 60 was liable for military duty and was expected to fight for his country. As a basic minimum he had to provide himself with a horse, saddle, bridle, rifle and 30 cartridges, and provisions for eight days.[3]

Conscious of his family responsibility as the breadwinner, the Boer was not a rash soldier. Nonetheless he was brave and hardy, and often fired by religious enthusiasm. Invariably he was an expert marksman armed with a modern rifle, often a Mauser and, on his pony, was highly mobile. The artillery forces of the Transvaal, built up by the Commandant-General, Piet Joubert, were superior in quality to Britain's. The Boers had proved themselves in the First Boer War to be formidable foes, and it was, therefore, curious that many British Generals were contemptuous of their fighting abilities. Hunter did not fall into this category.

Jan Smuts, Transvaal's young State Attorney, had proposed a 'blitz-krieg' campaign against the British garrisons at Mafeking and Kimberley and in Natal. The plan, in Natal, was to mount a three-pronged attack aimed at cutting off the troops in Dundee and then those in Ladysmith from the rest of the forces in Natal. To begin with the plan succeeded brilliantly, but British stubbornness and grit denied the Boers the fruits of their initial success.

Hunter left Durban the day after he arrived for Pietermaritzburg, the capital of Natal (see map L, p. 115). There he stayed with Sir Walter Hely-Hutchinson, the Governor. The two men had known each other in Barbados, where Hely-Hutchinson had been Colonial Secretary. Also Hunter had been best man to Hely-Hutchinson at his wedding. White landed at Durban on 7 October. He quickly came on up to Pietermaritzburg, where he stayed with Symons, who had been summoned down from the north for consultations. Hunter's orders from London had been to join White for the moment. Buller thought it would be useful if Hunter was employed on White's staff until his own arrival, when Hunter could join him in Cape Town and report on the position in Natal.

Success in his career had come quite late to Sir George White, now 64. He had done his soldiering on the frontiers of India and Burma, but had not had command of troops in action until he was 44 and still a Major. He had then won the VC and caught the eye of Lord Roberts who proceeded to push the younger man's career until in 1893 White succeeded his chief, over the heads of others, as Commander-in-Chief, India. After five years in this post he had spent two uneasy years as Quartermaster-General in London before being offered in the summer of 1899, the governorship of Gibraltar, a post usually reserved for distinguished Generals at the end of their careers. White had always set great store on physical fitness. But a riding accident when he was over 60 had left him with a gammy leg, the fracture having mended badly. Doubts were expressed whether he should go overseas with this disability, but he joked that his leg was fit for anything but running away. Temperamentally he was sensitive, and inclined to be shy.

The northern apex of Natal, in the days before the border was changed, jutted like an arrow head into Boer territory. The country was remote and

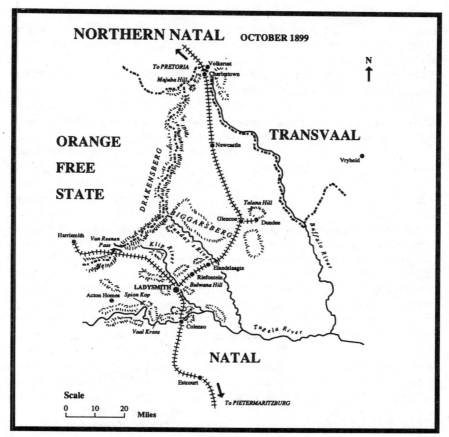

NORTHERN NATAL   OCTOBER 1899

Map M

mountainous and pierced by a single track railway running north to the Transvaal border at Charlestown and eventually reaching Johannesburg. Some 60 miles south of the border and about 40 miles from Ladysmith Symons had stationed himself at Dundee with about 4,000 troops. Between these men and the border the country was unguarded. White was immediately faced with a critical decision. How far forward should he place his forces to meet Boer thrusts which were likely to come from several directions? Buller had warned him not to keep his troops north of the Tugela river which meant evacuating Ladysmith. Likewise his two principal staff officers, Hamilton and Rawlinson, considered that it was strategically wrong for him to occupy Dundee, which had no protection on its flanks, or even Ladysmith. So White came to Pietermaritzburg with the intention of withdrawing his forward troops at least from Dundee. At one

119

stage the place favoured for concentrating his forces was Sunday's River Camp[4], a point just north of Elandslaagte and about 20 miles north-east of Ladysmith. This place would have commanded routes into Natal from both Boer republics.

On the evening of Monday 9 October White met Hely-Hutchinson to discuss the military position. Also present at the conference were Hunter, Symons and Beauchamp Duff, White's military secretary. A description of what took place at this conference, as seen through Hely-Hutchinson's eyes, is given in *The Times History of the War in South Africa*.[5] White put his case to the Governor for withdrawing his troops from Glencoe and Dundee to Ladysmith; they were militarily in a dangerous position and could not be reinforced. Hunter was then consulted, and said he agreed with White, as did Duff. But Symons was in favour of continuing to occupy Glencoe and Dundee. He was confident and felt there was no cause for alarm (in fact he always refused to believe that Boer farmers would attack British regular soldiers).[6] Hely-Hutchinson then explained his position. The primary object in occupying Glencoe was to make sure of the coal supplies there. From the political viewpoint withdrawal would have grave consequences. Loyalists, that is the Uitlander refugees from the Rand, would be disgruntled and discouraged. The effect on the Zulus numbering some 750,000 in Natal and Zululand might be disastrous. As yet they believed in British power. But they would look on a withdrawal as a British defeat. This must have been an awkward moment for White. Hunter was again consulted. He said that while retaining his opinion on the military situation it was a case of balancing drawbacks, and he advised under the circumstances that the troops should stay at Glencoe and Dundee.[7] This advice appears to have been decisive, for White decided to adopt this course. Hunter recalled in his evidence to the Royal Commission on the South African War some years later the Governor's special concern about the Zulus sitting on the fence to see which way the cat was going to jump, and added, though acknowledging it was somewhat presumptuous to do so, that he was practically asked to give the casting vote.[8]

It would have taken some courage on the part of White to disregard, after only a few days in the country, the policy being urged by the Governor. It is perhaps surprising to find that Hunter did not stick to his guns, but then the Governor was persuasive and Hunter too was a new boy who had not seen the terrain. It was a pity that, with his natural eye for country, Hunter did not have time to make a reconnaissance to Ladysmith and the frontier before the war began. In giving his views to the Royal Commission on what should have been done to defend Natal, he thought that it was a mistake in the first place not to have opposed the Boers up on the frontiers and did not agree with the policy of waiting for the Boers to come and find the British troops. To find the extreme north of Natal undefended, he believed, made the Boers jubilant. Their confidence increased and they became more aggressive. Expressively he asserted that '... if any enemy is going to invade your country ... the minute he puts his foot over your border, you ought to be able to stamp upon his toe.'[9] With the high calibre of troops available together with their adequate transport he considered that his scheme could have worked.

The conference had not ended until 1 a.m. So impressed was Hunter with its seriousness that before going to bed he wrote to Sir Evelyn Wood, the Adjutant-General, giving him a detailed account of what had happened in a letter running to several sheets of foolscap. When the Governor and Hunter met in the morning it transpired that the Governor had also sat up in the night writing a report on the meeting for his chiefs. Hunter asked Hely-Hutchinson to run an eye over his version to see whether it correctly described what took place. Apparently the two reports practically tallied.[10]

The very day the military men were in conclave with Hely-Hutchinson, the Transvaal Government, no longer held back by President Steyn of the Orange Free State, handed in its ultimatum at 5 p.m. to the British agent in Pretoria. The demands made by the Boers, to be met within 48 hours, were stiff and included: the withdrawal of British troops from their borders; the withdrawal from South Africa of all troops who had arrived since 1 June and a prohibition on any reinforcements. The terms of the ultimatum also ensured that the Orange Free State would join forces with her sister republic in any war.

The British government was not prepared to meet these demands, and so, on 11 October, as White and Hunter travelled by train from Pietermaritzburg to Ladysmith, the ultimatum ran out. The war was to last two years and eight months. It was to be a White Man's war, the Africans, essentially, not being involved in the fighting. It would be the first war since the Crimean War (excluding the short First Boer War) in which the British army had been pitted against white soldiers. It would account for deaths in action, or through disease, of some 30,000 soldiers and an unknown number of civilians and cost the British tax payer more than £200 million.[11] Hunter would serve in South Africa for some 16 months before being invalided home. But unlike most of the Generals who fought in South Africa his reputation would be untarnished when he left the Cape in January 1901.

On Thursday 12 October, on a cold and misty morning in the Drakensberg mountains, the Boers moved out of their laagers (camps) at Volksrust and crossed the border into Natal. Charlestown, the first settlement in the Colony, was occupied on 13 October and two days later General Daniel Erasmus, coming down the line of the railway, had reached the nearly deserted town of Newcastle 30 miles to the south. There was no opposition and Erasmus pushed on towards Glencoe. On his left Lucas Meyer struck west from Vryheid in southern Transvaal with a commando (mounted unit) of 3,000 men. He crossed the Buffalo river and made towards Dundee. On the right General Johannes Kock, in frock coat and top hat and with 1,200 men, was preparing to bypass Newcastle and head for the green hills of the Biggarsberg range. All these men came under the elderly and respected Commandant-General Piet Joubert, a man of French Huguenot stock with a huge flowing beard, who brought his wife along with him. By all accounts she was a formidable lady, not above directing the guns on to the targets she thought should be aimed at. Joubert had all told some 15,000 Transvaalers under his command. This well armed and highly mobile force now moved quickly to cut off the troops at Glencoe and Dundee from Ladysmith.

Down at Ladysmith White was now using Hunter as his 'chief staff officer', a post which Hamilton, three years older than Hunter but the junior in rank, had presumably expected to fill. Hamilton was an interesting soldier. Intelligent, debonair and personable, he wrote books and poetry. Like White he was both a Gordon Highlander and a protégé of Roberts. He had seen much active service and, never lacking courage, had done well. Intensely ambitious he was clearly set for a successful career. There is a suspicion that there may have been at times tensions between Hamilton and Hunter.

Patrols were sent out from Ladysmith and on 18 October contact was made with scouts from the forces of the Orange Free State, now also invading Natal, at Acton Homes some 20 miles west of the town. White, having heard on 15 October from one of his staff that the defences at Dundee were in a poor state, changed his mind about Symons, and at 3 a.m. on 18 October telegraphed him to fall back unless he could give assurances about his position and supply of water. Symnons could not give the assurances but wanted to remain. Finally White gave in, and telegraphed Symons that he 'fully supported' him.[12]

It was not long before the expected collision between the advancing Boers from the Transvaal and the British took place. Symons had badly misjudged the Boer as an enemy and consequently had neglected his defences. Thus no men had been posted on the high ground to the north and east of Dundee so that Meyer achieved surprise and was able to seize the unoccupied Talana Hill, an important feature, before dawn on 20 October. Determined to wrest Talana Hill from the Boers' grasp, Symons sent in his infantry. A sharp fight ensued which left the British victorious but at a heavy cost. There had been 500 casualties including Symons himself, mortally wounded. Further the cavalry, some 200-strong, became surrounded in broken country north of Dundee and were forced to surrender.

In the meantime, and some 25 miles to the south-west of Meyer, Kock had boldly reached Elandslaagte, less than 20 miles north-east of Ladysmith, and cut the railway there. The station master was forced to surrender his rifle but, such was the consideration shown at this stage of the war by the combatants, was given a receipt for it! Early the next morning Major-General John French, 15 years later to command the BEF in France, was sent by White with his cavalry to investigate what was happening on the railway and if possible clear the Boers from Elandslaagte. French quickly saw there was an opportunity to destroy what was a comparatively weak commando, and at once telephoned down the line to White for infantry reinforcements. White's first idea was to send Hunter to take command, for French was an unknown quantity as far as infantry work went. But Hunter thought the job was French's by right and that it would be unfair to deprive him of the command. White accepted this act of what has been described as 'self abnegation',[13] and instead sent Hamilton out to command the infantry brigade. Some cavalry and two batteries of field artillery, completed the task force which was rushed up the line by four trains. White could not resist seeing the battle and went up to the front where he remained a spectator. Hunter was left behind in charge at Ladysmith. Here he had to deal with a request for reinforcements from Major-General James Yule who had taken over command from Symons at Dundee. But no men could be spared.

At Elandslaagte a plan was quickly drawn up by French and Hamilton and an attack against the Boer position was launched. It was a bloody affair in which a bayonet charge finally broke the Boers. In the battle General Kock was killed and his commando decimated. At the end of the afternoon Hunter sent an urgent message out to White that there was a hostile advance on Ladysmith threatened from the north-west and that the force was required back at Ladysmith.[14] The following day White was able to contact Yule by telegraph over a line still uncut. He agreed that Yule should leave Dundee and try to march to Ladysmith by a 60-mile circuitous route through the hills to the east. The wounded, including Symons, were left in the army hospital in Dundee.

The forces of the Orange Free State under Martinus Prinsloo, their Commander-in-Chief, were now advancing steadily into Natal through the Drakensberg mountains via the Van Reenen pass and down the Klip river north-west of Ladysmith. Conscious of the need to prevent this force joining up with Joubert's and to stop the Boers interfering with Yule's march, White led 4,000 men north of Ladysmith on 24 October to Riefontein eight miles away, where the Orange Free Staters were dug in. Hunter went with him. During the operation the Natal Mounted Rifles and Border Mounted Rifles directed by Hunter did well in protecting White's left flank.[15] For the moment White achieved his limited objectives but could not dislodge the enemy from the row of hills they were occupying. The British troops withdrew to Ladysmith at 3 p.m. This was the first action against the Boers in which Hunter was involved. Also it was the first time that Christiaan de Wet, most indomitable of Boer leaders, fought against the British.

By Friday 27 October the Boers were reported, just a day after Yule's safe arrival in Ladysmith, to be four miles east of the town. White was now desperately looking for some way to deliver a major stroke against the forces threatening his position, but he found it difficult to decide what to do. At first White agreed to a night attack on Boer Headquarters, but later cancelled the operation as too risky. On the Thursday White had sent a message to Buller – he was still at sea and would not dock in Cape Town until the end of the month – asking for reinforcements. He also said he was short of staff officers and that Hunter was indispensable.[16] The same day he summoned Hamilton to discuss an attack on Pepworth Hill (see map N, p. 128), some three miles north-east of Ladysmith now held by Joubert's men. Hamilton was against it because it would be too costly in casualties. Hunter agreed and White gave up the idea.[17]

Two days later White conceived a plan on a much grander scale, involving two infantry brigades and other supporting forces. He proposed to storm Pepworth Hill with the same brigade Hamilton had successfully led at Elandslaagte. Another brigade on the right, led by Colonel Grimwood, was charged with taking Long Hill and thereby rolling up the Boers' left flank. This latter brigade was composed of the men who had marched from Dundee; they had to be in position by dawn. The attacks would be preceded by an artillery barrage and French's cavalry would be in support on the right. Finally, and this was the part of the plan particularly disliked by the staff, a column drawn from the Gloucesters and Irish Fusiliers under Carleton, CO of the latter regiment, would undertake a difficult night march through Boer lines to the vicinity of Nicholson's Nek north of Pepworth, and there take up station to cut off the expected retreat of the enemy after the assaults by the infantry brigades.

White took charge of the operation which began early on Monday 30 October. The day's fighting is sometimes known as the battle of Ladysmith. More often it is known as 'Mournful Monday', for White's plan failed totally, none of his targets being achieved. The operation began badly, for a part of Grimwood's brigade took up the wrong position with the result that the other parts found themselves unsupported. French's cavalry were also in the wrong place. It then became apparent that the Boers opposite the British right had changed their positions in the night and were now working around Grimwood's flank. Commentators have found it difficult to describe the disjointed action which took place over a large area that day. What is clear is that there was muddle and confusion among the British troops during the fighting.

In mid morning White sent Hunter up to Farquhars Farm on the right near the foot of Lombards Kop to report on progress by Grimwood's brigade. Hunter sent back word to White that the troops could make no headway and that the only thing to do was to withdraw them. So White ordered Grimwood to retire and told Hunter to superintend the operation. To quote Hunter, they then withdrew 'in a very orderly way.'[18] This is not, however, how others saw it. Nevinson, the war correspondent, described how the troops came back 'slowly, tired, disheartened and sick with useless losses.'[19] Some believed it was only the gunners who saved the retreat from becoming a rout. The artillery, both the 21st and the 13th Batteries, had played an important part in the day's fighting. Hunter had ordered up the 13th to the left of Grimwood's position with a view to creating an opening for a possible advance. It later took up a covering position to the rear of the infantry where it became a target for fire from both Boer riflemen and field guns. As the infantry withdrew, the gunners became totally exposed but stuck manfully to their task. Once Grimwood's brigade was safe, Hunter, who was walking about unconcernedly among the guns of the 13th, gave the order to retire.[20] That night he remained with the outposts and the next day was involved with Rawlinson in bringing in stragglers. A sketch was published of Hunter in the retreat giving succour to a wounded soldier by lifting him onto his own horse. The caption noted that '. . . his [Hunter's] name is synonymous for courage and kindness.'

On Mournful Monday the army gunners had been joined by the Naval Brigade who had come up from Durban under the command of Captain Hedworth Lambton of the Royal Navy. They had brought with them ten guns including two 4.7 inch guns with a range of up to 8,000 yards, and dismounted from HMS Powerful with commendable speed. These guns had gone into action as soon as they had arrived, hurling shells at long range at the advancing Boers. During the siege about to begin these naval guns would help to boost the morale in Ladysmith for they alone could begin to match the range of the Boers' Creusots. Unhappily, after the war the effectiveness of the naval gunners became a source of notorious acrimony between Hunter and Lambton which will be described in a later chapter.

One other disaster hit the British forces on that last Monday of October. At Nicholson's Nek Carleton's column, none of them mounted, was in dire straits. First, in the dark his pack mules with their mountain guns and ammunition stampeded and vanished. As dawn came the column found itself marooned behind the Boer lines. There was a fight but the men were surrounded. No relief came. Humiliatingly 954 officers and men surrendered. This catastrophe, soon followed by the encirclement of the town, had a profound psychological effect on White. He at once took the blame and in a cable to the War Office accepted full responsibility for what had happened. Badly depressed, he began to feel his troops were losing confidence in him and that he would be superseded. After Mournful Monday White tended to stay in his house and rarely went out among his troops.[21] This was to place much extra responsibility on Hunter's shoulders.

Buller had requested Hunter as his Chief of Staff to make a personal report to him on how matters stood in Natal. The report could not have made comfortable reading when Buller saw it at the beginning of November immediately after he arrived at Cape Town from England. In it Hunter stated that 'Ladysmith lies in a hollow commanded by heights too distant for us to hold and now possessed by the enemy. The Boers are superior in numbers, mobility and long-range artillery.'[22] It must have been clear to Buller that Ladysmith was going to be cut off, and that he would therefore have to change his original plan of striking first at Bloemfontein, capital of the Orange Free State, to relieve the pressure on Kimberley and Ladysmith. His presence instead was going to be needed in Natal to staunch the tide of Boer successes. As for the prospect of losing his Chief of Staff Buller seemed curiously indifferent.

Hunter, himself, must have seen the writing on the wall during the last week of October. He had though hoped up to the last minute that White would let him leave Ladysmith so that he could join Buller.[23] But it was not to be. White was in an obstinate frame of mind. For one thing, against advice strongly urged by both French and Hunter, he refused to send south his splendid force of cavalry[24]; in a siege they would have no role except that eventually the horses became a welcome source of food for the famished garrison. The last train out of Ladysmith left under enemy fire on Thursday, 2 November. Both French and his staff officer Douglas Haig were on it, at Buller's special request, but not Hunter. At 2.30 p.m. that day the telegraph line, the principal means of communicating rapidly in those days, went dead. Ladysmith was cut off and surrounded by the enemy, and the four-month siege had begun.

NOTES

1. RCSAW ev of Lt-Gen Hunter, 13 Feb. 1903 paras 14470–14687.
2. Pakenham *The Boer War* 106.
3. De Wet *Three Years War* 9–10.
4. RCSAW loc. cit.
5. TH II 128.
6. Symons *Buller's Campaign* 119.
7. TH II 129.
8. RCSAW loc. cit.
9. Ibid.
10. Ibid.
11. Pakenham 572.
12. OH I 127.
13. TH II 179.
14. OH I 171; TH II 195.

15. TH II 204.
16. Chisholm *Ladysmith* 110.
17. Hamilton *The Happy Warrior: A Life of General Sir Ian Hamilton* 136.
18. RCSAW loc. cit.; TH II 232
19. Pakenham 153.
20. TH II 233–4.
21. Symons 131; Pakenham 155.
22. OH I 197–8.
23. RCSAW loc. cit.
24. TH II 263.

CHAPTER 13

The Siege of Ladysmith

Ladysmith lies at a height of 3,268 feet on the northern edge of a sandy plain on the Klip river and is surrounded by high hills. In 1899 it was a town of some 4,500 inhabitants, the third largest in Natal. An unpretentious place, it consisted of two main streets with wooden fronted shops and houses roofed with corrugated iron. It had quite an imposing town hall and an hotel. The town was a military and transport centre with roads radiating in different directions from it; the railway from the south divided there. As a garrison town Ladysmith had a reputation for being hot, dusty and prone to disease. Into the town and its immediately surrounding area had poured a large number of troops and refugees. In addition to White's 13,500 soldiers, about 7,600 civilians had become victims of the siege including 2,500 Indians and 2,400 Africans. In all there were some 21,000 mouths to be fed. An extra strain on resources would be caused by the number of horses (there were 5,500 within the town's perimeter at the start of the siege) which White had insisted on keeping in Ladysmith. However, during the days preceding the siege innumerable trains from the south had brought into the place, besides extra military supplies, enough extra food to last those besieged for 90 days. There was no shortage of water, which came from the Klip river, but it had to be sterilised.

It had never of course been part of White's plan to allow himself to become besieged in Ladysmith, which was a far from ideal place to defend. In any case White's soldiers were supposed to be a field force engaged in active operations against the enemy and not bottled up virtually unable to move. By letting the Boers surround him White had left the country to the south sorely short of troops, a mere two battalions barring the way, in early November, to Durban. The position was a mess.

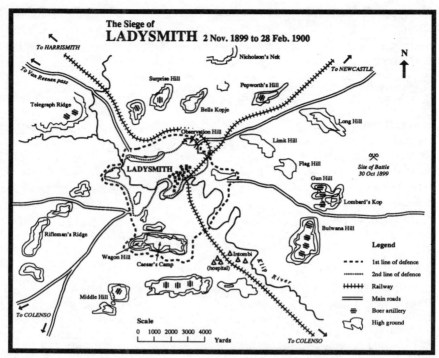

Map N

White's headquarters were in the local convent, a modest red-bricked bungalow perched on a terrace above the centre of the town. Hunter was there too and had a room next to White's. On 3 November Hunter wrote in his diary: 'cannot get officers to realise the true position.' By this he must have meant that it was not appreciated how perilous the military situation facing the garrison was, especially since relief could not arrive for some time to come. Nonetheless, Hunter believed that in the circumstances that had arisen there was no alternative to holding the town. Apart from the town's military significance, the fall of Ladysmith would have been, in Hunter's opinion, a signal for all the Boers in Cape Colony and the Zulus in Natal to rise.[1] As little had been done to prepare defences around Ladysmith work had to begin urgently to ensure that the Boers were prevented from obtaining an early lodgement in the town. Although the conditions were different, Hunter had of course practical experience of constructing defensive positions on the Atbara in the Sudan. In the event the organisation of the defence of Ladysmith largely rested, in the view of The Times History, on the shoulders of Hunter.[2]

First, a decision had to be made as to where to hold the line. Within the

128

defensive perimeter it was decided to include the high plateau to the south known as Caesar's Camp, some 2½ miles from the centre and some other eminences, but to exclude Bulwana, the highest point among the hills immediately circling the town 4½ miles away. Because the Boers put four pieces of heavy artillery on Bulwana commanding a good view of the whole garrison area this decision was sometimes regretted. Even so the perimeter ran to over 20 miles. It was divided into four sectors and commanders were appointed for each one. They were Colonels Howard, Knox, Hamilton and Royston. Hunter was lavish in his praise for the defensive works undertaken by Knox, nicknamed 'Nasty', because he was a disciplinarian. On his difficult eastern sector, where his men were particularly exposed to artillery fire, he had built up stone traverses and trenches capable of resisting fierce shell-fire. Hunter considered the fortifications in this sector were impregnable. Not all the defences were so adequate, as we shall see when the Boers launched a full-scale attack in January 1900 on Caesar's Camp in Hamilton's sector.

Besides the outer perimeter there was an inner scheme of defence, a kind of citadel into which Hunter moved ammunition and vital commodities such as flour and biscuits; holding this would depend to an extent on how long food supplies lasted. There was no shortage of small arms ammunition in the garrison; indeed when relief finally came there were still six million rounds unused in the reserves. Not all the troops were employed on defence of the perimeter and there was a central reserve of men who could be sent to sectors needing help.

Among the defenders was an assortment of troops. First, were the regular British soldiers described by Hunter as the flower of the army. Then came the naval brigade of 283 officers and men from *HMS Powerful* under Captain Lambton, their main role being to man the naval guns. For the two big 4.7 inch guns only 500 shells, instead of the 5,000 needed, could unfortunately be spared by the naval base at Simonstown (see map L, p. 115) so ammunition had to be severely husbanded[3]. Finally, there were the auxiliary and colonial troops, all volunteers and raised locally, such as the Imperial Light Horse and Natal Carabineers. Hunter spoke very highly of these men. The ILH, consisting of some 1,200 men, were the pick of the refugees from Johannesburg. Drawn from the ranks of mining engineers, managers and professional men, they were well-educated and motivated. Physically they were fine specimens. Hunter – he may of course have been exaggerating – thought that probably between 10 and 20 of them had incomes of £10,000 or more, a huge amount in those days. Speaking after the war he described the ILH as 'the finest corps I have ever seen anywhere in my life.'[4] In case the defences were overwhelmed Hunter had earmarked 200 Natal Carabineers as a kind of ultimate reserve with the task of smuggling White away from Ladysmith – probably in the dark – so as to ensure that he, an invaluable prize, did not fall into the hands of the Boers.[5] Another feature of the defence was the use made of the telephone. At headquarters there was a telephone exchange in touch with each sector commander, who in turn was in contact by telephone with his own sector outposts.

Against the defensive forces the Boers had at the start of the siege about 17,000 men camped around the town. The policy they adopted under their now ailing commander Joubert was a passive one. It was to sit tight, shell the town and hope the garrison would surrender. Although local attacks were made on 9 November on Observation Hill and Caesar's Camp, no effort was made for two months to mount a full-scale attack. Big guns, eventually numbering 24 or so, were placed on the hills circling Ladysmith and began a daily bombardment which usually lasted from early morning until dusk. The guns with the longest range, reaching up to 12,000 yards, were the French-made 6-inch Creusots which fired a 96lb shell. Each of these guns was given a nick-name by the defenders. Thus there was 'Long Tom' on Gun Hill, 'Puffing Billy' on Bulwana and 'The Meddler' on Middle Hill. The Boers also had 9-pounders, 12-pounders, 19-pounders and howitzers positioned on various heights. The garrison posted look-outs who blew their bugles as soon as the white puffs of smoke were seen coming from the Creusots. Then there might be 20 or 30 seconds in which to take cover. But the howitzers like 'Silent Suzie' fired smokeless shells and so avoiding action was not so easy. Soldiers took shelter from the shelling in their dug-outs while civilians had to spend time in caves excavated under the high banks of the river.

The bombardment, naturally enough, affected the morale of the besieged and was alleged to be the cause of a number of premature births. But in time people became used to being shelled. Casualties from the bombardment were not very high, though once a shell killed eight men of the Gloucesters and wounded nine more. Enemy gunners also hit the Town Hall which was being used as a field hospital. Just before Christmas White's headquarters received a direct hit but no one was killed; after this White and Hunter had offices in separate houses. Spent or dead shells became prized possessions and were sold for ridiculous prices. But as someone remarked to extract the fuse and withdraw the charge was a mad business for which a sledgehammer, chisel and coffin were indispensable!

At times the outposts came under Boer rifle fire. Once the Leicesters at Observation Hill, and the Rifle Brigade next to them, were made uneasy by severe sniper fire. Hunter then arrived on the scene. He deliberately stood up in the sight of the enemy saying to the men: 'Let us see whether the Boers can shoot or not.' Having exposed himself for a minute or two he then decided that they could not. The effect of his bravery, perhaps foolhardiness is the more appropriate word, on the troops was electric.[6] On the other hand, though personally rash at times, Hunter always wished to see casualties avoided where possible and this is one reason he applauded Knox for digging such effective defences.

White proved to be as passive in outlook towards the siege as his opponents. From the first he was disinclined to take any positive action. Hunter, together with both Hamilton and Rawlinson, would have liked to have seen far more active measures taken against the Boers. Eventually White approved an operation against Rifleman's Ridge, but he was indecisive and later cancelled it.[7] At long last, however, he gave rather grudging approval to a proposal to make a night attack on the guns on Gun Hill, which lay about $2\frac{1}{2}$ miles east of the perimeter, on condition that Hunter led the raid and took at least 500 men with him. Rawlinson asserted in his siege diary that the original idea was his, but then Knox too claimed the idea. Hunter produced a plan and his preparations went forward in great secrecy.

On the night of 7 December Hunter's party set off. With him went 500 Natal Carabineers under Colonel Royston, 100 men from the ILH under Lieutenant-Colonel Edwards, 18 men of the corps of guides under Major Henderson, White's Intelligence Officer, ten gunners and four sappers under Captain Fowke. The foot of Gun Hill was reached at 2 a.m., care being taken not to disturb a Boer picket close by, of whose existence Henderson was aware. The force divided into three. One party went to the left to protect the left flank and another under Royston went to the right to ensure that there was no counter-attack from the direction of Lombard's Kop. In the centre the assault party of 200 men was led by Hunter.

The storming of Gun Hill has been described on the first page of Chapter 1, and we will not repeat it. Mention should, however, be made of a nice story involving Hunter on account of his name being used as the pass word that night. During the early stages of the attack Sergeant (later Lieutenant) Finch-Smith of the ILH was annoyed by someone he mistook for one of his own men who would not keep his position. His suspicions aroused, he hissed at this man: 'Keep in your place'. When the man took no notice the Sergeant grabbed him by the throat and said: 'Who are you?' 'Oh, I'm Hunter' was the reply in a nearly strangled voice. 'I know damned well that Hunter is the pass word, but who the hell *are* you?' To the Sergeant's consternation the reply came: 'I'm Hunter, don't you know, General Hunter . . .' Hunter took no offence and found the episode amusing.[8]

When its objective had been achieved the raiding party returned to Ladysmith arriving at day-break. Casualties had been taken. Seven men, including Henderson, had received minor wounds. But one man, 6 foot 5 inches tall Trooper R. G. Nicol, had been shot through the spine and was mortally wounded. An ambulance Sergeant Charles Ligertwood, formerly a well known GP in Johannesburg, stayed with him all night on Gun Hill until both men were removed by the Boers at daylight. Trooper Nicol died in the Boer field hospital the following day.[9]

While the Boer howitzer was smashed beyond repair, the damage to the Creusot was not as great as had been hoped, though it was out of action for some time. The Boers repaired it in Pretoria and eventually put it back into service; its accuracy, apparently, was never the same again. The sortie was judged a success. White was full of praise for Hunter and his party, holding a special parade for them the next day and telling them that they were an honour to their country. In his diary White wrote about the sortie: 'I am so pleased not only because that gun was doing so much harm but also because H is such a delightful fellow and has done so well all through this siege.'[10]

The morale of the garrison received a boost by Hunter's sortie, and the public at home were warmed by his success. This did not prevent some mild criticism in the press that Hunter, as White's deputy, should have participated in such a hazardous operation, commenting that a chance bullet might have deprived the garrison of an officer whose loss would be an 'irreparable calamity'. The Boers themselves admired the cool daring of the raid. Christiaan de Wet wrote after the war: 'We all admitted that the English on that occasion acted with great skill and prudence, and that the courage of their leaders deserved every praise. Yet, if we had only been on our guard, we might have beaten off the storming party; but they caught us unawares . . .'[11]

Other night sorties followed Hunter's example. But the Boers had learned their lesson and surprise was not achieved. On 10 December the Rifle Brigade, in a party 500-strong, were intercepted on their way back from Surprise Hill and in a sharp fight lost nine men killed and 52 wounded. This was the last occasion when a night attack on Boer guns was sanctioned.

The main problem facing the garrison and civilian population before disease began to take a toll was boredom. White recognised this clearly enough when he told his staff: 'Gentlemen, we have two things to do – to kill time and to kill Boers – both equally difficult.'[12] To begin with there was plenty going on to keep people occupied despite the shelling. The women of Ladysmith gave tennis parties and there were gymkhanas. Cricket, football and polo (while the ponies were still strong enough) were all played. A military tournament was arranged by a committee of senior soldiers under Hunter's chairmanship. On the river there were races in tubs, and bathing parties were organised. Once, however, complaints were made to the Town Council that soldiers were bathing naked in the river and that this must be forbidden because the ladies enjoyed walking on its banks. For those with sociable tastes like Dr Jameson and Colonel Frank

Rhodes, brother of Cecil, the Royal Hotel provided a congenial meeting place at lunch time.

On Sundays there were always church parades and, very important, there was no shelling on the day of rest, at least to begin with. Personal behaviour between the warring sides was often courteous. For instance Joubert had sent a message of sympathy to Symons's widow. Then again there was thoughtfulness over medicines. Both sides did not take enough trouble over drinking water and the result was that dysentery flourished. The Boers asked the British side for chlorodyne, and a supply was at once sent over to the enemy lines with some brandy too! On the other hand the Boers exhibited a rather ghoulish attitude to the siege, and through their glasses the garrison could sometimes make out the Boer women, in their frocks and with their parasols who had come down by train to 'witness the torture of the doomed town.'[13]

Local papers began to appear and in the first issue of the *Ladysmith Lyre*, price 6d, a Christmas pudding was offered as a prize for the most miraculous escape from shell fire. A description of how this occurred was needed by the editor, whose decision presumably was final! For those with still more literary tastes a group was founded by some of the war correspondents who held readings from Shakespeare. Journalists and the rest of the garrison found communication with the outside world difficult. Native runners were used to carry letters and despatches through Boer lines, at a price, for this was hazardous. Carrier pigeons were also used. Military communication between Ladysmith and the British forces moving up from the south was made by heliograph, the Morse signals being bounced off clouds. By December the distance between these forces was tantalisingly small, Colenso, for instance, being a mere 12 miles as the crow flew from Ladysmith.

Arrangements were made by White and the chivalrous Joubert for the establishment outside the perimeter of a hospital (originally for civilians) at Intombi, nearly three miles to the south-east of the town. A train, always flying a white flag, was allowed to travel out and back to the hospital each day. There were also three field hospitals in the town itself. The 36 nurses available had to be shared around the hospitals. As dysentery and typhoid began to take their toll – Steevens the war correspondent and admirer of Hunter was one of the victims of the latter disease – the medical staff came under increasing pressure. Typhoid claimed 393 lives out of the total of 563 who had died from all causes during the siege. In early December Joubert complained that the privileges accorded the hospital at Intombi were being abused for military purposes. So White gave Hunter the job of holding an inquiry. During its course he discovered and corrected a few irregularities. He and Schalk Burger, the deputy Boer commander, held an amicable meeting when the latter accepted Hunter's report that the complaints were without serious foundation. White himself did not visit the hospitals but Hunter did. This became awkward because if Hunter tried to make inspections, White became a bit touchy and blamed Hunter for attempting to usurp his authority.[14]

The Boers had pushed south from Ladysmith during November though they had not mounted any real offensive towards Pietermaritzburg and Durban. But, as Pakenham points out in *The Boer War*, the Boers were fighting an essentially defensive war, though regarding attack as the best form of defence. By the end of November 50,000 British troops had arrived in South Africa as reinforcements and been dispersed by Buller to various parts of the front. The Commander-in-Chief saw the relief of Ladysmith as his first priority. He therefore assembled some 19,000 men in Natal, and on 15 December he made his first attempt at Colenso (see map M, p. 119) to break through the well-constructed Boer defences on the northern bank of the Tugela river. He failed dismally. For his part White had organised a large force as a Flying Column to break out of Ladysmith to the south and join hands with Buller's men coming north. But when the news of Buller's failure came through, the Flying Column stood down.

After Colenso Buller sent Lansdowne, the Secretary of State for War, a despondent telegram in which he said that he was not strong enough to relieve White and that he thought he 'ought to let Ladysmith go';[15] the precise meaning of these words has been picked over by historians. To White he sent a heliogram in which, having explained his position, he went on: '. . . I suggest your firing away as much ammunition as you can, and making the best terms you can. I can remain here if you have alternative suggestions but unaided I cannot break in . . .'[16] This gloomy message was followed by another one several hours later in which Buller reminded White that, whatever happened, he should remember to burn his cipher, code book and deciphered messages. It is hard to avoid the conclusion that Buller was inviting White to surrender. White replied robustly to Buller that he had food enough and that 'I will not think of making terms unless I am forced to . . . the losing of 12,000 men here would be a heavy blow to England. We must not yet think of it . . .'[17]

At an earlier moment Buller had conceived the idea of making his attack well west of Colenso. If he had succeeded in obtaining a footing on the north side of the Tugela his plan had been to signal the Ladysmith Flying Column to march out and meet him. In these circumstances he had planned to direct Hunter to supersede White, take command of the Ladysmith garrison and march south to link up with the British troops coming northwards. Buller obviously had more confidence in Hunter than in White. It is not surprising, however, that he did not state these plans to anyone before Colenso.[18] Buller paid dearly for his defeat at Colenso and his defeatist telegrams. Just before Christmas the Cabinet, without reference to Wolseley, appointed Lord Roberts as Commander-in-Chief in South Africa with Kitchener as his Chief of Staff.

White now fell ill with fever and took to his bed. He did manage, however, to go to the Christmas party for the 200 children in Ladysmith together with Hunter and other members of his staff. It showed how out of touch poor White was when he was heard to murmur: 'I had no idea there were so many children in Ladysmith.' There was a brief respite in the shelling over the festive season but on Christmas Day the Boers lobbed two shells into the town. They were found to be filled not with high explosive but with Christmas puddings! If you could find it there was still plenty of good food around. The 5th Dragoon Guards produced a menu with its main course 'Jambon au General Hunter (God bless the General for it) . . .'[19] And earlier Hunter had dined on St Andrew's night with the Gordons when dinner started with Scotch broth, and was followed by salmon and then haggis.

As Chief of Staff Hunter was in effect the chief administrator in Lady-smith. Many orders and notices were issued under his signature, covering a wide range of civilian as well as military matters. These included the payment of money due to contractors for supplies; the regulation of the water supply; the organisation of a postal service within the town ('money or valuables' were sent at the owner's risk!); the promulgation of traffic regulations ensuring vehicles drove on the left, and prohibiting any over-taking by vehicles in the main street. Hunter was determined life should go on in an orderly way despite the siege.

The civilian population came under military law and early on in the siege Hunter took pains to remind them of the dire penalties that awaited them if the law was transgressed. For instance anyone misbehaving or inducing others 'to misbehave before the enemy in such a manner as to show cowardice' might if convicted before a court-martial be liable for the death sentence. Hunter was not though the only person entitled to issue official notices affecting the civilian population. Both the Town Clerk and the Mayor continued to have a role to play, though no doubt under Hunter's eagle eye, and towards the end of the siege for example the Mayor was requiring everyone to hand over fowls and eggs to the military authorities for the sick and wounded.[20]

Early in the new year the Boers launched a major attack. At 2.45 a.m. on 6 January 1900 they assaulted Caesar's Camp, the southern plateau and its western extremity, Wagon Hill, both in Hamilton's sector. They also made two determined attacks that day against Knox's sector in the east and against Howard at Observation Hill. Heavy bombardments pre-ceded all the attacks. Knox and Howard successfully beat off the Boers. At Caesar's Camp the defences lacked trenches and obstacles to impede an attacker. Thus no barbed wire – there was plenty available – had been laid, and no field of fire cleared. Hamilton had relied on stone forts on the northern side of the plateau. The burghers managed to secure a foothold on the crest and the position, particularly at Wagon Hill, became critical. The

135

53rd battery, six companies of the Rifle Brigade, eight companies of the 60th Rifles and reserve companies of the Gordons were rushed to the scene. The battle swung back and forth all day and most of the British reserves were committed. Finally the tide turned at about 4 p.m. Hamilton made up for the deficiencies in the defences by personal gallantry during the battle. It was a day of many desperate deeds and five VCs were won. The British lost 17 officers and 158 men killed; 28 officers and 221 men were wounded, the brunt of the casualties being borne by the Manchesters, Devons and ILH. The Boer casualties were estimated at 184 killed and 380 wounded. Had the Boers succeeded in taking Caesar's Camp the holding of Ladysmith would not, in Hunter's view after the war, have become necessarily untenable, but the garrison would then have had a far more uncomfortable time.

The part played by White on this day is disputed. Hunter stated in his evidence to the Royal Commission that he, Hunter, was 'practically directing operations that day' because White was ill in bed and not in his office. This is not the version of the battle handed down in the chief chronicles of the day such as *The Official History* which has White very much on top of events.[21] White himself objected to what Hunter had said, and the latter was flatly contradicted by loyal supporters of White like Hamilton and Beauchamp Duff. We shall look at this contentious matter in more detail in a later chapter.

It is a moot point as to precisely where the responsibility lay for the inadequate defences at Caesar's Camp. Clearly, Hamilton has to take a great share of the blame, but then presumably White as the overall commander was ultimately responsible. And did White ever inspect the defences? If he did not, did he depute Hunter to look at them on his behalf? The answers to these questions are not known, but we have already seen that White was touchy about Hunter usurping his functions, so it seems perhaps unlikely that he delegated to Hunter powers to ensure that the defences were in order.

Rawlinson admired Hunter both as a soldier and as a man. He had seen him at close quarters in the Sudan and thought his real role was as a leader of men; he did not think at first that he would make a Chief of Staff. But he changed his view on this and did not believe that Hunter could have done better than he did at Ladysmith. 'The real soul of the siege', he asserted, 'is Hunter who is always about and always does the right thing at the right time.'[22] Hamilton, on the other hand, described Hunter as ignorant about being a Chief of Staff though admitted he was conscientious. Just a few days after the attack by the Boers Wolseley wrote to Queen Victoria and told her that there was 'a clever and able General' at Ladysmith called Hunter whom White was not making much use of.[23] This may not have been entirely fair to White who relied heavily on Hunter. White could not have been at peace with himself during the siege and his attitude to Hunter, for example over visiting hospitals, may at times have been equivocal. But after the siege he handsomely recognised the contribution Hunter made. And what did Hunter think of White? Duff said that Hunter did not care for White, and made no secret of this after an occasion when White found fault with him for issuing orders on his own authority.[24] It is possible, though this has to be conjectural, that Hunter found White's indecision and lack of grip irritating and in conflict with his own straightforward decisive approach to all matters.

The rest of January was a period of stagnation for the siege. Lord Roberts arrived in South Africa on 10 January and took over from Buller, who once again met with no success in trying to penetrate the Boer defences on the Tugela. Some 15 miles west of Colenso he had failed and been beaten at Spion Kop (see map M, p. 119) on 24 January when seemingly close to success. Buller was not always helped by his Generals, some of whom were eccentric. Thus Sir Charles Warren commanding the 5th division – when he was Commissioner of Metropolitan Police he issued his orders in rhyming prose – was said at Spion Kop to have snatched defeat out of the jaws of victory. And Sir Francis Clery commanding the 2nd infantry division dyed his sideboards blue and had a French chef with him.[25]

At the end of the month White accepted that there was nothing to do except await relief, which meant that the concept of a garrison Flying Column ready to go out and join hands with the relieving forces was at an end. The main effect of this was that the horses would no longer be required and that the animals therefore could be slaughtered and their carcasses used for food for the garrison. The resourceful Colonel Ward – called by White the best supply officer since Moses – was then able to invent a new food called 'Chevril' to help the diminishing rations in Ladysmith. A factory was set up and Chevril sausages became popular supplementing the daily allowance of $\frac{1}{2}$ lb of bread, two biscuits and minute quantities of tea, salt and sugar per person.

Morale in the town was falling. A man was sentenced by court-martial to hard labour for 'causing despondency'. People were dying daily from disease. Prices rose for food and commodities. Potatoes and eggs had become luxuries and cigarettes cost 1/- (5p) each. A case of whisky, somehow secreted away, was auctioned in February for £195. Behaviour began to deteriorate and there were cases of insubordination among the men. Stories circulated of officers cheating at cards and also stealing. In a siege diary – many were kept – Dr Kay admitted to stealing from a friend a milk tin full of candle droppings that had been collected to make a candle; this gave the thief an extra four or five hours of reading time. There was still some humour. The day after the 100th day of the siege the Boers signalled to the besieged '101 not out'. Quickly the Manchesters signalled back 'Ladysmith still batting'.[26] By February the investing force had been reduced to 5,000 men or even less. During that month an unsuccessful attempt was made by a German engineer to flood Ladysmith by damming the river Klip. Hunter would have been pleased to learn that the 2nd battalion of his regiment the King's Own Royal Regiment formed part of Buller's army. They did not forget him and heliographed him: 'The King's Own have come to get you out.' Hunter replied 'with God and the King's Own on our side we can not fail'.[27]

After yet a third failure, this time at Vaal Kranz some ten miles west of Colenso, Buller asked White for suggestions as to how the Boer defences might be overcome. White could offer none. As Hunter later explained, the soldiers in Ladysmith were singularly ill-informed about the physical features and characteristics of the surrounding countryside. He put this down to local Boer farmers being traditionally hostile, even before the war, to any attempts by soldiers to reconnoitre their land and the country for the purpose of acquiring military information or sketching maps and features.[28] But the long ordeal of the garrison was soon to be over. For Buller decided in the middle of February to attack this time the left flank of the Boer position, to the east of Colenso, and he began at last to make progress.

The breakthrough came after stiff fighting, and on 28th of the month, the 118th day of the siege, a relieving column rode into the town, the encircling Boer forces suddenly melting away to the north. When White met his deliverers he looked frail and stooped, walking with a stick. Hunter described him at the end of the siege as being a 'total wreck', but White and his garrison had somehow managed to keep the flag flying. There was a dinner to celebrate the relief that has been described by Churchill, who was of course quickly on the scene. They drank champagne and to eat there were tins of hoarded sardines. Hunter sat on White's right hand and was described by everybody as 'the finest man in the world'.[29]

On 1 March Buller arrived in Ladysmith. Two days later White received an address of thanks from the people of Ladysmith at the Town Hall. On this event Hunter noted in his diary: 'I declined a similar honour'. There was also that day a parade of Buller's troops. Hunter was on the dais, and as they marched by the men of the King's Own Regiment raised a special cheer for him. In addition, Hunter was remembered at home receiving telegrams of congratulation from both the Mayor of Lancaster and the Provost of Irvine. The scholars and masters of Glasgow Academy, his old school, also sent him a message, and at West Kilbride there was a torchlight procession through the village.

In his official despatch of 23 March White was generous in his praise of Hunter. He wrote that: '... I cannot speak too highly of [Hunter] whether for the performance of staff duties or for bold leading in the field. He is a most loyal and efficient Staff officer and I recommend him for advancement with the utmost confidence . . .'[30] Soon after the relief White went home and recovered his health, taking up his postponed appointment of Governor of Gibraltar. Later he would become a Field-Marshal, and be awarded the OM.

Hunter for his part was loyal to White after the siege, and in a speech at Kilmarnock in October 1901 said the credit for the defence of Ladysmith rested entirely with White, who owed none of his resolution or pluck to any heart but his own. The man could be summed up, Hunter said, in his own words: 'over my dead body'.[31]

Hunter wrote daily letters during the siege but some months after its conclusion, and to his great regret later, he burnt them all, thinking the letters worthless.[32] He also kept a siege diary, but handed it in. This diary has never come to light.

NOTES

1. RCSAW ev of Lt-Gen Hunter (see Note 1 Ch. 12).
2. TH IV 312.
3. Sharp *The Siege of Ladysmith* 3.
4. RCSAW loc. cit.
5. Ibid.
6. Wilson *With the Flag to Pretoria* I 498.
7. Hamilton 142.
8. Gibson *The Story of the Imperial Light Horse in the South African War 1899–1902* 75.
9. Ibid. 70–5; also see for a description of the Gun Hill sortie OH II 546; TH III 167 and Wilson I 498–9.
10. Sharp 54.
11. De Wet 31.
12. Symons 143.
13. Conan Doyle 165.
14. TH III 163; Pakenham 355.
15. Pakenham 239.
16. OH II 551.
17. Ibid.
18. Durand *The Life of Field-Marshal Sir George White* II 132.
19. Griffith *Thank God we kept the Flag Flying* 169.
20. Lines *The Ladysmith Siege* 20 et seq.; and information supplied by the Ladysmith Historical Society.
21. OH II 563.
22. Maurice (biography of Rawlinson) 56.
23. RA P5/55.
24. White Collection MSS Eur F 108 BA4/20 Beauchamp Duff–White 1 Nov. 1903.
25. Pakenham 302; Symons 108.
26. Griffith 48.
27. Cowper 226.
28. RCSAW loc. cit.
29. Churchill *London to Ladysmith* 465.

30. White Collection MSS Eur F 108 58 despatch of 23 Mar. 1900.
31. *Kilmarnock Standard* obituary of Hunter Jun. 1936.
32. DHD 193.

CHAPTER 14

Mafeking Relieved

For the part he had played in defending Ladysmith Hunter was quickly rewarded. On 6 March 1900 he was promoted Lieutenant-General for 'distinguished conduct in the field' and given command of the newly formed 10th division at Elandslaagte. Under him came the 5th brigade (Major-General Hart), the 6th brigade (Major-General Barton), three batteries of field artillery, a company of Royal Engineers and the Imperial Light Horse as divisional cavalry. If, however, he thought that, free at last from the deadly confines of the Ladysmith perimeter, he would soon be launching his troops against the enemy, he was wrong. The Boers were well entrenched in the Biggarsberg range and Roberts had given orders to Buller, difficult at this distance to understand, to go onto the defensive.

Apart from the duties connected with his new appointment, there were other matters commanding Hunter's attention. First the farewells. The Naval Brigade, a popular arm during the siege, left for the south by train and Hunter went to see them off. White left too, still unwell. Both Hamilton and Rawlinson had been summoned over to the Cape to join Roberts. Rawlinson said that his one regret on leaving Ladysmith was parting from Hunter, for whom he had a high regard.[1] Hunter always had a big mail. Now there were heaps of letters to read and to answer. In a letter to Wingate, who the previous December had become Sirdar of the Egyptian army in place of Kitchener, he wrote that he sometimes wished himself back but 'most times I am thankful to have got clear of Egypt.'[2] Presumably to satisfy his curiosity, Hunter paid a visit to the top of the great hill Bulwana to the east of Ladysmith, and took with him Major Prince Christian Victor, Queen Victoria's favourite grandchild, who was serving on the staff and had just arrived. He visited too, for the second time, Gun Hill. And he lunched with his new chief Buller, a man with whom he had rapport. His old friend the distinguished surgeon Sir William MacCormac was in Ladysmith visiting the hospitals, and was also present at the lunch.

Early in April Hunter and his 10th division were ordered to the Cape. He left Ladysmith on 9 April with his ADC Major King and en route to Durban, he stayed two nights with his friend Hely-Hutchinson, the Governor of Natal, at Pietermaritzburg. Another guest was Major Aylmer

Haldane, who had just escaped from the prisoner of war camp at Pretoria. It had been Haldane who had commanded the armoured train in which Churchill rode as a war correspondent. Now four months later Haldane was still blaming Churchill for persuading him to take the train on into what was to prove a trap set by the Boers and which resulted in their both becoming prisoners. Hunter noted in his diary that Haldane was 'furious with Winston Churchill'.

On 13 April Hunter sailed from Durban for the Cape on *T S Bavarian* with some of the 6th brigade. At East London they were told to proceed to Cape Town where Hunter received orders to go at once and meet Roberts at Bloemfontein. The position in South Africa had certainly been transformed in the first three months of the year, ever since the energetic Roberts had arrived. Kimberley had been relieved and the battle of Paarde-berg had been won, though at some cost. General Piet Cronje and over 4,000 men, both Transvaalers and Free Staters, and 50 women had surren-dered there. Then Bloemfontein, expected to have been stoutly defended by the Free Staters whose capital it was, had fallen without a fight. Presi-dent Steyn had fled 120 miles up the railway to Kroonstadt. At this stage of the war Roberts believed in the velvet glove approach and had offered an amnesty to armed Free Staters, except for their leaders; under its terms they were required to return home, take an oath of allegiance and surren-der their arms.

Roberts's plan was now to thrust north with his main army and strike at Pretoria 280 miles away. For the moment he decided not to deal with de Wet, the new Commander-in-Chief of the Orange Free State Army (his predecessor Ferreira had been accidentally shot dead by one of his own sentries) and the sizeable force of Free Staters, who would be behind his line of advance. He believed that once Pretoria fell, Boer morale would be broken and the war would end. Buller, whom Roberts would have liked to send home but did not quite dare to, was to be given something of a side show in Natal. Roberts also had plans to raise the siege of Mafeking as soon as possible, and this is where Hunter came in.

Hunter saw Roberts at breakfast time on 19 April. He was given by the C-in-C a free hand to organise at once the relief of Mafeking[3] which showed the confidence Roberts placed in Hunter. The siege had to be raised by 18 May, the date given by the Garrison commander, Colonel Robert Baden-Powell, after which supplies of food would run out. Hunter, predictably enough, wanted to command the relief column himself, but Roberts would not let him. Instead, Colonel B. Mahon, a cavalryman who had done well in the Sudan, was placed in command of the column.

The next day Hunter set off for Kimberley by train, travelling third class in a carriage with no doors or windows. The 6th brigade was ordered to join him there but the 5th had been diverted for other duties. During the last ten days of April Hunter was hard at work assembling the relief

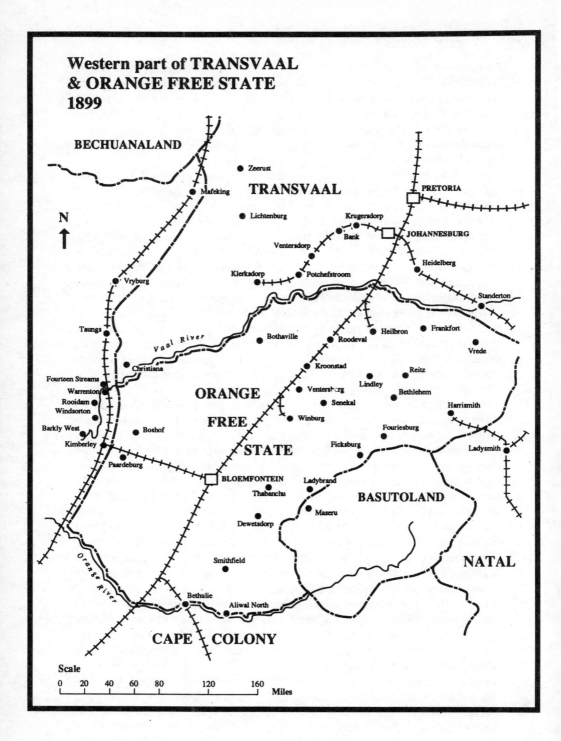

Western part of TRANSVAAL & ORANGE FREE STATE 1899

BECHUANALAND

TRANSVAAL

N

Zeerust

Mafeking

Lichtenburg

Krugersdorp

PRETORIA

Bank

JOHANNESBURG

Ventersdorp

Heidelberg

Klerksdorp

Potchefstroom

Vryburg

Standerton

Taungs

Vaal River

Bothaville

Roodeval

Heilbron

Frankfort

Christiana

Kroonstad

Vrede

Fourteen Streams

Warrenton

ORANGE

Reitz

Rooidam

Windsorton

Ventersburg

Lindley

Bethlehem

FREE

Senekal

Harrismith

Barkly West

Boshof

Winburg

Kimberley

STATE

Fouriesburg

Paardeburg

Ficksburg

Ladysmith

BLOEMFONTEIN

Ladybrand

Thabanchu

BASUTOLAND

Maseru

Dewetsdorp

Orange River

Smithfield

NATAL

Bethulie

Aliwal North

CAPE COLONY

Scale

0   20   40   60   80   120   160
                                            Miles

column and planning its route. Speed was of the essence and so he looked to raise a force along the lines of a Boer commando. He believed that irregulars, who had served him well at Gun Hill, were best suited for the purpose in mind. The column would be only 1,000 strong with six guns. It was comprised of: 900 men of the Kimberley Mounted Corps and the ILH, 100 picked infantrymen from Barton's Fusilier brigade, divided equally between men from England, Scotland, Wales and Ireland and 100 men of the RHA to man the 12-pounder guns. There were also two machine guns and 52 supply wagons, each with a team of ten mules.[4] War correspondents attached to the column were made by Hunter to sign an oath of secrecy about its destination and composition.[5]

Many of those riding in Mahon's column were former members of the Jameson raid who had, some years before, set out to overthrow Kruger's republic from the same Mafeking they were now about to relieve. Hunter knew many of the men from Ladysmith and it may have caused him some wry amusement to send them back to Mafeking to settle a score with their old enemy. Preparations, made to a high standard, were completed and the column left on their mission from Barkly West on 4 May. Their adventure was not without risk as there were some 1,500 Boers under Snyman besieging Mafeking and there were around 2,000 Boers under General du Toit in the area of Fourteen Streams and Christiana (see map O, p. 142). Finally, there were Boers to the west of Kimberley who had invaded the western districts of Cape Colony.[6] Mafeking, itself, lay isolated on the railway to the north in the middle of nowhere and on the fringe of desert regions leading to the Kalahari.

The general advance north had been resumed by Roberts's forces, including Hunter's division, the day before Mahon left on his mission. Its objective was Pretoria. The C-in-C had 38,000 troops under command, spread over a huge front some 150 miles across. Roberts himself thrust up the railway from Bloemfontein with two divisions. On his right Ian Hamilton, in high favour and now advanced in local rank to Lieutenant-General, commanded another division. On his left was Lord Methuen aiming at Boshof and on the extreme left was Hunter.

Hunter's plan was to draw the Boers away from Mahon, and with this in view he crossed first the Mafeking railway and then the Vaal river near Windsorton. He now advanced up the west side of the river. Just south of Rooidam Hunter's leading troops the 5th Imperial Yeomanry, a unit which had been borrowed from Methuen, were halted at about 9.30 a.m. on 5 May by du Toit's men who had come south to bar Hunter's progress. This move by the Boers suited Hunter's purpose admirably since it enabled him to deal with the foe while Mahon drew away to the north in comparative safety.

The Boers, reinforced and numbering a good 1,000 men with two guns, had occupied a series of rocky hills running north-west to south-east over

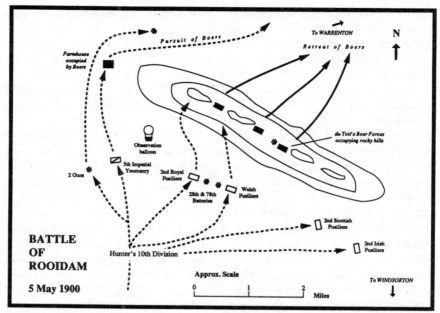

Map P

some four miles. After the Yeomanry's patrols under Colonel Meyrick had drawn fire, Hunter sent two battalions, the 2nd Scottish Fusiliers and the 2nd Irish Fusiliers, to the east to guard against the Boers moving down to Windsorton in his rear. Then the 2nd Royal Fusiliers and Welsh Fusiliers under Barton, together with the 28th and 78th batteries, pressed on until they reached the Boer front at about 11.30 a.m. Hunter now decided to deploy his forces on his left to try and turn the Boers' right flank, using the Yeomanry and two guns. A farmhouse on this flank was seen to be the key feature; possibly it had been noticed by an observation balloon which apparently was 'hovering at a great height over the battle'.[7] The Boers were driven from the farmhouse by Meyrick who at once saw that he was enabled to look round the Boer position. The guns were called up and began to shell the enemy, enfilading their positions on the reverse slope of the high ground they were occupying. At about noon the infantry began their advance through thick bush and scrub, attracting fire from the defending Boers, but they did not attempt to cross the open ground below the hills until the artillery from a range of about 2,800 yards had spent some time shelling the enemy. When the final assault was ordered, Barton was able to push his men forward against the extended Boer right, seize the rising ground and begin to turn the enemy's right flank, supported in this by the guns on his extreme left. The final advance began at

3 p.m. by which time the defenders had had enough. They fled from their positions fearful of having their line of retreat cut off, and were pursued for some three miles by the Yeomanry who took prisoners. The Boers suffered over 50 casualties from the action, and on the British side one officer and 6 men were killed, and there were 38 wounded.[8] Hunter had, of course, considerable numerical superiority over his opponents at Rooidam, but nonetheless *The Official History* described the battle as a 'brilliant engagement'. This was the first major action in South Africa which Hunter directed. It showed him to be well able to adapt his tactics to new circumstances.

As a result of this action the Boers fell back before Hunter, who reached the Vaal at Warrenton. Here the Boers had destroyed the multi-span railway bridge crossing the river to Fourteen Streams, which on 7 May Hunter occupied without opposition. He was now joined by most of Hart's 5th brigade, and at once set to work to construct a temporary bridge. A week later he marched his division north-east to Christiana, the surrender of which he took from the mayor and public prosecutor. He thus became the first of Roberts's troops to enter the Transvaal. The mayor was asked to furnish Hunter with a daily report on: 'the state of affairs in your District; the tranquillity of its inhabitants; the number of arms, stating their manufacture, handed in to you . . . and anything else of importance which comes to your knowledge.'[9] Here were echoes of Hunter relishing the role he had played in the past as a military Governor. At about this time Hunter offered a Boer flag he had captured to Roberts. The C-in-C at once telegraphed him to send it to Lady Roberts for safe keeping!

Hunter now returned, perhaps somewhat unexpectedly, to Fourteen Streams to complete the 1330-feet temporary railway bridge. It has been suggested that the operation against Christiana was a feint to keep the Boers guessing and to distract them from interfering with Mahon's column. There may be some truth in this, but at the same time it is surprising that Hunter did not take at least part of his force up the railway north towards Vryburg and Mafeking in active support of Mahon. The explanation presumably is that he felt he could secure his rear better from Fourteen Streams and also he did not wish to split his force at this stage.

In the event the Boers were unable to prevent Mahon from making rapid progress; in 12 days he covered some 230 miles through hostile territory. Since Taungs, Mahon reported to Hunter, the column had had a Boer commando on their right flank[10], but Mahon had marched by night and this helped to keep the enemy at bay. There had been one sharp fight and the column lost five men killed and 21 wounded. Finally at Massibi some 30 miles west of Mafeking Mahon joined forces with Lt.-Col. (later Field-Marshal) Herbert Plumer who had been operating with a small column from Rhodesia. They at once began a move to relieve the besieged town. But Mahon first had to warn Colonel Baden-Powell at Mafeking of his own relative weakness and he did this by inventing a school-boy code which began 'our numbers are Naval and Military Club multiplied by ten [94 Piccadilly × 10 = 940] . . .' and ended 'our supplies the OC 9th Lancers [Lt-Col Little = few].'[11] To Boers intercepting the message it would be double Dutch, as it was meant to be.

General De la Rey had now arrived on the scene from the east and with 2,000 men he tried to stop the relieving forces gaining their objective. There was some stiff fighting, but the cordon was broken and Mahon entered the town on 17 May. The siege had lasted 217 days, easily the longest of the Boer war. As it turned out the garrison could have held out until 1 June by which date, had it been necessary, Hunter's whole division could have reached Mafeking.[12]

The undoubted hero of the siege was the garrison commander, B-P as he was known, the future Chief Scout, an independently minded soldier as Hunter was soon to find out. None could say that B-P had not commanded his small force with flair. During the opening weeks of the siege he had held at least 6,000 Boers at bay with his tiny garrison of about 1,000 men including civilians pressed into service.[13] There is little doubt that this had helped to take some pressure off the hard-pressed British troops in Natal. Almost more than any other episode during the Boer war the relief of Mafeking captured the public's imagination. In London when the news of the relief came through there were indescribable scenes of fervour among the huge crowds in Piccadilly.

Hunter received news of the successful relief of Mafeking on 20 May while still at Fourteen Streams. He at once wrote to Mahon to congratulate him on his achievement and to inquire when he would be rejoining the 10th Division. Mahon replied on 28 May that he would come as soon as B-P 'allows me to leave'.[14] B-P himself had written to Hunter on 25 May, assuming he came under Hunter's command (which he did not), and asked if Mahon's force could remain with him to help in the pacification of the Western Transvaal. Before he had heard from Hunter, he had then sent out the ILH under Lieutenant-Colonel Edwards, one of Hunter's officers, to support Plumer at Zeerust some 40 miles to the north-east. He had also, according to Mahon, appointed Edwards to be a District Commissioner in that area, and had also commandeered into the bargain some of Mahon's transport. Hunter, in fact, had already conceived other plans for Edwards. The least stuffy of commanders, he nevertheless is likely to have seen all this as rather high-handed action on the part of B-P. At any rate he wrote to B-P ordering Mahon's force back[15] including the ILH. On 28 May B-P wrote again to Hunter to say that it would be 'unsafe' to withdraw Edwards and the ILH from Zeerust because Snyman and De la Rey were within 25 miles of the place. He hoped that Hunter would allow him to retain the ILH under his command, otherwise he would have to withdraw Plumer. Finally he mentioned too that the rest of Mahon's force was on its way to rejoin Hunter[16]. According to *The Times History* Mahon's column including the ILH rejoined Hunter at Lichtenburg in early June.[17]

Once the railway line and the bridge at Taungs, also damaged by the retreating enemy, had been repaired Hunter and his division continued their advance, entering Vryburg on 24 May. Meanwhile Roberts and the rest of his army had been making spectacular progress to the east. Kroonstad had fallen 12 days earlier and Roberts was poised to cross the northernmost border of the Orange Free State. He now proceeded to annex the Boer Republic and to rename it the Orange River Colony. Roberts kept in close telegraphic contact with his Generals, and had agreed with Hunter that they would converge on Pretoria with Hunter's division undertaking a sweeping flank march on the left. This plan never came off, for the Transvaal Boers were falling back swiftly and in confusion. In doing so they had suffered a loss in morale, and the surrender of Johannesburg was offered to Roberts by Commandant Krause on condition that Roberts allowed them to withdraw their army from the town. Roberts had been worried that the retreating Boers would sabotage the mines of the Rand but Krause assured him that the mines would be left intact provided the burghers could make good their escape. In this way street fighting would also be avoided.[18] So Roberts halted his divisions and permitted the Boer soldiers to leave without interference. Roberts, anxious to bring the war to a speedy and humane end, believed that Boer resistance was on the verge of collapse. It certainly looked like it. Kruger fled from Pretoria which, undefended, Roberts entered on 5 June. And 3,000 British prisoners of war were at once released from their camps in the Boer capital.

For a time it must have looked to Hunter as he came up from southwestern Transvaal on his flank march to Pretoria that Boer resistance was collapsing. At the same time as he was trying to 'settle' the country he was also accepting the surrender of large numbers of burghers. At Lichtenburg, reached on 3 June, 400 gave themselves up with their arms, ammunition and horses. The arms were destroyed and the horses served as remounts for Mahon's exhausted relief column. But now there came a change of plan because of the absence of Boer opposition to Roberts, and the 10th Division were ordered to take Potchefstroom, 75 miles to the south-east. On the way Hunter accepted the surrender of 1,800 Boers with their arms at Ventersdorp, while Mahon went to Potchefstroom, where 150 Boers gave themselves up. At Klerksdorp 350 men under the Boer leader Andries Cronje surrendered to Hunter's troops.[19] The rifles taken were always burnt.

It was reported to Hunter that Cronje was ill. So he suggested to Roberts[20] that in the circumstances it would be 'judicious' to promise him good treatment. Also the people of Klerksdorp were agitated because Cronje might be sent to St Helena, now a regular destination for Boer prisoners, or away from his neighbourhood. In reply Roberts told Hunter that he could promise Cronje every consideration, and if his health necessitated it, he would be able to remain in his own home.[21] The next day Hunter wrote to Cronje placing the services of his Medical Officer at the disposal of the Boer leader and saying, rather touchingly, that he hoped Cronje 'would now regard him [Hunter] as his friend.'[22] Hunter's sense of chivalry may have paid off for later in the war, like some other Boer leaders, Cronje fought on the British side. Earlier, while at Lichtenburg, Hunter had been able to render a kindness to Mrs De la Rey the wife of the Boer General who was to remain in the Western Transvaal, a thorn in the flesh of the British for two more years. It seems that two of Mrs De la Rey's horses had been confiscated. Hunter for some reason thought this was unjust, and had them returned to her. She wrote and thanked him handsomely.[23]

But despite Roberts' optimism – maybe understandable since he was occupying the capitals of both Boer republics – the war was by no means over. The final surrender of the Transvaalers had not taken place. Indeed, having managed to extricate themselves successfully from Johannesburg, they were now being reorganised east of Pretoria by Botha and Smuts who had been encouraged by the moral support of President Steyn and de Wet. The latter had struck a telling blow on 7 June at Roodewal station when in an audacious raid with 800 mounted burghers he had captured 500 British soldiers and a mountain of supplies, before disappearing in the direction of Lindley. De Wet was serving notice of the kind of warfare that the British must now expect.

The tranquillity with which Hunter's advance had been received by the people was about to prove deceptive. Hunter's 10th Division had been obliged to leave garrisons, taken from Barton's brigade, in its wake as it progressed through the Transvaal. Its strength depleted it advanced on Krugersdorp, just west of Johannesburg to find the railway had been blown up at Bank station, and the telegraph cut.[24] Hunter's diary entry for 17 June was cryptic. It reads: 'Arrived Bank. Killed the telegraphist.' Ahead Krugersdorp described by Hunter as the cradle of Boer independence was giving trouble, and Mahon, on Hunter's behalf, gave the town an ultimatum: either surrender or be shelled. At the last minute it decided to surrender, and at least 1,000 prisoners were taken.

On 17 June Roberts sent telegrams to his principal commanders, including Hunter, in which he explained his plan to subjugate the Orange River Colony. First he planned to provide adequate garrisons for the principal towns and vulnerable points on the railways. Next he was organising four Flying Columns to be constantly on the move in the Colony under Methuen, Hamilton (based on Heidelberg), Clements and MacDonald.[25] Hunter at Krugersdorp asked Roberts for orders, and consequently was summoned to Johannesburg where on 23 June he met both Roberts and

1. Family group, 1877. AH aged 20 on extreme right (Author's collection)

2. AH aged 25 taken in Plymouth (King's Own Royal Regimental Museum, Lancaster)

3. AH in group at Wadi Halfa with Daisy Low on his left, March 1895 (Duncan Doolittle)

4. Fort Handoub, Suakin (Author's collection/SAD)

5. Drummers and Buglers, 12th Sudanese battalion (Author's collection/SAD)

6. Osman Digna, the Dervish leader (N J Russel)

7. Five Sergeants of the crack 9th Sudanese battalion, ca.1910 (Orders and Medals Research Society)

8. A rifleman of the 10th Sudanese battalion (Author's collection)

9. View of Akasha (SAD)

10. The battle of
    Atbara, 8 April
    1898. The Anglo-
    Egyptian troops
    storming
    Mahmoud's
    zariba. (SAD)

11. Gunboat being
    hauled over the
    second cataract
    (from a
    watercolour by
    P Komarnyckyj.
    H Keown-Boyd /
    Leo Cooper)

12. The bombardment of Metemma, October 1897 (SAD)

13. George Hunter (Author's collection)   14. Duncan Hunter (Duncan Doolittle)

15. General Sir Reginald Wingate
    (Author's collection)

16. Hunter with officers of the 2nd
    Battalion, The King's Own Royal
    Regiment at Lichfield, 19 January
    1899 (King's Own Royal
    Regimental Museum, Lancaster)

17. The assault on Abu Hamed,
    7 August 1897 (from a watercolour
    by P Komarnyckyj. H Keown-Boyd/
    Leo Cooper)

18. Hunter helping a wounded soldier,
    Ladysmith, 30 October, 1899
    (Author's collection)

19. Prinsloo's last stand at Slaapkranz,
    July 1900 (Author's collection)

20. Hunter as Colonel of the Regiment with the officers of the 1st Battalion, King's Own Royal Regiment at St James's Palace, 12 June 1913
(King's Own Royal Regimental Museum, Lancaster)

21. Hunter with his bride, Mazie Inverclyde, 1 November 1910 (Author's collection)

22. Hunter with King George V at Frensham, 1915 (N J Russel)

Kitchener. The outcome was that his 10th Division was disbanded. Hunter with a column of troops, including the 5th brigade, was sent to Heidelberg so as to release Hamilton's column[26] for its new role. Hunter's orders were 'to be ready either to stretch out a hand to General Buller at Standerton, or to move upon the left flank of any enemy attacking Pretoria from the east.'[27]

At this stage in the war the position was very fluid, and orders and plans were apt to be changed at a moment's notice. Looking back over the previous seven weeks must have been a cause of some satisfaction to Hunter. He had led his division over 400 miles of country and demonstrated an ability to take rapid action. His had been the main responsibility for relieving Mafeking and he had then taken the surrender of some 3,500 men. Less satisfactory had been the uncertain business of 'settling' the country. For instance the prisoners he had taken were allowed, in accordance with prevailing policy, to go free on oath. In his diary Hunter commented 'what folly!' He must have already been wondering how effective this policy was going to be. Nonetheless these must have been exhilarating times. Crossing the open spaces of the veldt and being almost constantly on the move with plenty of hard riding was what Hunter liked. But, Rooidam apart, there had been hardly any fighting.

Fate at this moment decided without warning to intervene. Ian Hamilton, at Heidelberg, had an accident on 25 June in which he fell from his horse during a skirmish and broke his collar bone. Roberts ordered a switch. Hamilton would take over Hunter's column, and Hunter Hamilton's. Hunter had been provided with a new opportunity. He seized it. The next six weeks would be among the most exciting and rewarding of his military career.

Notes

1. Maurice (biography of Rawlinson) 59.
2. DHD 195.
3. AHd 19/4/00.
4. OH III 181 and appendix V.
5. *Morning Post* 26 Jun. 1900.
6. TH IV 216.
7. Wilson *With the Flag to Pretoria* II 590.
8. OH III 110, 182; TH IV 217.
9. Hamilton Collection 24/7/11 AH letter book 17 May 1900.
10. NR Mahon–AH 15/5/1900.
11. Pakenham 415.
12. TH IV 222.
13. Jeal *Baden-Powell* 228, 245.
14. NR Mahon–AH 28/5/1900.
15. Jeal 313, 314; NR Baden-Powell–AH 28/5/1900.
16. Ibid. (NR).

17. TH IV 224.
18. TH IV 152.
19. AHd 3/6/00 and 8/6/00.
20. WO 105/17 AH–Roberts (R) 13/6/1900.
21. WO 108/239 R–AH 14/6/1900.
22. Hamilton Collection loc. cit. AH–Kronje 15 Jun. 1900.
23. NR Mrs De la Rey–AH 6/6/1900.
24. OH III 232; TH IV 345.
25. OH III 135.
26. NAM 7101-23-114-1 R–Secretary of State 24/5/1900.
27. OH III 308.

CHAPTER 15

De Wet Escapes – Prinsloo Surrenders

Roberts's long lines of communications stretching back 1,000 miles to Cape Town were highly insecure with thousands of active Free Staters under de Wet in his rear. His plan was now, in June 1900, to drive from the west and north against de Wet, whose burghers were concentrating in the area of Lindley and Bethlehem. For this task he would use the four recently formed mobile columns, one of which was commanded by Hunter. These columns would try to sweep the enemy southwards against the line Ficksburg to Winburg already held by Lieutenant-General Sir Leslie Rundle with his 8th and Colonial divisions and towards the Wittebergen mountains and the Basutoland border (see maps O and Q at pp. 142 and 152). Roberts' plan was ambitious. Its central aim was to capture de Wet, fast becoming the most menacing of Boer leaders, and eliminate from the war the flower of his army. Roberts himself would leave the handling of the operations to his commanders on the ground, over whom he would exercise supervision through the telegraph system despite its vulnerability to sabotage by the enemy.

Hunter left Heidelberg on 27 June with his column. It consisted of the 21st Infantry Brigade under Major-General Bruce Hamilton, the 2nd Mounted Infantry Brigade under Brigadier-General Ridley, the 2nd and 3rd Cavalry Brigades under Brigadier-Generals Broadwood and Gordon respectively, the Rimington Guides and divisional artillery. The Rimington Guides were a small force 200-strong raised locally by Major Rimington, and mainly used in a scouting role. To these men were added two squadrons of Scottish Yeomanry from the disbanded 10th division, making in all a total of 7,312 men, 3,942 horses and 30 guns.[1]

As he went south through the open rolling downland on both sides of the Vaal river Hunter cleared the country of all horses and supplies. Roberts had instructed him not to burn down the houses of the enemy; this form of collective punishment did not begin to be used widely until some weeks later. But he could take forage without paying for it and was entitled to warn people that their property might be confiscated.[2] The enemy was about but made no real effort to interfere with his progress.

Hunter had no difficulty in quickly getting on terms with the men in his new command. Pakenham, the historian, has observed that he had a gift like Buller for making ordinary people feel that he cared about them. March Phillipps, a young officer in the Rimington Guides, said that Hunter had a way of looking at people 'as if he felt the most friendly interest in you. And he does; it is not a bit put on.' Once, Phillipps related, there was a halt on the march for a smoke and Hunter gave the order to mount. One of the orderlies, a trooper in the Lancers, jumped up in too much hurry and left his pipe behind. Hunter saw the dirty but precious object, picked it up and put it in his pocket. At the next halt he went up to the trooper and gave it back to him.[3]

On 3 July Hunter reached Frankfort, nearly 60 miles on, where he was joined from Heilbron by his old comrade from the Sudan Major-General Hector MacDonald and his column. This included the Highland brigade, the 5th field battery and Lovat's Scouts, in all some 4,000 men. The Lovat Scouts had been formed by Lord Lovat from among the ghillies and stalkers of his Beaufort estates. The original idea had come from Mac-Donald, the son of a crofter. These Scouts were men entirely after Hunter's heart and would be invaluable to him in the weeks ahead. At Reitz which he reached on 7 July Hunter detached Bruce Hamilton with the 21st brigade and some supporting troops with orders to take a convoy of empty wagons to Heilbron and to return with supplies for the force.

There was a sense of urgency in the air and Hunter drove his men on at speed. Away to the south there was now the sound of heavy firing from the direction of Bethlehem. Broadwood and his cavalry were at once despatched towards the sound of the guns followed by Hunter himself and the mounted infantry. On 9 July Hunter reached Bethlehem to find that Major-Generals A. H. Paget and R. Clements coming in from the west had succeeded in taking the town.

In accordance with Roberts's orders Clements with his 12th brigade some 2,500-strong had earlier marched up from Senekal to join forces at Lindley with Paget and his 20th brigade about 2,000-strong. Lindley was a desolate little town, prey to every passing force, be it British or Boer, and it had changed hands on no less than seven occasions during the last fortnight of May.[4] The two columns had moved from Lindley in parallel south-east to Bethlehem, which they found to be defended by de Wet. Initially the Boer General put up a fight but then he changed his mind and decided to retreat to the south, anxious that his right flank should not be cut off

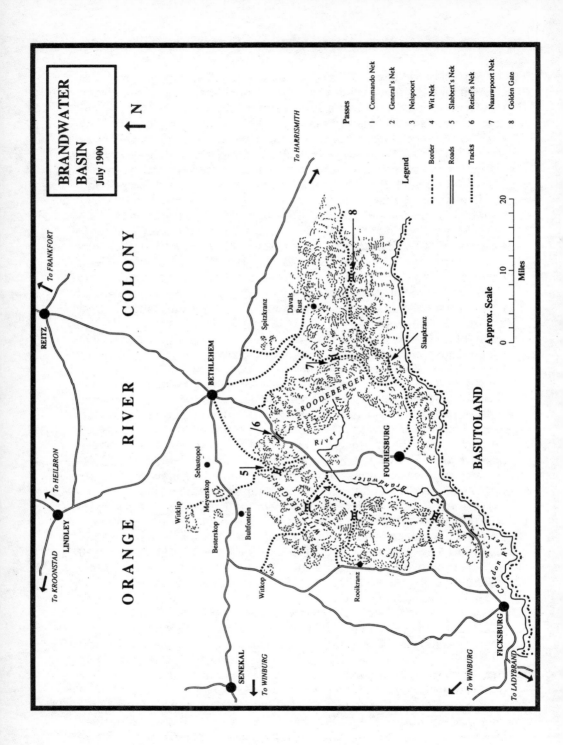

Map Q

152

by Hunter's advance from Reitz. For some reason Clements did not pursue the enemy with his mounted men. Steyn and his entourage had already preceded de Wet, and withdrawn through the mountains to establish their seat of government at Fouriesburg close to the Basutoland border.

The Free Staters, numbering over 6,000 men and with some 20 guns, now took up strong defensive positions in the Wittebergen and Roodebergen ranges. These wild and tangled mountains, spurs of the mighty Drakensberg, run continuously from just north of Ficksburg for some 75 miles eastwards, roughly in the shape of a horseshoe and in the direction of Harrismith. They enclose a fertile plain watered by the Brandwater and Caledon rivers. Entry into this plain was apparently possible through just six passes suitable for wheeled transport: Commando Nek, Wit Nek, Slabbert's Nek, Retief's Nek, Naauwpoort Nek and finally far over to the east the Golden Gate. Across the Caledon river to the south of the area rose the main Drakensberg range whose peaks at this time of the year were snow-capped. The Brandwater Basin, as the place was known, might on the one hand be regarded as a sanctuary guarded by almost impregnable defences. On the other, and this looked more likely to military men, it might seem like a trap from which escape could prove difficult. Clearly many Boers, de Wet as we shall see excepted, felt themselves to be safe there, and did not expect British troops to be able to penetrate their fastness, least of all as quickly as they eventually did.

Sitting in his Pretoria Headquarters Roberts now realised that with so many different columns of troops operating in the area he needed to appoint an overall commander. Only in this way could full advantage be taken of a situation in which a large force of Boers had become apparently bottled up with nowhere to go. He chose Hunter, and on 11 July gave instructions to him that Rundle's troops as well as the Clements/Paget force were to come under his command. At the same time Roberts spelt out the task. This was to block the enemy within the Brandwater Basin, to prevent his escape and if possible to force his surrender.[5]

No sooner had Hunter arrived in Bethlehem than a letter was brought to him, under a flag of truce, from his opponent de Wet. It was a reply by the Boer General to a letter that Paget had written charging the Boers with:

(1) using explosive bullets against British troops;
(2) shooting the wounded on the ground;
(3) shooting coloured people.

De Wet rejected these complaints. He countered Paget by saying the Boers had captured from the British cases full of all kinds of dumdums for Lee Metford rifles (Dumdums are soft nosed bullets which expand on impact with horrific effect; their use was proscribed at the Hague Conference in 1899). The Boers, he said, would continue to use these bullets until assurances were received that strict orders against their use had been issued by the British. On the second complaint de Wet found it incredible to be charged with such barbarity without any facts being produced. The same applied to the third complaint.

On his arrival at Bethlehem various problems exercised Hunter's mind. Perhaps the most immediate was the question of supply. At this stage in the war not many British troops were living off the land, and in the hostile country around Bethlehem Hunter was having to obtain his supplies from distant centres such as Heilbron and even Winburg, both on the railway. This meant sending heavily escorted supply convoys to these places, which of course depleted the forces available for offensive action. The round journey from Bethlehem to Heilbron was some 130 miles and oxen travelled at only one to two miles an hour. The time such journeys took can be imagined. Until the return of Bruce Hamilton and his supply column Hunter only had supplies, at $\frac{3}{4}$ rations, to last him until 18 July. Another absentee was Clements, who had left Bethlehem to obtain supplies in Winburg via Senekal on the very day of Hunter's arrival there. It is not clear whether Hunter sent him off or whether he chose to go on his own initiative and before they could discuss the military situation and requirements.[6]

In a long telegram sent on 11 July Hunter now gave the C-in-C his views on the situation.[7] As the enemy were in such strong positions at Naauwpoort, Retief and Slabbert Neks, he thought initially that their positions in the Basin could only be turned at the southern end of the front from Ficksburg or at the distant eastern end from Harrismith although he had not ruled out the use of Slabbert's Nek. Also he would need to coordinate plans with Rundle who was 55 miles away to the south-west. The country, Hunter decided, was not suitable for cavalry and he told Roberts that he was therefore sending back Gordon's 3rd cavalry brigade to Heilbron. He also explained about the supply position.

Though this was a matter not specifically mentioned to his chief Hunter was beset by an absence of information about the enemy's numbers, dispositions and plans. In those days there was virtually no War Office information about the physical features of the Wittebergen mountains and their passes, and the existing maps of the Brandwater Basin were sketchy, the Intelligence Branch still having no information about the roads and tracks in the area. A few locals provided some information as did a prisoner. It is not surprising that in the circumstances, therefore, Hunter advised Roberts that for the present 'we limit ourselves to keeping de Wet where he is.'[8]

Two days later after further reconnaissances had been made Hunter revised his plans as to how he would conduct offensive operations. He had decided to force a passage through Nelspoort, a minor pass on the west side of the Wittebergen, now reported to be passable for wheeled traffic. For this task he would use Clements's troops when they had returned from obtaining supplies. Rundle would block Commando Nek while he himself would block Retief's Nek, currently held by de Wet.[9] But this plan was quickly overtaken by events.

Some important intelligence had reached Roberts which he passed on to Hunter in two telegrams both dated 14 July.[10] In these Roberts referred to information received from Sir Godfrey Lagden, the British Resident in Maseru, Basutoland. According to Lagden the enemy was proposing to force his way out of the Brandwater Basin. One report said this would happen 'south of Ficksburg', and the other said it would be 'through the line Witkop–Ficksburg.' Boer forces were said to be at Commando Nek, eight miles from Ficksburg, and their wagons – always a good indicator of their line of advance – at General's Nek a few miles to the east. Assuming the information to be correct – it was not – Roberts urged that Rundle's mobile units should be moved to meet the threat. He finished his message by exhorting Hunter to use every endeavour to prevent a breakout. These reports were not the only ones received by Hunter on the subject of the Boers' intentions. Rumours had also been reaching him that the enemy were intending to break out in a southerly direction. Hunter acted at once on the information from Roberts. He told his chief that he was reinforcing Rundle at Witkop with 400 mounted infantry and a gun from Clements.[11] In addition Rundle was not to operate against Slabbert's Nek, but to keep his forces south of Nelspoort; this seemed logistically a sensible decision as Slabbert's Nek was much nearer to Hunter than to Rundle. The latter, a highly reliable soldier despite his nickname Sir Leisurely Trundle, took other appropriate steps to ensure that the Wit Nek pass was covered, and moved his Headquarters towards Rooikranz which he found to be held in force by Boers.

Another important move was made by Hunter on the next day, 15 July, for he sent the 2nd Cavalry Brigade under Broadwood, and the 20th Infantry Brigade with eight guns and the 14th and 15th Imperial Yeomanry all under Paget, along the Bethlehem to Senekal road to head off the enemy if an attempt was made to break out to the north-west, and to pin him down until Hunter could attack his rear. That day Paget arrived after dark at Sebastopol about nine miles from Bethlehem and about ten miles from Slabbert's Nek due south.[12] What, of course, Hunter had not done, and he would be criticised afterwards for this omission, was to seal off the two critical passes, Slabbert's Nek and Retief's Nek, both strongly held, by posting troops directly opposite them. According to *The Times History* Clements and Paget thought the passes should be blocked off. But Clements, as we have seen, had gone off to Senekal for supplies on 9 July and was not present at Bethlehem to back up the representations apparently made by Paget to Hunter on the subject.[13]

All was not well among the Boers behind their commanding ramparts. De Wet did not care for the position in which he found himself, hemmed in by the mountains. He considered that if his troops stayed there long they would be annihilated by the immense forces of the enemy.[14] A secret council of war was therefore held by the Boer leaders presided over by Steyn, and a decision was taken that the burghers would break out of the Brandwater Basin. The Boers would divide into three columns. The first one about 2,600-strong under de Wet, mainly consisting of the Heilbron and Kroonstad commandos and half the Bethlehem commando, and accompanied by Steyn, would leave on the night of 15 July and travel north-west towards Kroonstad and Heilbron. The second column, 2,000-strong, was entrusted to Paul Roux and would leave the following day in the evening in the direction of Bloemfontein. The last column of about 500 men would leave the same day under Crowther and march to the north of Bethlehem. The small balance of men remaining, under Prinsloo, was left to hold the passes against the British.[15]

It was a bold plan and the first part of it succeeded brilliantly. On the night of the 15th de Wet left as planned with his force plus four guns and no less than 460 wagons, and passed unchallenged through Slabbert's Nek. They headed north. But what of Paget? His men had spotted during the afternoon of that day a small laager in Slabbert's Nek, but following this discovery Paget had taken no particular precautions. Thus the Nek was not reconnoitred again, nor were pickets posted any distance from where Paget's men spent the night at Sebastopol.[16] As de Wet's long column passed close to Paget's men the camp fires of the British could be seen in the distance.

The escape of the Boers, though it was not at once known which commandos and which leaders were involved, was discovered quite soon the next day. Hunter immediately sent Broadwood and his brigade and also Brigadier-General Ridley with 800 mounted infantry in pursuit. The latter was ordered to join up with Broadwood. But despite Broadwood's efforts the wily Boer and his men were not to be caught.

However, the Boer column due to follow de Wet never moved out of the Basin. For one thing they would not now have been able to achieve the same measure of surprise as de Wet had managed. But much more significantly once the iron hand of de Wet was removed, the Boers dithered and the remaining Generals and leaders began to quarrel among themselves about their seniority and plans for escape. We shall return to this presently.

However much he regretted it, Hunter did not let the escape of de Wet throw him out of his stride. Plans for attacking the remaining Boers in the Basin went steadily forward. Bruce Hamilton arrived back in Bethlehem with his supply wagons, and was sent off with his column, reduced somewhat in numbers, and consisting of the Camerons, 550 mounted infantry and the 82nd battery, to seize Spitzkranz a hill some 10 miles south-east of Bethlehem which overlooked the long approach to Naauwpoort Nek. There he encountered some 400 Boers but succeeded the next day in driving them from the hill. On the western side of the Wittebergen, Clements took over the approach to Wit Nek from Rundle, who was thus enabled to tighten his holding line down to Ficksburg. Paget was by now at Bultfontein and Hunter with four battalions was covering the area between Paget and Bethlehem.

The Boers opposite Hunter's forces were distributed as follows. 2,500 men of Prinsloo's and Roux's commandos held Slabbert's Nek and Retief's Nek. Some 1,500 commandos under Crowther faced Rundle on the west, and to the east 400 men under Haasbroek were in the Naauwpoort Nek area. Far over to the east commandos from Harrismith and Vrede (see map O, p. 142), who had been slow to answer the call to assemble in the Basin, were in the neighbourhood of the Golden Gate. They numbered some 1,500.[17]

Final plans and reconnaissances had been made. Good work had been done in difficult country by the Lovat Scouts. March Phillipps described the mountainous country which they were about to enter as 'poisonous'. He hoped that Hunter with his great reputation as a fighter had not bitten off more than he could chew. But then he had to admit that he 'looks as if he could chew a good lot.'[18]

The attack would go in on 23 July. The objectives at this stage were to break into the Brandwater basin and to capture Fouriesburg. While Rundle's forces would demonstrate, or feint, on the west side of the Wittebergen range, carefully coordinated assaults would go in simultaneously at Slabbert's Nek using the Clements/Paget force and at Retief's Nek, probably the tougher of the two passes, under the command of Hunter himself. While he had under his present command, according to *The Times History*, in all some 18,500 men and 72 guns, quite a number of these men were on garrison duty, such as Rundle's troops at Ladybrand and elsewhere, and others were guarding supply convoys.

At 11 a.m. on 22 July Hunter left Bethlehem with MacDonald's Highland brigade, two 5-inch guns, the 5th and 76th field batteries, the Rimington Guides and the Lovat Scouts. He had also sent for the 1st Sussex and the 81st battery to join him the next morning from Meyerskop, a few miles to the north-west of Retief's Nek. With the idea of deceiving the enemy his force started towards the south-east as if they were going to the assistance of Bruce Hamilton in front of Naauwpoort Nek. Hunter then changed direction and arrived at Boshoffs Farm among hills just three miles short of Retief's Nek, but not before his mounted troops were engaged with some 200 Boers at the close of the day. Hunter's ruse succeeded, for the Boers at Retief's Nek detached some troops and sent them east to reinforce their men at Spitzkranz.[19] The weather was vile and the troops bivouacked during a night of rain, snow and intense cold.

The Boers' position at Retief's Nek was formidable. The approach to the pass was funnel-shaped and was bordered on either side by huge rock faces. From the mountain mass spurs jutted down into the plain, which itself was broken by rocky outcrops, a feature of this part of the Orange River Colony. The range extended in depth for some two or three miles before the interior valley of the Caledon river was reached. The physical features at Slabbert's Nek were not dissimilar.

At 8 a.m. on 23 July Hunter's field batteries and two 5-inch guns began shelling the pass at Retief's Nek and the heights on either side of it. An hour later the 2nd Black Watch with the Rimington Guides and Lovat Scouts moved forward to occupy a conical hill and crest to the left of the front with the object of turning the Boer position. They did well against heavy fire and by nightfall had occupied the hill and crests adjacent to it, almost turning the Boer line. Progress by other units was less successful. The Sussex regiment supported by the 81st battery arrived on the scene in the early afternoon and were sent to take a lofty hill on the right near Tuifelberg, a notable landmark in the immediate vicinity. While they were able with difficulty to obtain a footing on the slopes, they came under fierce fire and were eventually compelled at dusk to fall back. The Highland Light Infantry had in the meantime been sent against the rocky crags in the centre and had gained a precarious footing on the spurs below the cliffs. Helped by the fire of the gunners they just managed to hold on until nightfall. In his diary Hunter admits that his progress had only been slight – perhaps he was unduly pessimistic – and commented that his men had been baffled by the precipitous nature of the Boers' position. He reported to Roberts that his attacks had been 'strongly opposed' and that the enemy 'strongly entrenched had fought stubbornly.'[20]

Somehow a way through the tangled mountains had to be found. It was left to the intrepid Lovat Scouts to find it. The Scouts had been carefully studying the terrain during the day and at nightfall three men set off into the crags, and discovered that a peak which looked like the rock of Gibraltar and which lay between the position occupied by the Black Watch and the summits at which the Highland Light Infantry were aiming was unoccupied. The Scouts scrambled down and reported this to Hunter; they were at once ordered to retrace their steps and to lead two companies of Highland Light Infantry up to the peak. The summit was occupied in the dark and before the Boers had time to resume the position which they had temporarily abandoned during the night. On 24 July Hunter gave up his attempt on the right to take the Tuifelberg. He now concentrated all his efforts in exploiting the advantage won by the Black Watch and the Highland Light Infantry. So MacDonald was charged with taking the Seaforths and four guns of the 76th battery in a wide turning movement

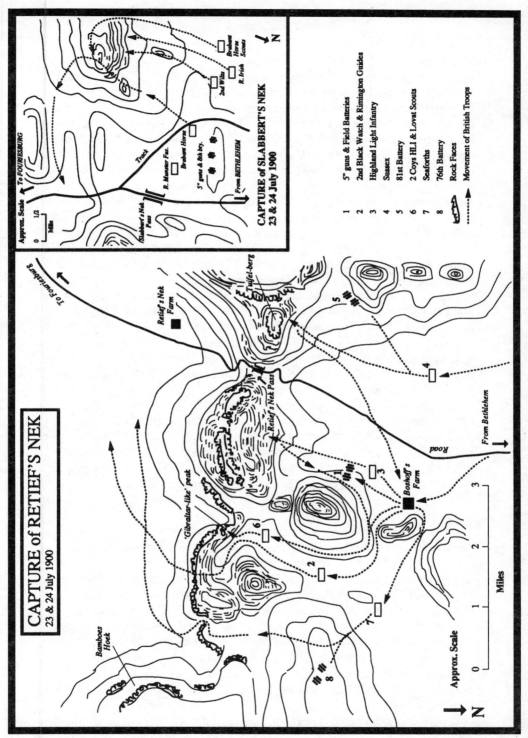

CAPTURE of RETIEF'S NEK
23 & 24 July 1900

To Fouriesburg

Bamboes Hoek

'Gibraltar-like' peak

Retief's Nek Farm

Tafel-berg

Retief's Nek Pass

Boshoff's Farm

Road

From Bethlehem

N

Approx. Scale

Miles
0   1   2   3

CAPTURE of SLABBERT'S NEK
23 & 24 July 1900

N

To FOURESBURG

Slabbert's Nek Pass

Track

R. Munster Fus.

Brabant Horse

5" guns & 8th bty.

From BETHLEHEM

2nd Wilts

R. Irish

Brabant Horse Scouts

Approx. Scale
0   1/2
Miles

1   5" guns & Field Batteries
2   2nd Black Watch & Rimington Guides
3   Highland Light Infantry
4   Sussex
5   81st Battery
6   2 Coys HLI & Lovat Scouts
7   Seaforths
8   76th Battery
   Rock Faces
   Movement of British Troops

to the left of the Black Watch. This move was highly successful and the Boer defences were overcome with great gallantry west of Bamboes Hoek, the high ground being won just before noon. This enabled the Seaforths and the Black Watch to descend on the south side into the valley of the Brandwater, thus finally turning the Boer defences. These had already been partially compromised by the winning of the summits, with their commanding field of fire, by the Highland Light Infantry in the night. The enemy saw their position was lost and evacuated the pass to avoid being trapped between Hunter and Clements, for the latter's troops were now swarming over Slabbert's Nek three miles to the west. Soon after 1 p.m. Hunter ordered his guns and baggage to move through Retief's Nek and within two hours they were bivouacking at Retief's Nek farm in the open valley beyond. The enemy had vanished in the direction of Fouriesburg. In two days' fighting Hunter's column had sustained 93 casualties, mostly occurring on 23 July, 12 killed and 81 wounded.[21]

Clements, marching on 23 July from Bester's Kop some ten miles from Slabbert's Nek, had joined forces at 10 a.m. with Paget who had camped just $2\frac{1}{2}$ miles from the pass. As the senior of the two Generals Clements took charge, and at once obtained a good position for his artillery, which was able to bombard the enemy's trenches and silence his guns. On the left centre he proceeded to use the Royal Munster Fusiliers as a containing force, while his main effort was made on the right. In time the Wiltshires and Royal Irish gained a footing on some high ground and after some adventurous scouting in the night, this time by the Brabant Horse, unoccupied high ground was discovered and seized towards the end of the night with the help of some cover obtained by low cloud. From this commanding height the enemy's position could be turned and by 11 a.m. on 24 July the Boers had left the Nek. Clements's and Paget's men suffered 42 casualties, 8 killed and 34 wounded.[22] There is no record of Boer casualties during the fighting for the two passes.

As soon as he reached the rich pasture land of the Basin, Hunter lost no time in detaching MacDonald and his Highland brigade. He was sent off at 8 a.m. on 25 July, together with the Lovat Scouts, 5th field battery and the 5-inch guns, to join Bruce Hamilton in blocking off the other exits by which the Boers might leave the Brandwater Basin. There were two passes to seal: first Naauwpoort Nek, and second, 25 miles away on the eastern side of the mountain chain, the Golden Gate pass. In his diary Hunter wrote: 'I must avoid pushing enemy back too fast so as to give my "stop-gaps" time to get into position. One can flatter one's enemies as well as one's friends.'

The role given to Rundle's forces on the western side of Wittebergen was much less dramatic than the one accorded to the forces assaulting the two north-facing passes. He carried out admirably his part of the battle plan. Demonstrations against the Boers were made without any serious attempt to carry enemy positions with the exception that the Boers were driven back through Wit Nek. This pass turned out to be a narrow and rough exit, quite unlike its misleading representation on the War Office map which showed it as a fine broad thoroughfare; no doubt this is why an exaggerated importance had been attached to it as a potential exit for Boer forces. On 25 July Rundle received word from Hunter that he and Clements were inside the Basin, and that the Boers had fled south. Rundle at once vigorously pushed forward, seized Commando Nek and continued on into the Basin.

Hunter made steady progress in the direction of Fouriesburg. His force was now small and consisted merely of the Rimington Guides and the 81st field battery. March Phillipps saw Hunter ride forward in the afternoon and after watching through his glasses for a while the figures of Boers in the distance, returned to his men with a smile on his face. Instead of ordering an advance as the impetuous ones expected, Hunter led the column back the way he had come for several miles and then camped.[23] He was simply in no hurry, and had good tactical reasons for not dashing after the enemy.

The next afternoon, 26 July, Hunter rode into Fouriesburg and found that Rundle had already taken possession of the little town after a forced march of 25 miles from Commando Nek. Sixty-nine British prisoners of war held there were released, and a huge supply of Mauser ammunition for Boer rifles was found. Hunter and Rundle called on Mrs Steyn who with her two children and servants had been left behind, first by her husband the President when he had escaped from the Basin and then by the retreating Boers as they fell back to the east. She told Hunter that President, Generals and burghers meant to fight on to the bitter end with or without foreign intervention, and she predicted the eventual destruction of the British forces. Hunter passed this on to Roberts with the comment that Mrs Steyn was 'a pleasant and plausible woman who made no secret of her side's resolve to win the war or die in the attempt.' She asked leave to proceed to her farm near Bloemfontein,[24] a matter for Roberts to decide (permission was given a few days later).

Throughout 27 July Hunter's forces kept lightly in touch with the enemy who withdrew towards Slaapkranz. Hunter was concerned about MacDonald's lack of strength and sent him an extra 300 Mounted men and the Sussex. He hoped that by now he and Bruce Hamilton had been able on the other side of the mountains to block the remaining passes. Communication between Hunter and his subordinates was not easy; there were no telegraph lines round the hills to the north and reliance had to be placed on messengers, who were slow. So Hunter could not be sure of the position. In fact the situation to the north in difficult country was not entirely satisfactory. MacDonald had succeeded by the evening of 26 July, after working his way round from Retief's Nek, in closing Naauwpoort Nek. Bruce Hamilton nearby had been held up by the Boers who fought a rearguard action at Daval's Rust. But MacDonald, instead of proceeding to close the last exit at Golden Gate, wasted, according to the account in *The Times History*, a whole day on the 27th, and did not start for the most easterly of the passes until the next day.[25] He then decided on 28 July that, as he was making slow progress owing to the terrain, he would return to Naauwpoort Nek and leave it to Bruce Hamilton with about 850 men and six guns to struggle on towards the Golden Gate. The enemy was continuing to show plenty of fight and twice that day offered stiff resistance to Bruce Hamilton, who was still short of his objective.

The main force of Boers in front of Hunter continued to retreat during 28 July up the valley from Fouriesburg towards the mountains, and fought tenaciously all day. To outflank the enemy Hunter was ready, as he put it, to 'violate' the Basutoland border. He telegraphed Roberts about this. Clements led the advance and the enemy was gradually driven back from ridge to ridge to Slaapkranz. This was a position with high and difficult cliffs on either side of the road. As at Retief's Nek progress at first was slow. Rundle's infantry consisting of the 2nd Scots Guards, 1st Leinsters and some of the 2nd Royal West Kents tried hard but could make no real headway. Hunter wrote in his diary at the end of this day: 'To advance further would cost too many lives. advise wait till nightfall and give him [the enemy] the bayonet. Select Romilly's battalion, 2nd Scots Guards, for the job. I should like to go myself but Generals must not lead battalions.'

The plan worked, for the Scots Guards exploited a mistake by the Boers, who gave up a central height owing to a confusion of orders, and by midnight the pass had been won. Hunter remarked that 'Rundle and Clements handled their troops with splendid judgement. My artillery was beautifully worked and my staff is perfect.'[26] During the day, there had been 34 British casualties, including four men killed.

By now the Boers had become despondent. Not only had they endured a series of military reverses but they were also suffering from acute problems of leadership, though this was of course unknown to Hunter at the time. After de Wet had left the Basin on the night of 15 July – a move for which he has been criticised on the basis that the Commander-in-Chief is not the first to leave from a dangerous situation – disputes began as to who was the new commander of the men left behind. At first it appeared to be Paul Roux but since some men were dissatisfied it was decided to hold an election. This took place at a council of war on 27 July near Slaapkranz. The result was unexpected. Martinus Prinsloo, a rich and influential elder of the church in Winburg, who had been in command of the Free Staters earlier in the war in Natal, was elected over the younger Paul Roux. But the confusion that had existed earlier was not dispelled because the votes of the more distant commandos were not received.

Nonetheless Prinsloo thinking himself elected and having given up hope of defeating the British, sent an emissary to Hunter at 7.15 a.m. on 29 July to ask for a four-day armistice, to apply to the whole fighting line. Its object was to enable Prinsloo to enter into peace negotiations. Hunter refused the request. The emissary chosen by the Boers was S. G. Vilonel once regarded as a young and progressive commander. It was an odd choice. Vilonel had once tried to induce some of his comrades to surrender. He was tried in the field, found guilty of treason and sentenced to five years' hard labour. Thus he was in disgrace. Why Prinsloo chose him as an emissary remains something of a mystery.

Messages between Prinsloo and Hunter went back and forth under a flag of truce, while the fighting continued beyond Slaapkranz. In answer to Prinsloo's initial request for an armistice Hunter sent Lieutenant-Colonel Philip Le Gallais, his Chief of Staff, to the enemy camp to demand unconditional surrender of all men, arms and ammunition. Prinsloo forthwith sent a second message, received at 10.30 a.m., requesting that the horses, saddles, bridles and other possessions belonging to the burghers should be guaranteed to them, and moreover that they should be free to go home. To this Hunter repeated his call for unconditional surrender. He urged Prinsloo to accept that his people would receive every consideration and kindness which it was possible to bestow upon them as prisoners of war. Hunter added that he wished to avoid any further bloodshed and unless he, Prinsloo, was willing to abide by whatever Lord Roberts decided he would be compelled to continue the fight. Back at about noon came the answer with Prinsloo asking for more time to discuss matters with his officers. Prinsloo also said that Vilonel was authorised to enter into discussions. The latter proceeded then to argue for better terms giving religious reasons for them. Eventually Hunter refused to have any further discussions, whereupon Vilonel drew from his pocket another letter from Prinsloo, which he had had on his person all the time, in which Prinsloo agreed to unconditional surrender.[27] Rundle and Hunter's staff all witnessed this unusual event. This scene has been described in picturesque terms. One account has Hunter calmly taking out his stop-watch and telling the Boer emissaries that they had 20 minutes to make their decision on whether or not to accept unconditional surrender. When the time ran out he gave immediate instructions to his orderlies for the 5-inch guns to open fire on Boer positions. This made Vilonel produce his final letter smartly.[28]

Hunter immediately wrote to Prinsloo – it was now 4.30 p.m. – and confirmed that he would allow each burgher to ride his horse to the point of the railway, and that he did not intend to confiscate private property or the personal effects of the men. The burghers, however, would become prisoners of war until the peace and would have to give up all arms and ammunition: also horses, wagons, carts, oxen and mules would all be confiscated.[29] The formal surrender, Hunter stated, was to take place at 9 a.m. on the next day, 30 July. Hunter ended by begging Prinsloo to accept his and his men's admiration for their foes' 'loyal and gallant conduct while acting against us.' He then began arrangements to stop the fighting; this included sending a message to MacDonald through the enemy camp.

Hunter had been careful to keep Roberts fully posted during all these developments, and had received confirmation from the C-in-C that his approach to the Boers' demands had been correct.[30] The fact that the telegraph to Pretoria was not always working properly possibly told to Hunter's advantage. Off his own bat he was enabled to offer the Boers concessions about private property and personal effects not being confiscated (except horses). This may have helped the surrender process.

The next day at 9 a.m. Prinsloo and Crowther came with their men to lay down their arms to a place which became known as 'surrender hill'. It was near to a farm named appropriately enough Verliesfontein ('verlies' means 'loss'). The setting in the sparkling air 5,000 feet up must have been breath-taking. The surrounding peaks, unsurpassed in their wild grandeur, were bathed in a golden light and below the valley floors were lost in a hazy blue. Hunter and Rundle with their staffs were waiting for their foes by a tall flag-pole from which floated the Union Jack. In the place of honour on the right were the Scots Guards. The Boers approached between the lines of British infantry, standing with their bayonets fixed, and threw down their weapons. They were a mixed crowd. White-haired grandfathers and sometimes young boys mingled with those of fighting age. They rode small ponies with bright coloured rugs. Their clothes were of rough country cut, with here and there a khaki tunic taken obviously from some captured British soldier or, worse, from a corpse. They seemed glad to be out of the war. That day the Ficksburg and Ladybrand commandos, 879 men with one Krupps gun, surrendered. The next day the Senekal and Winburg commandos, 354-strong, came in with their leaders. At the same time to the north Bruce Hamilton took the surrender of 1,298 men under three Commandants.

But not all the Boer leaders accepted Prinsloo's authority to command their surrender. After telling Prinsloo on the evening of the 29th that *he* had been elected Commander-in-Chief, Paul Roux went to Hunter to say that he was the rightful Boer commander and that the surrender was all a mistake. Hunter was unimpressed. Eventually Roux accepted that he was bound by Prinsloo's action, and came in with 1,200 men. De Wet comments in his autobiography that Roux's behaviour must have afforded Hunter much amusement. Haasbroek was one of the Boer leaders who did not accept the surrender, and with as many men as he could collect together he went to the Golden Gate. There he found Olivier and others trying to make a last stand. But the men were no longer willing to fight.

Olivier, however, persuaded some 1,500 of them to march off in the direction of Harrismith. In his diary Hunter wrote that these men escaped from 'under MacDonald's nose', making it clear whom he privately thought was responsible for this escape. MacDonald was sent in pursuit of Olivier, but the Boer and his men for the moment evaded capture. Hunter regarded Olivier's conduct as a dishonourable breach of faith and held him personally responsible for failing to surrender.[31] A week later Hunter sent him an ultimatum. Unless he surrendered, all concessions made by Roberts to the burghers who had just given themselves up would be withdrawn.[32]

On 30 July Hunter despatched Major King, still his ADC, with one of Prinsloo's staff officers to try and find de Wet, quite a difficult task in itself. They were to deliver to him a letter from Prinsloo (who signed himself Commander-in-Chief) with information about the surrender. In addition the letter, according to Hunter's diary, was to advise de Wet that a continuation of the struggle was useless. But this additional bit is missing from the text of Prinsloo's letter that appears in de Wet's book. Hunter must have thought this exercise was worth while for he commented that it 'might do good, can't do harm.'[33] Upon the formidable de Wet the message from Prinsloo had no positive effect at all. The capitulation of his fellow-countrymen filled him with disgust. In replying briefly to Prinsloo, de Wet acidly asked him by what right he usurped the title of Commander-in-Chief.

The figures given for the number of Boers surrendering in the Brandwater Basin vary. The usual one quoted is 4,140 men though by 9 August the figure had risen to 4,314. In his diary Hunter gave the figure as 4,800 men which seems on the high side. In the haul were three Generals (Prinsloo, Roux and Crowther) and ten Commandants. The prisoners would go to camps in Ceylon (Sri Lanka). Over 4,000 horses and ponies, 2,800 head of cattle and a vast number of sheep were collected as well. The huge quantity of rifles handed over and about 2,000,000 rounds of ammunition were destroyed. The number of field guns surrendered, only three, two of them captured earlier from the British, was disappointing. Others were destroyed and some hidden away before the surrender while a few were dragged off to Harrismith.

The Boers' surrender to Hunter was the climax of a highly successful military operation for which Hunter is entitled to much credit. *The Times History* calls it 'one of the greatest military achievements of the war.'[34] It may not have had a major effect on the course of hostilities for already the hardliners had decided to adopt a guerrilla strategy which would prolong the war for nearly two years more. But on the other hand about half the fighting strength of the Free Staters had been knocked out as a result of Hunter's operations. Certainly at no other time during the Boer War did so many Boers surrender at one time – the number even exceeding those who had capitulated at Paardeburg earlier in the year (where the figure was 4,069). On the British side the casualties amounted to 275 men of whom 33 had been killed.[35] It was therefore a victory obtained at a comparatively small cost.

How does Hunter emerge from this episode? His plan for the break-in was well conceived, and the operation once under way was conducted with determination and speed over difficult country. His leadership was outstanding. His tactics and the handling of his forces, taking into account the special problems of communicating with his commanders, were highly effective. He was much concerned about avoiding too many casualties. His management of the surrender negotiations showed skill in balancing firmness and conciliatoriness. The victory was unfortunately marred by his failure to prevent the escapes of de Wet and Olivier. He recognised these failures very frankly in his report to the Chief of Staff dated 4 August, a despatch which was published in the *London Gazette* on 8 February 1901. How many commanders would have been so honest? It is something of a puzzle why Slabbert's Nek was not properly blocked earlier. It clearly should have been, and Hunter was here at fault. Also Olivier's escape might have been prevented if MacDonald had not lingered. We do not know what action, if any, Hunter took to urge MacDonald and Bruce Hamilton to move faster to the Golden Gate. On the other hand, with difficult communications he was very much in the hands of his subordinates on his northern front.

Hunter has been criticised for sitting around too long in Bethlehem. It has been said for one thing that he was over-preoccupied with his supply positions. This is arguable. To ensure that he had enough supplies for a campaign in the mountains which could have lasted much more than two weeks was surely to err on the right side. Also it was sensible on arrival there not to rush headlong towards the mountains, but take stock, wait for his troops to concentrate and in the meantime try to find out about the enemy's dispositions.

Hunter had some interesting observations to make in his report. Always they were forthright and to the point. He had nothing but praise for the Rimington Guides and Lovat Scouts, commenting on them respectively: 'they have never disappointed me . . .' and 'they are a splendid band of Scotsmen which is the highest compliment I can pay them'. The gunners too received praise. But the infantry came first in his estimation and of them he said: 'Everybody knows how highly Napoleon appraised British infantry and since then they have not changed except to improve. Generals, Regimental Officers and men have learnt how to minimise losses against magazine rifles, and smokeless powder in defensive positions; now they threaten flanks and turn positions.' His one criticism was the callous indifference displayed by many officers and men to the danger of grass fires and the necessity of at once putting them out.

The Boers' reputation he put into context. Some he admitted were 'crack shots' but 'man for man their shooting is not as good as ours. Their mobility is the main point where they excel us'. Thus they were always ready to take up a new position or reinforce their flanks. Other aspects of the way the enemy conducted warfare to their advantage struck him equally forcefully: their mastery of three languages and ability to obtain information from all people; their not wearing uniform which meant that one moment they could pose as peaceful farmers, the next prove themselves as active soldiers; their secret supplies of arms and ammunition; their universal skill with horses and transport, and their local knowledge of the country.[36] Some of this may be obvious enough but it points to the author's grasp of warfare in all its facets.

Hunter and his men received warm praise from Roberts, who according to his biographer James was never disposed to blame him for the failure to take de Wet.[37] Certainly Roberts signalled back to the Secretary of State giving his opinion that Hunter had shown marked ability and judgement in his conduct of the operations and that there were good local reasons connected with the terrain for the escape of de Wet and of Olivier.[38]

NOTES

1. WO 105/10 AH–COS 4/8/1900.
2. WO 108-240 Roberts (R)–AH 30/6/1900.
3. Phillipps *With Rimington* 180.
4. TH IV 302.
5. WO 105/10 loc. cit.
6. WO 105/17 AH–R 11/7/1900; AHd indicates that Hunter sent Clements off to obtain supplies. But the TH at IV 319 states that Clements left Bethlehem before Hunter's arrival there.
7. WO 105/17 loc. cit.
8. Ibid.
9. WO 105/17 AH–R 13/7/1900.
10. WO 108/240 R–AH (tels 2749 and 2760) 14/7/1900.
11. WO 105/10 loc. cit.; WO 105/17 AH–R 14/7/1900.
12. OH III 295; TH IV 321; WO 105/10 loc. cit.
13. Ibid. (TH) 312.
14. De Wet 161.
15. OH III 295; TH IV 316; de Wet 162.
16. TH IV 321.
17. Ibid. 326.
18. Phillipps 146.
19. TH IV 328.
20. WO 105/17 AH–R 23/7/1900.
21. WO 105/10 loc. cit.; OH III 200; TH IV 327–30.
22. WO 105/10 loc. cit.; OH III 299; TH IV 330.
23. Phillipps loc. cit.
24. WO 105/17 AH–R 26/7/1900.
25. TH IV 335; the OH (at III 303) has on the other hand both MacDonald and

Bruce Hamilton marching 'with all speed' to the Golden Gate. The TH version is preferred.

26. AHd 28/7/00.
27. NR Prinsloo–AH and AH–Prinsloo letters all dated 29 Jul. 1900; WO 105/10 loc. cit.
28. Wilson *After Pretoria the Guerrilla War* I 32.
29. NR loc. cit.
30. NAM 7101-23-114-1 R–AH 29/7/1900.
31. WO 105/10 loc. cit.
32. WO 105/17 AH–R 6/8/1900.
33. AHd 31/7/00.
34. TH IV 343.
35. WO 105 Box 10 126/144: list of casualties.
36. WO 105/10 loc. cit.
37. James *Lord Roberts* 333.
38. WO 105 Box 10 126/144 R–Sec of State forwarding AH's despatch of 4 Aug. 1900.

CHAPTER 16

Guerrilla War

After his triumph in the Brandwater Basin Hunter had another six months in South Africa before he was invalided home. These months were not distinguished for him by any outstanding action in the field. The first three of them were spent chasing Boers round the Orange River Colony without much success. The rest of the time he was Governor of Bloemfontein and commanding all forces in the Orange River Colony. There was though an unhappy development during these months and that was Hunter's disillusionment with the military policy followed by Roberts. Basically Roberts believed the war to be virtually over while Hunter did not accept this and considered there was a long haul ahead. His relationship with Roberts has a bearing on our story, and this is something we must examine shortly.

Hunter's victorious forces dispersed quickly in early August. Bruce Hamilton and Paget and their men were placed in charge of the prisoners and set off with them to march to the railhead at Winburg, 80 miles away. They left on 2 August. Clements and his column were required in the Transvaal, and proceeded to Kroonstad. Rundle received orders from Roberts to resume his independent command and was directed to Harrismith to follow Olivier, while Hunter himself returned on 5 August to Bethlehem.

Five days later, with a force consisting of MacDonald's Highland brigade, half the Bedfords, the 6th and 15th Yeomanry battalions, the Lovat Scouts, the 5th and 82nd field batteries and one 5-inch gun, Hunter set off in the chase to prevent Olivier joining de Wet in the mountains of Western Transvaal. On 12 August he received the following orders from Roberts:

'You should remain for the present in neighbourhood of Lindley, visiting Heilbron, Reitz, Frankfort, or any place you think the enemy is concentrating. Keep enemy constantly on the move and try and restore confidence among people. Get hold of horses, cattle, etc, paying for them when desirable.'[1]

The next day this telegram was amended stating that Hunter's base should be Heilbron. It is not too easy to follow what Roberts meant by 'restore confidence'. He was presumably thinking about the need to protect inhabitants regarded as loyal to the British crown. But most people, as was being patently demonstrated, were against the British, perceived by them to be invaders. The burnings of farms and houses being used increasingly as a punishment and also the confiscation of animals was hardly likely to create confidence.

On 14 August just beyond the Rhenoster river some 12 miles south of Heilbron Hunter encountered a Boer force of 1,800 men with six field guns and two machine guns under Froneman. They were holding a position about five miles long parallel to and on the right of the Lindley to Heilbron road near Witpoort. The force contained other Boer leaders including Olivier, Haasbroek and Fourie, all wishing to join de Wet. An engagement began at 11.15 a.m. when the Boers fired on Hunter's leading troops. At once Hunter attacked, having to execute a change of front to his right as he did so. Pinning the enemy down with his 5-inch gun, the 5th battery and half the Black Watch, he sent the Highland Light Infantry, the Lovat Scouts and the 82nd battery to turn the Boer left. At first they pushed the enemy back before the Commandos stood firm. Hunter then threw in his reserves, the Bedfords, placing them on the ground won. This enabled the Highland Light Infantry, despite heavy shrapnel and rifle fire, to sweep along the ridges previously occupied by the Boers. At 4.40 p.m. the Black Watch and Seaforths covered by the 5th battery made a frontal assault aiming at a high hill towards the enemy's right. At dusk the Boers fell back and retreated to the south-east. It had been quite a stiff fight, in which a Second Lieutenant and three men were killed and 42 soldiers wounded.[2] As usual there is no record of Boer casualties.

The following day Hunter occupied Heilbron, where he spent the next week. He described his life on the veldt to his sister-in-law Abby in one of the few surviving letters he wrote during the war. Everybody was 'in rags, no tents, weary men, and thin horses, but we can move fast enough to puzzle the Boers sometimes . . . our men are splendid. No crime in great

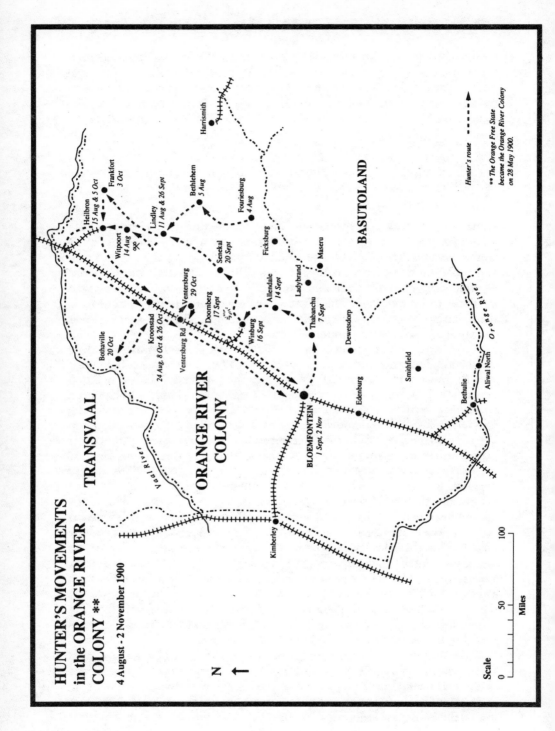

HUNTER'S MOVEMENTS in the ORANGE RIVER COLONY **

4 August - 2 November 1900

N ←

TRANSVAAL

ORANGE RIVER COLONY

BASUTOLAND

Harrismith

Heilbron
15 Aug & 5 Oct

Frankfort
3 Oct

Lindley
11 Aug & 26 Sept

Bethlehem
5 Aug

Fouriesburg
4 Aug

Witpoort
14 Aug

Senekal
20 Sept

Ficksburg

Maseru

Ladybrand

Allendale
14 Sept

Bothaville
20 Oct

Ventersburg
29 Oct

Doornberg
17 Sept

Thabanchu
7 Sept

Dewetsdorp

Kroonstad
24 Aug, 8 Oct & 26 Oct

Ventersburg Rd

Winburg
16 Sept

Vaal River

Smithfield

Orange River

Edenburg

BLOEMFONTEIN
1 Sept, 2 Nov

Bethulie

Aliwal North

Kimberley

Scale
0   50   100
Miles

Hunter's route

** The Orange Free State
became the Orange River Colony
on 28 May 1900.

Map S

temptation . . . some terrific marching.' Mail was intermittent for when the Boers raided trains and intercepted mail bags these were burnt. But now his 'table and little camp bed are strewn with letters', and most of the pile had to be answered before he was off again. There were some sentimental bits too in his letter for he had just heard from Daisy Low which 'has set me pining for a look at you all again.' He mentioned rumours that he was to become eventually Military Governor of the Orange River Colony or Transvaal but jokingly added he would 'rather go to China'. He thought South Africa had the makings of a grand country and would develop under a good government.[3]

De Wet was causing great unease again. From the western Transvaal he had crossed over the Vaal river on 23 August with 300 men and was marching south. The enemy's intentions were uncertain but their ambitions could include the capture of Bloemfontein and even the invasion of Cape Colony. Hunter went down to Kroonstad. Suddenly there was positive news. Olivier with 1,000 men and two guns had appeared nine miles north of Winburg and had surrounded a party of 220 men under Lieutenant-Colonel H. M. Ridley. Hunter was told by Roberts to direct operations to relieve Ridley, but that in doing this Heilbron might have to be given up.[4] Bruce Hamilton raced with his column to rescue Ridley and succeeded in extricating him and his men from a tough spot. They all withdrew to Winburg which was then attacked by Olivier. During the operations Olivier and his three sons fell into a trap and were captured by eight men of the Queenstown Volunteers led by a sergeant. Hunter must have felt a lot better now that Olivier was 'in the bag.'

During August military requirements in the Transvaal, where Roberts was conducting operations towards Komati Poort on the Portuguese East Africa border, had reduced Hunter's command to MacDonald's Highland Brigade, Bruce Hamilton's column and Le Gallais' mounted troops.[5] At the end of the month Hunter went down to Bloemfontein to confer with Lieutenant-General Thomas Kelly-Kenny, the Military Governor there, on the general situation in the Orange River Colony. Bruce Hamilton together with Le Gallais had been despatched to Ladybrand whose small garrison was reported to be surrounded by some 3,000 Boers under Fourie. A constant feature of the campaign now was for garrisons holding small towns to become hostage to marauding commandos, who could strike at will and withdraw rapidly. Even if the countryside was mainly bare of vegetation and trees, it was at least intersected with rocky hills and outcrops providing cover for guerrilla forces. The arrival of Bruce Hamilton foiled the Boers who withdrew northwards in the direction of the hilly area of Doornberg, north of Winburg.

No doubt thinking he saw an opportunity comparable to that provided by the Brandwater Basin, Hunter decided to try to surround the Boers in the Doornberg hills. Rundle's 8th Division was put at his disposal and came up from the east. During the first two weeks of September the British columns began to close in on the hills where the Boers had gone to ground. To begin with, things looked promising and on 15 September Hunter took part in a midnight march which caused him 'much excitement and some trepidation'.[6] But the well-planned operation fizzled out, for while there were some minor engagements with the enemy, the Boers were not willing to become entrapped and by 18 September it became clear that the Boer forces in the Doornberg had dispersed. To prevent the area from being used again as a sanctuary Hunter determined, in accordance with the prevailing policy, to lay waste the surrounding country. The appropriate orders were therefore given to Rundle and MacDonald. At the same time Hunter himself headed east towards Senekal in pursuit of the main enemy force which, however, highly mobile as usual, was not to be caught.

Roberts, still optimistic about the war though with less cause, now ordered the adoption of a new scheme in the Orange River Colony to counter Boer tactics. In effect he was reverting to his earlier methods which he had introduced on 17 June whereby certain centres would be garrisoned, while mobile columns, based on them, roved about destroying all subsistence for the enemy. Hunter was directed to exercise general control over the forces in the north of the Orange River Colony, keeping Le Gallais' mounted troops with him, and going wherever he could best supervise the operations.[7] According to his diary this was a scheme which Hunter had suggested to Roberts. The C-in-C gave explicit instructions to clear the whole area of supplies. If the people chose to listen to de Wet then they and their families would be starved. This was the mailed fist approach, though it was not to have the desired effect of cutting off the Boer troops from their food and forage. Gradually as their policy was not seen to be producing results the British became more ruthless and there was greater resort to the burning of farms and houses. The war was in fact becoming nastier.

Tirelessly Hunter covered his area. On 20 September he was at Senekal. On the 26th at Lindley. On 3 October at Frankfort, once again for a time occupied by the British. On 5 October he went to Heilbron, and on the 8th he was back, by rail, at Kroonstad. And so it went on, without very much being achieved in terms of suppressing the guerrilla war.

While at Kroonstad Hunter learnt that the enemy was using Bothaville, nearly 50 miles away to the north-west, as a base for operations against the railway and telegraph. He determined to investigate this himself, having heard that 1,600 Boers were moving on the town. He left Kroonstad on 16 October taking with him Bruce Hamilton's column plus half the 39th Field Battery and 70 mounted men. The 3rd Cavalry Brigade as well as the Rimington's Guides and Le Gallais' troops were also to co-operate. As ever the Boers proved elusive and only small numbers of them were encountered. Bothaville was occupied without resistance on 20 October.

In the houses supplies of ammunition were found secreted away. The inhabitants were boastful of the part they had been playing in raids on the railway. Hardening his heart Hunter therefore resolved to take severe punitive measures which he saw in the circumstances as his duty. Some 45 houses were burnt down on 23 October. But he did not burn the church – its pulpit had been used to conceal telegraph instruments – the manse, public buildings and houses used for Red Cross purposes.[8]

After the burning of Bothaville it was reported that the Boers were threatening the railway at Ventersburg Road station. An exchange of telegrams took place between Roberts and Hunter. Hunter was asked what action he was proposing to take, and Roberts was asked whether Ventersburg and Lindley too, both Boer strongholds, should be burnt. Roberts's advice, not seemingly an instruction, was that every house belonging to a Boer who was absent should be burnt.[9] In the event Bruce Hamilton took in hand the destruction of the houses and farms of suspects in the area. The practice of burning houses and farms caused outrage in England. Consequently, Roberts was obliged to modify his policy and in November to amend his instructions to his commanders so that houses could be destroyed only if there had been an act of treason by their owners or if the houses had been used for firing upon troops or in operations against them.[10]

During the operations at Ventersburg at the end of October Hunter planned to ambush the Boers and placed his troops close under a hill which it was thought was free of the enemy. In the early morning it was some 300 Boers on top of the hill who sprang the surprise on the British below. All was confusion for a time as fire rained down on the British. A major was shot dead and horses, mules and oxen stampeded. In the middle of all this Hunter, described by a correspondent as 'the equal of any VC hero that ever existed', strolled calmly among the soldiers restoring order, and then organising a counter-attack. 'Let it rip, boys. Don't give the beggars breathing time . . .' The men of the Sussex battalion went forward boldly, charged the hill and put the Boers to flight.[11] This may well have been the last action in the Boer War in which Hunter was personally involved.

When Hunter returned to Kroonstad he found a telegram dated 25 October from Roberts awaiting him. It read: 'I was under the impression that you would not care to serve [on] in South Africa and proposed to let you return to India when the war was over . . .'[12] It was true that Hunter had become disenchanted with serving in South Africa. This is quite clear from letters he wrote on 28 October to Duncan and to Wingate. He told both of them that he had asked not to be included in the list of soldiers to be left permanently in South Africa. He hoped to return to India. As for the war, he disagreed with those, like Roberts, who said it was practically over. As early as August Hunter had written to Wingate to say that

Roberts would not finish the war in a 'month of Sundays'. He thought there was 'too much Rawlinson and Hamilton and not enough Buller and Kitchener'. Two months later, again to Wingate, he wrote that the vitality of the Boer cause had been underestimated. 'We have annexed a country without conquering it'.[13]

He was of course right about the war and being a forthright man he did not conceal his views from his superiors. With the hit and run tactics being adopted by the Boers, Roberts faced difficulties in deciding which of the smaller towns should be garrisoned. On the advice of Major-General Charles Knox he decided to abandon Lindley. On 31 October Hunter sent a telegram to Roberts which shows the frustration he felt over what was being done. It read:

> 'Districts are upset by policy of vacillating and changes. Withdrawal after occupation is jubilantly accepted by the inhabitants as a confession of our inability to do otherwise and is magnified by Boer leaders into military success . . .'[14]

Hunter went on to give his opinion to Roberts that Lindley, which was in his area and not Knox's, should have been held. Also he felt that Knox's views should have been referred to Roberts through him.[15] Hunter's telegram was certainly outspoken, but was it rashly phrased? The word 'vacillating' seems almost to reprove the C-in-C, and calls to mind the rebuke he gave Kitchener in the Sudan in 1896 about the 'death march'. We do not know what Roberts's reaction to Hunter's telegram was but it may have been irritation or worse.

The state of personal relations between Roberts and Hunter is not known. At any rate on his arrival in Bloemfontein in early November to take over from Kelly-Kenny as Military Governor, Hunter wrote to Duncan complaining in an almost savage manner about Roberts whom he described as 'so weak and vacillating; so short sighted in policy and given to favouritism; and so ruled and badly advised; that I would gladly get away from him, for I never want to serve a day under him again. Buller, Kitchener, or even I would have finished the business now. As it is the damage is done and it will take time, a long time, to get things straight . . .'[16]

Hunter was not flattering about those who were running the war and took a mighty swipe at them when he went on to comment that he had been 'repairing the sins of omission of other people' ever since he had been in South Africa. He declared with a little humorous exaggeration that it was 'just like going round with a broom in the wake of a dirty housemaid.'[17] He felt in duty bound to give vent to these feelings and this did not make him popular. Not surprisingly he did not expect, he confided to Duncan, to prosper when Roberts went home to become C-in-C in London. Here he was correct. Lord Esher, that grey eminence of the establishment with a finger in every military pie, wrote in his Journal in January 1901: 'He [Roberts] has changed the order of merit in which he classes his Generals. Hunter no longer holds first place. Ian Hamilton and Smith-Dorrien take precedence of him.'[18]

What made Roberts change his mind about Hunter? It is unlikely that this came about as a result of any military failure on Hunter's part. On the contrary Hunter had done well and Roberts does not seem to have blamed him for de Wet's escape. It is much more likely to have been because of Hunter's criticism of the conduct of the war. For instance he never hid his feelings when he thought that men's lives were at stake or had been wasted. In addition Roberts could not have been pleased to read an article in the *St James Gazette* quoting, on 14th August 1900, a special correspondent in Pretoria who unfavourably compared Lord Roberts's methods of conducting the war with Hunter's. The paper criticised Roberts for how he dealt with prisoners (at first he had let them go free on oath), and his efforts to make 'war and peace in the same breath'. The inference was that this would not have been Hunter's way. It then went on to describe how Hunter, a 'humane' man, whose unselfish disposition, courage and resource 'inspire confidence and affection' recognised how important mobility was to the Boer. This was why, quite apart from insisting on the surrender of Mausers, Hunter had confiscated every cart, wagon, horse, mule or ox on which he could lay his hands. Again the inference was that Roberts was blind to this need.

We may reasonably conclude therefore that Hunter's views – not that he would have given them to correspondents – were not welcome to the Field-Marshal and significantly contributed to Hunter's loss of favour. Hunter's outspokenness did not always serve him well. The pity of it is that we do not know what precisely Hunter would have done to overcome the Boer. He did not care for any form of vacillation. Certainly Roberts's mixture of the velvet glove and mailed fist approach would not have appealed to him. Total war against the Boer or else a sensible political settlement would have been more his style. But this is speculation. So far as is known he never committed his views to paper.

Hunter was still confident enough in his star to believe that Roberts could not damage his prospects for long and that his day would come. But he ruled himself out of participation in the reform of the army, which he saw would have to come about once the war was over, correctly anticipating that Roberts would not wish to involve him in it.[19] Hunter's military career was highly successful but he never achieved the ultimate accolade of the Field-Marshal's baton. Was Roberts in any way responsible? There is no specific evidence for this. Roberts's term as C-in-C ended in 1904 though he may, off stage, have continued to exert some influence for a time. Hunter's career, on the other hand, continued to prosper for some years after that date.

The three months Hunter spent at Bloemfontein as Military Governor and commander of troops in the Orange River Colony were not conspicuous for their high drama. They seem to have been almost lack-lustre days. The job certainly must have been more administrative than operational. Hunter was no longer chasing Boer columns over huge distances. Roberts handed over his command to Kitchener on 29 November and sailed for home soon after. Hunter now knew where he stood. Kitchener apparently valued his opinion on the war in the Orange River Colony. According to Major (later Field-Marshal) William Birdwood, then Military Secretary to the C-in-C, Kitchener was in the habit of having a direct 'talk' over the telegraph wires with Hunter about the situation.[20]

There must have been some doubts about Hunter's health towards the end of the year. Roberts, in a telegram, had regretted that 'another operation is necessary but trust you will be able to hold on for a few months.'[21] This must have been his arm playing up again for we know that he had it X-rayed when he went home. Also, Roberts in writing a valedictory letter to Hunter – as he wrote to all his senior commanders – said that 'if your health requires change there is really no necessity for you to continue longer in the field. I know from what you have told me and what I have heard from Lord Kitchener that you require rest and treatment'.[22] Some time towards the end of the year he developed malaria and when he came to leave South Africa he was invalided home.

While Hunter was at Bloemfontein the central figure on the enemy side continued to be de Wet, who had again eluded capture in early November in the north of the Orange River Colony. In the fighting, the courageous and able Le Gallais had been killed, to Hunter's sorrow. They had fought together since the Atbara. Towards the end of the month de Wet made a swift descent with 1,700 men into the south of the Colony with a view to invading the Cape and causing havoc there among the Boers, who had as yet not joined the ranks of those opposing the British. The lightly garrisoned town of Dewetsdorp fell to de Wet who then, after posting a strong cover behind him, moved swiftly south through Smithfield towards Aliwal North just over the border into the Cape. But he was unable to make a crossing of the river against the defences in place and his plan to invade Cape Colony was thus foiled. Hunter had gone down to Smithfield and was there on 28 November, though there is no evidence that he assumed command of any troops in the field. Nor can we estimate the precise role he played in thwarting de Wet. Kitchener too was at the scene of operations at Bethulie in early December before de Wet did a disappearing trick back to the north. There is a family story that Kitchener and Hunter, ill-escorted, were riding out together on some reconnaissance during the war, and were nearly captured by a party of Boers. Hunter's quick-thinking apparently saved the day. No more details have been handed down and Kitchener's biographers do not mention the incident. If there is truth in the story it must have taken place at about this time in the south of the Orange River Colony when the two men were together.

That Christmas Hunter remembered Mrs Steyn, wife of the fugitive President of the former Orange Free State, living on her farm outside Bloemfontein. He sent her children some sweets. It was a typical gesture of the man.

In the New Year, on 21 January, Hunter was relieved by Major-General Tucker and handed over his command. He left Bloemfontein for Cape Town on the 24th, and there stayed for four days at Government House with Milner before sailing on the last day of the month for England. In his own words he felt that 'he had not done badly out here' and he hoped he would be fully employed again.[23] The army was sorry to see him go. In the words of Arthur Conan Doyle, who had been a doctor in Bloemfontein in the war: 'The gallant Hunter . . . to the regret of the whole army was invalided home'.[24]

NOTES

1. NAM 7101-23-114-1 Roberts (R)–AH 12 Aug. 1900.
2. OH III 330–1; AHd 14/8/00.
3. DHD 226.
4. NAM loc. cit. R–AH 25 Aug. 1900.
5. OH III 470.
6. AHd 15/9/00.
7. OH III 476.
8. OH III 482; WO 195/17 AH–R 23 Oct. 1900.
9. NAM loc. cit. R–AH 26 and 28 Oct. 1900.
10. TH IV 493.
11. Wilson *After Pretoria the Guerrilla War* I 187; *Liverpool Daily Post* 2 Dec. 1900.
12. NAM loc. cit. R–AH 26 Oct. 1900.
13. SAD 270/10/22 AH–Wingate 28 Oct. 1900; and SAD 270/8/28 AH–Wingate 22 Aug. 1900.
14. WO 105/18 AH–R 31 Oct. 1900.
15. WO 105/18 loc. cit.; TH IV 489.
16. DHD 230.
17. Ibid.
18. Brett *Journals and Letters of Reginald Viscount Esher* I 273.
19. DHD 230–1
20. Birdwood *Khaki and Gown* 121.
21. NAM loc. cit. R–AH 25 Oct. 1900.
22. Ibid. R–AH 27 Nov. 1900
23. DHD 233
24. Conan Doyle 414.

CHAPTER 17

Interlude in Scotland

Hunter's journey home from Cape Town to Southampton by *RMS Briton*, beginning just a few days after the death of Queen Victoria at Osborne on 22 January 1901, took 16 days with a stop at Madeira. On 2 February in the middle of the Atlantic ocean Captain Griffin stopped the ship's engines. To coincide as far as possible with the arrival of the funeral *cortège* at Windsor, he read the Burial Service to the assembled company. The sea voyage may have restored Hunter to health, for there is no information that he was ill or indisposed when he arrived home and took some well-earned leave.

At the end of March he was chosen to go on a Mission led by the Duke of Abercorn as its Special Ambassador to announce the death of Queen Victoria and the accession to the throne of King Edward VII to the Courts of certain countries in northern Europe. First visits were made to Copenhagen, Stockholm and St Petersburg, where Hunter met Czar Nicolas II and the Czarina. Next in Berlin he rode with Kaiser Wilhelm II. After the visit to the court of the King of Saxony Hunter returned home. It was felt that with the state of the Boer War it would be better if he did not accompany the Mission to the Hague in case he was offered insults.[1]

On his return, Hunter was summoned to Sandringham, where the King wished to hear from the Duke of Abercorn about his Special Mission. The King was immensely interested in all matters relating to foreign affairs, the army and the navy[2] so he would have enjoyed pumping the Duke and Hunter. His interest in military affairs extended to being informed of proposed appointments to senior posts, and even to signifying his approval of them. This is well illustrated with what now happened to Hunter, who was expecting to return to India. On 25 April just three days after staying at Sandringham he was offered command of the Scottish District. Two days later his Diary entry reads: 'Told I must accept Sc. Comd. King's wish: not mine.' There was nothing he could do. But Hunter had been lucky hitherto in his career as a senior soldier. This was the first appointment he was given which he did not care for.

Two months earlier Hunter had become the Honorary Colonel of the 2nd Volunteer battalion of the King's Own Royal Lancaster Regiment. Perhaps thinking that the time was opportune after his recent contact with his Sovereign, he wrote in June to Sir Francis Knollys, the King's Private Secretary, proposing that the King become Colonel-in-Chief of the King's

Own Regiment. This he judged would have a good effect on recruiting in Lancashire. Presumably he had the agreement for taking this action of General Sir William Cameron who was then the Colonel of the Regiment. The King decided to speak about this to Lord Roberts, the Commander-in-Chief, to whom Hunter also wrote. Roberts, however, did not favour the idea.[3] Maybe it was too soon after the King's accession to put up such a proposal. Nonetheless in March 1903 the King did become Colonel-in-Chief of the Regiment and was followed in this position on his death by his son, George V.

Towards the end of 1901 an event occurred which caused something of a sensation in army circles, and which had an indirect effect on Hunter's career. Sir Redvers Buller had returned from South Africa to resume his old command of the army corps at Aldershot, probably the most important post in the army outside London. Goaded by his detractors, he virtually admitted at an official luncheon that he had advised Sir George White to abandon Ladysmith. Roberts had never liked Buller and this gave him the opportunity to have him dismissed. But before Buller was sacked Roberts sent a telegram to St John Brodrick, the new Secretary of State for War, as follows:

> 'When Buller goes I would strongly recommend French be appointed to succeed him. Hunter has not the necessary experience as an instructor of British troops. Moreover Hunter is well placed where he is. He is popular in Scotland and in that part of the Kingdom he will be able to do exceptionally valuable service in working with Militia and Volunteers, most essential to the success of our Army Corps Scheme.'[4]

Hunter, therefore, was in the running for the key Aldershot post but was not sufficiently in favour with Roberts to obtain it. There was irony in Roberts's reasoning given the role which Hunter was to assume later as the chief trainer of the new armies in World War I. In the event French, a cavalryman, went to Aldershot, and in a career sense never looked back for he became CIGS in 1911 and was given command of the British Expeditionary Force in 1914. As far as senior appointments went Roberts may well have been inclined to blow hot and cold. According to Ian Hamilton, who as his Military Secretary was in a position to know, the C-in-C was considering the possibility at some stage in 1901 of sending Hunter back to South Africa as Kitchener's Chief of Staff. Hamilton, not a supporter of Hunter, did not think him suitable.[5] In fact it was he, Hamilton, who in the event was sent out in November to do the job. His career, which often seemed to be in some competition with Hunter's, steadily prospered until he was appointed Commander of the Gallipoli expedition in World War I. But he was blamed for the failure of that campaign, and that effectively was the end of his career.

The job of commanding Scottish District, the Headquarters of which was at Castle Terrace, Edinburgh, was not one which particularly appealed to Hunter. He told Duncan that after his active life 'this command is not going to be any great shakes,' and that there was 'no Army in Scotland.'[6] His work was much involved, as Roberts had pointed out, with units such as the Volunteers and the Yeomanry which in course of time would become part of the Territorial Army. It was really a sideshow, with for instance, an emphasis on inspections, the opening of drill halls and shooting ranges. At least Hunter had the satisfaction when opening the Kilmarnock range of taking first shot and scoring a bull's eye!

Hunter may have been a bit lonely in Scotland. His friends were even advising him to marry, not that he contemplated taking their advice. Certainly there was no shortage of social life for him. He hunted and stalked. He always went to the Derby and Grand National. There were country-house parties and regular visits to London and its theatres. A gregarious man, he would keep in touch with his wide circle of friends. He valued friendship and it was said of him: 'he never spoke ill of any man, was always seeking to do others kindnesses and never forgot a friend.'[7]

Honours still came his way and he received Honorary degrees from Glasgow and Cambridge Universities. Also he was made a Freeman of the burgh of Kilmarnock.

For the first time since he was a young man Archie Hunter was living quite close to his mother Mary Jane and sisters, and he saw more of them. Soon after his return from South Africa it must have given Archie great pleasure to see Duncan who was over from the United States on a business trip. Their meeting would hold poignant memories for Archie, for it was the last time he saw his brother. In September 1902 Duncan contracted diphtheria and died quite suddenly while on holiday in Maine. Archie and the whole family were devastated. Duncan's mother, Mary Jane, hardly stirred from her house for days unless it was to attend to her hens (Rhode Island Reds) which had been hatched from eggs sent by Duncan.[8]

Archie himself wrote a tender and loving letter to his sister-in-law Abby. He told her that he could 'barely see the paper I write on. Yet not a word I write can help you . . . You are to be loved and admired for your brave courage.' He offered to come over at once to the States if it would help Abby, and said too she must come and stay with him.[9] For the moment though they did not meet. Always they would remain the closest of friends.

Later in the year Hunter renewed his acquaintance, in somewhat unusual circumstances, with the German Emperor. Kaiser Wilhelm II had been visiting Lord Lonsdale at Lowther Castle and was on his way back to his yacht lying at Queensferry on the Firth of Forth. His special train arrived at Dalmeny station, where he was met by Lord Rosebery and a Guard of Honour formed by the Black Watch. As the Emperor's carriage was about to move away from the station its horses were suddenly frightened, shied and began to bolt. Happily, Hunter was on the spot. With great presence of mind he averted an almost certain accident by quickly stepping up and seizing the bridles of the horses, bringing them under control. But for Hunter the carriage could have careered away and overturned with resultant injury or worse to its illustrious occupant. The Kaiser remembered Hunter and, as an expression of gratitude, presented him with a Mauser pistol. On the outbreak of World War I, Hunter was so disgusted with the behaviour of the Emperor and Germany that he sent a telegram to his sister Ann telling her to throw the pistol into the Thames. The family story is that she cannily wired back: 'Telegram received.'[10] The pistol survives and is today in the possession of Senator John H. Chafee of Rhode Island, a grandson of Duncan Hunter.

The Khedive of Egypt, Abba Hilmi II, invited Hunter to attend as his guest the opening in December 1902 of the new Assouan dam. Hunter made a leisurely journey out to Egypt, leaving London on 26 November and spending nearly two months abroad. In Cairo he stayed with the Cromers and, of course, saw his brother George. On his way to Assouan he visited the excavations at Luxor and met Howard Carter, the Egyptologist. After the opening of the dam he went on south with Wingate, the current Sirdar, and revisited the temple of Abu Simbel and the site of the battle of Abu Hamed, where he saw the graves of Major Sidney and Lieutenant Fitzclarence.[11] He then continued on to Khartoum where his old battalion, the 9th Sudanese, formed a Guard of Honour for him. There he visited the new Gordon College set up with so much foresight as a centre for higher education, which had been opened a few weeks before by Kitchener. It was a project close to Hunter's heart. The return to these scenes of past triumphs would not have been complete without a visit to the battlefield at Omdurman. The state of the country was now generally peaceful, and that too would be gratifying to Hunter.

The Boer war had finally come to an end with the peace treaty of Vereeniging signed on 31 May 1902. The British army had not covered itself with glory. It was not that the soldiers had not fought well. They had and against a difficult enemy. But Britain had not been properly prepared for war, the organisation of the army and the War Office was a mess and too many elderly Generals had been incompetent. Reform was in the air. As a start a Royal Commission on the South African War was set up under Lord Elgin and began its hearings late in 1902. Hunter was called to give evidence on 13 February 1903, after Roberts had given his evidence but before Buller and White had given theirs.

Lord Esher was, as might have been expected, a member of the Commission. An astute observer of the passing scene, he was impressed with the straightforward way in which Hunter gave his evidence. He at once wrote to King Edward whose confidant he was, about the evidence that he had heard given that day and told the King that Hunter 'is a somewhat unusual type of officer; far more "professional" than most of his contemporaries – with somewhat advanced ideas of army reform.'[12] He went on to make the point that Hunter would be 'a useful coadjutor should any bold attempt be made to reorganise the War Office and the Army.'

Some months later Esher relayed to Knollys the King's Private Secretary what Repington, at that time an up and coming Lieutenant-Colonel, told him about the Boer war. So far as the personal valour of the Generals went he gave 'the palm to Hunter. No combination could be better . . . than Kitchener to plan a campaign, and bring the troops to within touch of an enemy and Hunter to direct and lead the actual fight.' He instanced the earlier battle of Atbara as a prime example.[13]

Hunter's evidence to the Royal Commission, which was held at St Stephen's Hall, Westminster, is important for three reasons. First, it throws light on the role he played at the conference White held with the Governor at Pietermaritzburg just before the war and his thinking about how Natal should have been defended; these are matters that we have already considered. Second, he gave his wide-ranging views about the state of the army and certain reforms he thought necessary. Third, he became involved, essentially through lack of thought and his injudicious use of words, in two serious scrapes, which may not in the long run have done him any good.

On the state of the army Hunter clearly enjoyed giving evidence. In answering the questions put by his interlocutors he was both constructive in his ideas and decisive in his opinions. Some of his evidence was by way of enlarging on a written submission already sent by him to the Commission before he was called which was published as an appendix to its report. On recruits to the army, he thought pay was still too low and that men should be paid extra for achieving skills in, for example, scouting, marksmanship, signalling and so on. Better pay he felt would attract a more intelligent recruit. On training, he made a plea for a more practical approach and for more manoeuvres 'over large tracts of varied country under experienced officers who are neither too fat nor too old . . .' Also, taking a leaf out of the book of continental countries, he considered the landing of troops off ships on a coastline should be practised; in this he was envisaging the need for combined operations. NCOs, Hunter felt, should be better trained and he went so far as to make the novel suggestion of setting up a staff college for them.

As for officers they should be 'caught young', as in the navy, be better educated and paid more. There should also be a selection system so that all officers were divided into those fitted for promotion to field rank and above, and those who were not. 'Neither Duke's son, cook's son nor son of a millionaire', Hunter ventured, should go beyond the rank of Captain unless fitted to be entrusted with the lives of other men.

He was in no doubt that the sappers and gunners at Woolwich received a superior education to that meted out to the infantry and cavalry at Sandhurst. Some of Hunter's ideas were perhaps too optimistic; for example, he was unrealistic over the average officer's capacity for languages, but the great thrust of his arguments was that the army and its officers should be far more professional in outlook and training. On specialist arms, he believed transport should now be treated as a separate branch.[14]

On motor cars he was in advance of his times in foreseeing their developing role. He would have liked to have attached to every Volunteer unit, Militia or Yeomanry regiment in Scotland, some motor transport so that the country could be toured and thoroughly explored. This would help in countering any possible invasion threat. In due course he thought the practice of moving guns around with 'motor carriages' would be brought to a 'high state of perfection'. Liddell Hart, the military historian, wrote that Hunter was one of only two Generals in the Boer War who had a vision of the value and future use of motor vehicles in war.[15]

On questions of army organisation at the War Office, he offered no opinion. But then he did not speak on matters of which he had no knowledge. Hunter's views were always forward-looking and often imaginative; they might be contrasted with the views, for instance, of Douglas Haig, who, professional soldier that he was, unbelievably was arguing as late as about 1908 for the retention of the lance as a cavalry weapon.[16]

In some ways Hunter's evidence was a *tour de force*. But he tripped up badly twice. The first time concerned what he said about the performance of the guns of the naval brigade at Ladysmith commanded by Hedworth Lambton. Invited to comment on this subject, he began by telling the Commission that 'the gun-laying in the Army . . . was infinitely better than the gun-laying in the Navy'. In his opinion the naval gunfire had 'produced a moral effect [on the Boer guns], but it produced no other effect. I think they hit one gun.' Admitting that he was treading 'on very delicate ground', he asked the chairman whether it was in his province to go on. He was told it was. So he ploughed on, even commenting as he did so, that his words 'will raise a tremendous storm of indignation.' He continued: '. . . the practice made with the naval 4.7 was – I do not wish to use too harsh a term – well, it was such that I offered to take the girls out of the school to come and serve the guns and make as good practice.'[17]

There it was. In so many words he had compared the naval gunners to a crowd of school girls. He could hardly expect not to attract some opprobrium from the Senior Service. It came sharply enough from Hedworth Lambton, the son of Lord Durham and now a Rear Admiral (later an Admiral of the Fleet), when it was his turn to give evidence a month later. Asked to comment on what Hunter had said, he lost no time in firing a broadside calling Hunter an extremely ignorant man. Almost in the same breath he said that he was 'a very gallant man but it is bravery and stupidity combined in his case'. Hunter, Lambton supposed, had never seen a big gun before and knew nothing about shooting. He should not have compared naval and military shooting, and he was wrong to say that the ranges of the naval guns firing from a fixed platform never varied. Lambton then quoted at great length a number of war correspondents and others who had been at Ladysmith and who testified to the accuracy and great value of the naval guns during the siege.

When the report of the Royal Commission was published during the summer of that year, a rapid piece of work by any standard, the fat was really in the fire. Lambton struck out wildly. He wrote on 5 September a very angry letter to the Secretary of the Admiralty referring to the 'premeditated and impudent attack' on the naval guns by Hunter. The 'insult' had become public, he said, and there should be a public 'atonement'. Moreover, he asserted that 'until this business is cleared up no Naval officer will care in the future to go to the assistance of the Army, when in distress'. There was more about 'Hunter's slanders'. In a pointedly personal attack, Lambton said that Hunter's charges have 'no surer foundation than the ignoble envy of an ungenerous, ungrateful nature . . . it is equally clear that his retention in high command will be a continual insult to the Navy.'[18] He also posed the question as to whether what had happened was an 'individual aberration' on Hunter's part or whether there was a 'conspiracy to rob the Navy of the laurels she won' in the war. It was an intemperate letter and he sent a copy to Hunter.

The affair escalated rapidly. First the Adjutant-General became involved, then Roberts, the C-in-C, and finally the King was informed. Hunter remained cool under fire. But he was ready to make amends and to apologise for the unfortunate expressions he had used in his evidence. Hunter's letter of apology was written from Edinburgh and dated 27 September. While he properly expressed his regrets, he adhered to the opinion he had formed about the effectiveness of the naval guns because this was based on what he saw with his own eyes. For his part, Lambton was required to withdraw the personal remarks he had made about Hunter. The whole correspondence was then published by the Admiralty and the hatchet was considered buried. Roberts wrote to Knollys telling him what had been agreed about this 'very disagreeable affair' and hoping that the King would be satisfied with the outcome.[19] Looking back, the responsibility for this rather ridiculous business must be shared. No doubt Hunter was to blame in the first place for the rash way he had criticised the naval gunners, but Lambton overreacted and, showing a marked lack of judgment, made his recriminations personal. In a sense, however, the last word rested with Hunter. For, soon after Admiral Sir John Fisher became First Sea Lord in 1904, he acted with speed to correct what he believed to be the unsatisfactory state of naval gunnery.

The other scrape in which Hunter became involved as a result of his evidence did not attract the same public attention as the affair of the naval guns, but it might have affected his credibility more in the longer term. It concerned Sir George White and the question of the command at Ladysmith on the occasion of the big Boer attack on 6 January 1900. Hunter told the Commission:

> 'On that day I was practically directing the operations, because, I think, on that day Sir George White was in bed – at any rate, he was not at the office; I went to him at various times during the day and told him how things were going. It was, I suppose, the first instance . . . of a fight over a considerable area ever being directed by the telephone.'[20]

Hunter should have realised that what he had said would lead him into trouble – and it did. White, now Governor of Gibraltar, saw his reputation at stake, and he was determined to defend it. So he wrote to Hunter questioning his evidence. Hunter at once replied in a long letter on 29 September 1903, giving his recollection of the facts. He began by saying that early on the 6th each commander of the separate defence sectors was clamouring for reserves and that:

> 'I went at least twice to your house and found you there: that as far as I recollect you were in your bedroom and I think in bed: that I reported the situation as I understood it. I distinctly remember working the telephone, asking many questions and getting the answers myself over it so as better to judge the local situation and in your absence from HQ directing the necessary moves.'[21]

Hunter conceded that it was under White's orders that certain reinforcements were sent to Wagon Hill and to Caesar's Camp and that White himself wrote some heliograph messages from his bedroom. But he went on to refer to the many messages which he, Hunter, had received and to the orders he had sent out during the changing fortunes of the day from the verandah of HQ house without immediately referring them to his Chief. He believed that he 'correctly stated to the Commission that I practically directed operations: it might be more correct to say some or many operations.'[22] Later in the letter, slightly weakening his case, Hunter stated that in White's absence from Headquarters House he was certainly 'accountable for some of the steps taken to stem the assaults' on Ladysmith that day. Hunter also reminded White that there were days during the siege when he, White, was too ill to leave his bed. Strictly speaking, Hunter maintained, the command devolved on those occasions onto his shoulders. The letter was perfectly polite, but it was clear that Hunter while making some concessions generally stuck to his guns.

White sent a copy of Hunter's letter to various people on whose support he could count. He obtained it. Beauchamp Duff, his Military Secretary at

Ladysmith and now Adjutant-General in India, loyally went to the defence of his old Chief. 'Hunter must be mad, as mad as a march hare!' he stated in a carefully written letter from Simla on 1 November.[23] Then quoting from his diary Duff indicated that Hunter had exaggerated White's illnesses and that, while he had been ill in Ladysmith in December, at the end of January and again at the beginning of March, there were no other occasions when he was seriously incapacitated.

Turning to the day of the big attack, Duff said that he woke White just after 3 a.m. to tell him of the assault, and that Hunter arrived very shortly afterwards to ask for orders. White gave him these and reinforcements were sent off to the points threatened which at that time were Caesar's Camp and Wagon Hill. Duff considered that Hunter was right in saying that he saw White in bed but that this had happened at 3 a.m. According to Duff's account, when Hunter left White got up and dressed remaining for a time at his house. Duff thought it possible that Hunter might have made a second visit to his chief. When the real gravity of the situation became apparent White came over to the HQ house probably immediately after daybreak. In Duff's view White remained there directing operations until the close of the action in the evening.

Duff went on to say that every important movement of troops during the day was ordered by White personally, though the orders naturally were issued through Hunter as Chief of Staff. He accepted that Hunter worked the telephone but he was wrong to indicate that orders were given on his responsibility. Hunter's memory, Duff asserted, had played him false on this. Interestingly, Duff told White in a separate shorter letter that 'Hunter disliked you' and made no secret of this after an occasion when White had found fault with his Chief of Staff for issuing orders on his own authority. Duff thought the 'misstatements' made by Hunter might be ascribed to 'his vanity – always his weak point . . .' which had led him to believe what he had said.[24]

Another who came strongly to White's defence was Ian Hamilton. As he was not at Headquarters on 6 January, being engaged on the ground in repulsing the enemy, he was not an entirely satisfactory witness as to how the command was exercised that day. Hamilton asserted that, while he had spoken to Hunter on the telephone at 1.30 p.m. in the apparent absence of White, he had received no order of any sort from Hunter all day, though many orders and messages came to him from White sometimes via Rawlinson. He also wrote that he never saw White fitter than he was on that day, and that 'some strange mental aberration or delusion must have possessed Hunter' when making his statement to the Commission. Hamilton conceded that Hunter was a man 'not capable of knowingly being untruthful'. His travesty of the facts had been unconscious and due to self-delusion. He also commented that Hunter 'has got such a curious fanatical twist in his mind that he is capable of almost anything in the way of assertion provided this particular temper has been roused in him.'[25]

Hamilton may have been guilty of some exaggeration in what he said about Hunter's temper, but there may have been an element of truth in his assertion as will be seen when we come to examine Hunter's behaviour as Governor of Gibraltar.

Other people too wrote supporting White, including Dr Treherne, though he admitted that his patient had 'indispositions' during the siege. Lambton also weighed in – incidentally there is no evidence that he was at Headquarters on 6 January – beginning his letter in the same vein as Duff: 'Is General Hunter mad . . .' He went on to say that he began to understand how it was that after Kitchener's celebrated victory in the River War it was put about that 'Hunter and not Kitchener was the man who ought to have the credit',[26] implying clearly enough that this was Hunter's doing. This was grossly unfair to Hunter. There is no evidence that Hunter was responsible for putting out any such suggestion. On the contrary Hunter was an essentially modest man and not known to have been boastful about his role in battle or in past campaigns.

It is a pity that we do not have the advantage of Rawlinson's view on the matter of the command, as he was at Headquarters all that day. His diary which is so informative on the siege sheds no light on the matter, though he does refer to a minor tiff between Hunter and White a few days after the big attack.[27]

Hunter may have been careless or injudicious in his use of words about the command on 6 January, just as he had been over the naval guns. Indeed, in his letter to White he engaged in a bit of back-pedalling. If we were to accept Duff's evidence, then White was at his Headquarters from daybreak onwards. This seems to leave Hunter in control at Headquarters from just after 3 a.m. until daybreak. He may well have felt during those critical hours as if, in his own words, he 'was practically directing the operations'. Also where was White at 1.30 p.m. when Hamilton rang asking for him? Presumably – though this would conflict with Duff – he was not at Headquarters, otherwise he would surely have come to the telephone. In comparing the personalities of White and Hunter and their respective performances during the siege, it is not difficult to imagine that, with Hunter's decisiveness and confidence in contrast to White's uncertainty and lack of confidence, the real decisions at Headquarters that day were in effect made by Hunter. At any rate this seems to have been the view taken by Pakenham, for in his history of the war he considers it was on 'Hunter's shoulders, and Rawlinson's, that the main burden of saving Ladysmith depended that day'.[28]

The two scrapes flowing from his evidence to the Royal Commission show that Hunter could not always number tact among his qualities. This was partly because he was fearless, morally as well as physically, sometimes to the point of rashness. He could, nonetheless, be perfectly tactful or diplomatic when occasion demanded it. The trouble was that when he conceived it as his duty to speak out – for instance to expose inefficiency or to correct what he saw as a wrong impression – he seemed ready to be deliberately tactless. It was a fault that he was either unwilling to correct or which in his enthusiasm was unable to check.

Towards the end of April 1903 Hunter received a letter from Kitchener, now C-in-C in India, from Nuski in Baluchistan, saying that he had mentioned his name to Roberts for an Indian command. Hunter of course jumped at the opportunity of returning to India. Roberts duly approached Hunter in July offering him an army corps, which turned out from a follow-up letter from Kitchener to be the Bombay command.[29] So it was all settled and before the tiresome questions arising from his evidence to the Royal Commission came to embarrassing notice.

Before he left for India Hunter attended the big manoeuvres lasting four days, and the first to take place for five years, held in the south of England. The first Army corps of 26,000 men commanded by French was opposed by a force of 20,000 men commanded by that old warrior, Sir Evelyn Wood. These forces, the first marching west from Aldershot and the other north-east from Bulford, were destined to clash on the Marlborough and Wantage downs. It was of course a pity that the command of the Bulford forces was given to the 65-year-old Field-Marshal whose career was virtually at an end. It would have been more imaginative to have given it to a younger man like Hunter, who had to content himself with being the senior umpire on French's side.[30] But the manoeuvres did at least ensure that Hunter was quite up to date with the army's thinking on battlefield tactics when he set sail for Bombay on 8 October.

NOTES

1. AHd 22/3/01 to 17/4/01; DHD 234–5.
2. Magnus *King Edward the Seventh* 277 and 325.
3. NAM 7101-23-191-11 Roberts' (R) reply to AH's letter of 25/6/1901.
4. NAM 7101-23-124-1 R–Sec of State 12/10/1901.
5. DHD 239.
6. Ibid. 238 and 240.
7. *Dictionary of National Biography* 1931–40 ed 456–8.
8. DHD 246.
9. Ibid. 244–5.
10. Ibid. 247.
11. AHd 13/12/02.
12. RA W 38/71.
13. RA W 38/110.
14. RCSAW: ev of Lt-Gen Hunter (see Note 1, Ch. 12).
15. Liddell Hart *History of the First World War* 35.
16. De Groot *Douglas Haig 1861–1928* 100.
17. RCSAW loc. cit.

18. RA W 56/55.
19. RA W 56/93.
20. RCSAW loc. cit.
21. White Collection MSS Eur F 108/69 AH–White 29 Sep. 1903.
22. Ibid.
23. Ibid. Beauchamp Duff–White 1 Nov. 1903.
24. Ibid.
25. Ibid. Hamilton–White 29 Jan. 1904 and 30 Jul. 1905.
26. Ibid. Lambton–White 22 Sep. 1903.
27. Rawlinson Diary NAM 5201-33-7-1 Jan. 1900.
28. Pakenham 273.
29. AHd 7/7/03; DHD 250.
30. *Daily Telegraph* 9 Sep. 1903.

CHAPTER 18

Indian Command

On his first posting to India in 1899 Hunter was in the country a mere 132 days before leaving for Durban and the Boer War. When he arrived in Bombay on 24 October 1903 he was to spend just over five years on the sub-continent, apart from home leaves. For more than $3\frac{1}{2}$ years he commanded the Western Army Corps with his headquarters at Poona and for the rest of his time he commanded the Southern Army. Hunter was keen on soldiering in India, because according to the conventional wisdom of the time, it was there that the gravest military threat to the Empire lay. In 1903 therefore, from a career point of view, India looked to be a good place in which to serve. Hunter's star again seemed to be in the ascendant.

All through the Victorian era the Indian government had been preoccupied with the Russian menace looming across the mountains of Afghanistan. This after all was the way Alexander the Great had reached the Indus valley as had Babur, founder of the Mogul dynasty and descendant of Genghis Khan. Under Czar Alexander II Russia had been gradually expanding into central Asia. She had seized Tashkent in 1865, and then swallowed up the surrounding khanates. From India it looked as if she was encroaching ominously on Afghanistan which was considered to lie within Britain's sphere of influence. With their serious misgivings about the intentions of Russia, the British believed that their position in India would best be protected by a chain of buffer states around its northern frontier, Afghanistan being the most important. In 1880 at the end of the Second Afghan war a new Emir, Abdur Rahman, was installed in Kabul. Although he proved to be well disposed towards the British, fears of the Russian threat did not decline, especially in view of the military railway

189

being built from the Caspian sea to Samarkand. In 1885 the Russians occupied the little known oasis of Pandjeh, north of Herat, and close to the Afghan border, and the two countries edged towards war. The crisis passed, having provided Gladstone with a reason to abort the Gordon Relief expedition. But the 'Great Game' continued to be played by these two major powers in the remote regions between the Indus and Asiatic Russia.

A new Viceroy appeared on the scene in 1898. He was the ambitious and brilliant 39-year-old George Nathaniel Curzon. He was an ardent Russophobe, having some years earlier made an extraordinary journey to Samarkand and Tashkent which convinced him that the Russians had their eyes on India. Curzon believed too in a 'forward policy' which involved posting troops on the Indian borders, and of controlling at the same time the tribesmen who lived a lawless life in this frontier country.

Curzon considered that the Indian system of defence needed overhauling, and soon decided that Kitchener was the man for this task. Kitchener, involved in the Boer War, did not reach India to assume his new post of Commander-in-Chief until November 1902. On arrival he found that his troops were distributed around the country in penny packets, organised apparently for purely internal defensive purposes, a hang-over no doubt from the Indian mutiny, 45 years before. Kitchener, like Curzon, believed that the Russians might invade India,[1] and he therefore decided that the army must be reformed to counter this or any external threat. To meet this requirement the army needed to be converted into a modern force based on the division system (in India, unlike Britain, the division was some 18,000 to 20,000 strong), and to be properly concentrated at certain places. At the same time he considered that staff organisation was unsatisfactory and the railway system ineffectively utilised for military needs, while mobilisation procedures, supply, transport and the medical services all needed overhauling. Also, more needed doing to promote recreational facilities for the soldiers. Finally, more modern equipment was required.[2] There was a lot to be done, and early on during his seven-year tenure as C-in-C, Kitchener decided that Hunter, well proven as an energetic leader of men, could help him to carry out his task.

Unfortunately for all concerned, Kitchener found that he could not work with the Viceroy. They were both self-willed men. Soon they were quarrelling over who was to control the army. This quarrel was to have far-reaching consequences, and we shall return to it in due course.

Running the Indian army was firmly in the hands of British officers, 12 of whom were allocated to each Indian battalion. Service in the Indian army was always popular with the British. Subalterns' pay was slightly better in India and soldiers worked harder there than at home, even in the heat. The outlook was more professional, and there was often the chance of a scrap on the North-West frontier. The first decade of the century was, as it turned out, a relatively peaceful one for India, and there were no major expeditions mounted against recalcitrant tribesmen.

Hunter's command covered a large area, extending up to Baluchistan in the north-west on the Afghan and Persian frontiers, and included his old District of Quetta. Under him he had three divisions, the 4th, 5th and 6th, made up of both British and Indian troops. In command at Quetta of the 4th division was Hunter's trusted old friend, Major-General Smith-Dorrien, destined to be an army commander in World War I. Major-General Sir O'More Creagh VC commanded the 5th division at Mhow, midway between Bombay and Agra; he would in 1909 succeed Kitchener as C-in-C (when he became known as 'no more K'). Finally at Poona, Major-General G. Richardson, a keen big game hunter like his chief, was in charge of the 6th division.

As might be expected, Hunter began his tour of duty with a thorough programme of inspections. In his command there were many famous British regiments including the Royal Scots, the Yorkshire and Lancashire, the Cheshires, the Argyll and Sutherland Highlanders, the 10th Hussars and so on. All of these were inspected as were many other regiments and units including batteries of Royal Field Artillery, the forts at Bombay and of course Indian army regiments. They must all have been kept on their toes, anxious that Hunter's eagle eye would not spot weaknesses. For as March Phillipps had observed during the Boer war 'nothing escapes him'.[3] Best of all he loved to be up on the Afghan frontier, and Smith-Dorrien recalled with pleasure two long tours there with Hunter. He spent most of April 1904 in what is now Pakistan, visiting Sind, and then Quetta and distant border posts like Fort Sandeman, familiarising himself with the terrain, the tribesmen and the military problems on the frontier. Although the conditions were different and the enemy much less visible it may well have evoked memories of Wadi Halfa and defending Egypt. Later his tours of inspection would take him as far afield as Aden and its hinterland, Socotra and the tiny Kuria Muria islands off the coast of Oman.

But much of Hunter's time was taken up perforce with military administration and implementing Kitchener's reforms. This work varied as leaves from a surviving letter book show. Here is a sample of matters dealt with in one week: accelerated promotion of promising officers; requesting divisional commanders to give attention to the frequency with which men, particularly NCOs, had to do guard duty (Hunter thought it was too frequent); rebuking his Deputy Adjutant General for not bringing to his notice some important papers; reporting to his chief on a decline in the incidence of venereal disease; canvassing ideas for improving the performance of a regiment he judged to be slack, and requesting his commanders to improve the cleanliness of barracks.

This last point may be a dull one but is worth mentioning for the light it shows on Hunter's outlook. For him the cleanliness of the men and their barracks was paramount. He demanded excellence and was therefore disappointed when expected standards were not reached. Of course as has been seen from his days in the Sudan, Hunter had something of a 'thing' about cleanliness.

Early in 1904 an event occurred in the Far East which was to change profoundly the attitudes of the Asian peoples to the European powers. The Japanese were worried the Russians were making a puppet of Korea. Also they were concerned by the movement of some 170,000 Russian troops into Manchuria where the Russians, with the Boxer rebellion fresh in their minds, feared for the safety of their newly-constructed Trans-Siberian railway.[4] On 8 February, without warning, the Japanese struck at the Russian naval base at Port Arthur. The war which followed was savage and lasted 18 months. The Japanese forces had been completely modernised but were something of an unknown quantity. Their army had been modelled on the German army and their navy on the Royal Navy. How would they perform? It soon became clear that the Japanese had turned their forces into a formidable fighting machine, which by the middle of 1905 had inflicted a series of crushing defeats on their opponents. Port Arthur surrendered after a long siege and Mukden was captured, while the Russian navy suffered disastrously at the hands of Admiral Togo at the battle of Tsushima Straits. Hunter as a professional soldier was deeply interested in the war, and how it was being fought. He asked Kitchener in the early summer of 1904 if he might be considered for accreditation as a Military Attaché to the Japanese army.[5] Ian Hamilton was already there in that capacity. When the time came to find a replacement for Hamilton, Hunter's name was considered in January 1905. The King was consulted but expressed doubt as to whether Hunter had the required tact for the post.[6] In the event, Hamilton was given an extension, and so Hunter's application came to nothing. It had begun to look as if his clumsiness in giving evidence before the Royal Commission on the South African war was coming home to roost.

A crisis had arisen between Russia and Britain during this war in the Far East in the most bizarre of circumstances, which well illustrated the delicacy of the relationship between the two countries. In October 1904 the Russian Baltic fleet was en route to the Far East to reinforce their fleet already badly mauled there by the Japanese. In fog on the Dogger Bank fishing grounds the Russians unbelievably mistook a fleet of trawlers from Hull for Japanese torpedo boats, and opened fire. A trawler was sunk and there were casualties. There was a great public outcry and war between the powers was narrowly averted. Hunter took a bullish line and thought it should have been war. Even before the Dogger Bank incident, it appears that he had been infected by the prevalent climate of opinion in India against Russia and her designs.

In due course Ian Hamilton on his way home from Manchuria stopped off in India and reported to Kitchener and some of his senior commanders on the war. He was a good observer and Hunter listened attentively to what he had to say. Within a few days he sent a long memorandum to his three divisional commanders covering the salient points made by Hamilton. Hunter was particularly struck by the tactics of Japanese infantry. If checked in their advance they went to ground and dug in using the entrenching tools they carried, provided they were not less than 600 yards from the enemy. When resuming the advance that distance was covered in a surging non-stop charge. He also noted points about the Japanese use of cavalry (their attitude to this arm was negative) and artillery, their communications systems, such as telegraph and field telephones, and their organisation. Hunter thought that several things observed by Hamilton about the Japanese soldier deserved recognition and admiration: '[his] simplicity of living, hardihood . . . high sense of military honour . . . good discipline, cleanliness, sobriety, fearlessness of pain and death'.[7] The Russians, Hamilton said, were brave and not inferior physically. But they were poorly led and careless over the preparation of defensive works. Hunter saw no lessons there.

Russia had suffered a great humiliation at the hands of the Japanese and experienced, too, serious unrest at home. What then of the Russian threat to India? Arthur Balfour the Prime Minister had warned the House of Commons rather bombastically in May 1905 and before the conflict ended that although Russia appeared 'prostrate to the world', she would recover and would again threaten the British position in India. When the Liberals came to power at the end of that year they were determined to improve relations between the two countries and an Anglo-Russian Convention was signed in St Petersburg in 1907. In the accord the Russians formally acknowledged that Afghanistan lay outside their sphere of influence. The old threat from Russia to India receded, though this may not have been recognised for a time.

We must now turn to the quarrel between Curzon and Kitchener which continued on through most of Hunter's first two years in India. What is not well known is that Hunter played a part, if only indirectly, in the dispute. The government of India in those days was totally autocratic. The Viceroy in Council reigned supreme as the country's executive authority. On this Council, which was something like the British Cabinet, sat two soldiers, each with a separate raft of responsibilities. One was the Commander-in-Chief, who was of course the executive head of the army. He was responsible for recruitment, promotion, organisation, training, mobilisation, operational planning and for directing the army in war. The other was the Military Member who was in charge of the Military Department and acted rather as the Secretary of State for War did at home. He was responsible for military administration covering supply, transport, ordnance, stores, military works and, very important, military finance including the budget. He was entitled to criticise freely any plans or projects coming up from the C-in-C. Perhaps surprisingly, the Military Member – in rank he was only a Major-General – attended *all* meetings of the Viceroy's Council whereas the C-in-C by tradition attended only those in which he was directly involved. The system of 'Dual Control', as it was known, was according to Curzon only a division of labour. It had worked well in Roberts' day. But to Kitchener it was anathema. He wanted complete military power and found the prevailing system unworkable. Predictably, he soon had differences of opinion with Sir Edmond Elles, the incumbent Military Member who had been rather taken under Curzon's wing. In 1903 before Hunter's arrival, Kitchener produced a paper demanding the abolition of the Military Member, which was rejected. There followed a pause during which Kitchener undertook with Curzon not to bring up again the thorny problem of Dual Control for a year. When he did return to the subject he was well prepared and had produced a 32-page document setting out his full reasons for the abolition of the Military Member and his Department. He sent this memorandum which was dated 1 January 1905 to all those of the rank of Major-General and above in India, Elles excepted, inviting their comment. Hunter's response ran to just six lines. An extract reads: '[Your memo] must carry conviction to the minds of all men who have had any practical experience as a leader in war . . . I regard your arguments and conclusions as unanswerable . . .'[8]

The drama between the two Titans mounted. Curzon saw the issue as principally constitutional. On 10 March his Council gave him overwhelming support in rejecting Kitchener's memorandum. In fact, the C-in-C found himself in a minority of one. At home partly as a result of Kitchener's clever lobbying tactics Balfour and St John Brodrick, the new Secretary of State for India, tended to side with Kitchener. There was almost deadlock. A partial compromise was proposed in London and endorsed by the Cabinet whereby the Military Supply Member, as he would be known, retained his seat on the Council but lost most of his power. Elles was required to step down. Kitchener had in effect achieved what he wanted. On 25 June an important meeting took place between Curzon and Kitchener about the Cabinet's decision. The discussion grew warm. Curzon threatened to resign unless the Military Supply Member reverted to his previous title. At this point Curzon is supposed to have burst into tears.[9] Kitchener, embarrassed for once, gave way. Anyhow, he thought the point was trivial. In August there was a final showdown when Curzon was not allowed to appoint Major-General Sir Edmund Barrow, his nominee as the new Military Member. Curzon, humiliated, had had enough, and his resignation was announced on 21 August 1905. He left India in November, a wounded man, and was succeeded by Lord Minto.

In his short period in India in 1899 Hunter had observed the Dual

Control system and did not like what he saw. During the Boer War he several times discussed Indian military administration with Kitchener, and impressed on Kitchener, who had never served in India, that the Military Department was unnecessary and should be swept away.[10] Kitchener clearly agreed with what Hunter had said and thought abolition would be a simple matter. He even spoke to Balfour and Lansdowne about it before leaving for India.

When he returned to India Hunter came to know Lovat Fraser, editor of *The Times of India*. Often he lunched or dined with him when in Bombay. On 22 June 1905, according to Fraser, the two men met accidentally at the Bombay Yacht Club, and lunched together. Afterwards they had a conversation lasting two or three hours during which Hunter told Fraser the whole story of the Curzon–Kitchener controversy from the point of view of army headquarters. For Hunter the worst feature of the existing system was its wastefulness, large sums of money being squandered by the Military Department. Hunter told Fraser that throughout the dispute Kitchener consulted him and sent him 'every single paper for his advice and suggestions'.[11]

Lovat Fraser wrote a memorandum to Curzon dated 26 January 1908 on what Hunter had told him. He described Hunter as 'the soul of honour and incapable of the slightest prevarication'.[12] He was a responsible and discreet journalist, was on good terms with Curzon and was an author of repute. In his book *India under Curzon and After* Fraser makes no reference to his conversations with Hunter. There is no reason to doubt the accuracy of what he has passed down in his memorandum, which was one of several he wrote to Curzon on the dispute. Given therefore the validity of what Lovat Fraser wrote, Kitchener would perhaps have had another reason for wishing to have Hunter with him in India, once his initial effort in 1903 to have the Military Member and his Department abolished had failed. On rare occasions, such as before the battle of Atbara, Kitchener showed uncertainty on what course of action to pursue. With Hunter at hand he would have a useful sounding board and a strong supporter to boot.

Just before going home on leave Hunter comes, tantalisingly, into view once more on the subject of the dispute. His diary is silent on the issue except for one entry. Against 1 July 1905, just a few days after the tempestuous meeting between Curzon and Kitchener described above, he wrote:

'Lunch Viceregal Lodge, Simla. Lord and Lady Curzon one ADC Governess children and self. Have messages from Lord Curzon and from Lord Kitchener a propos of their differences, for the Prime Minister and Secretary of State for India.'[13]

What is perhaps odd is that Curzon should have entrusted Hunter, obviously well-known as a supporter of Kitchener, with a 'message' for the Prime Minister. Was it oral or written? It says a lot for Hunter that his relations with Curzon were such that, at the height of the quarrel, he could receive an invitation to lunch *en famille* and even be asked to carry a message back home. It would, on the other hand, be no surprise that Kitchener had asked his trusty subordinate to carry back a message to the Secretary of State, though he had already written a letter about the meeting with Curzon to the Military Secretary at the India Office on 26 June.[14] At any rate a week after the lunch at Simla Hunter sailed from Bombay for three months' leave. On arriving home he went straight to London and stayed there a few days. There is no mention of whether he saw Balfour or Brodrick. We can only speculate on whether or not he had some kind of role to play on behalf of one or other of the protagonists, or both of them.

By the time Hunter returned from leave Kitchener had 'won' his battle. In effect, the military had overcome the civilians. Many people were unhappy with the outcome. Roberts, for instance, did not side with Kitchener. In India the press were almost unanimous in blaming the Cabinet in Britain and Kitchener for what had happened. In his autobiography Smith-Dorrien considered Kitchener had gone too far. On the other hand Magnus, Kitchener's biographer, believed that the system of military administration which Kitchener destroyed in India was obsolete and on the point of breaking down.

Early in 1905 Hunter had suffered a blow. On 1 February his mother died suddenly at the age of 71 at home in Scotland. She had outlived three of her 11 children and her three husbands. The family story is that she wanted to marry a fourth time but Archie, by then a General, took rapid action to prevent this. Three husbands is enough, he is reputed to have said. Undoubtedly she was something of a character with extravagant tastes and sometimes odd behaviour. Her bank manager told his staff not to leave him alone with Mrs Boyd in case she managed to wheedle him into agreeing a further overdraft! On her death she left over £4,000 in debts though there were just enough assets to pay these off.[15]

It is difficult to judge what kind of a relationship Archie had with his mother since he became so self-reliant at an early age. He may have been made uneasy by her prodigality and her occasional eccentricities. He did not though seem to have the affection for her that his brother Duncan perhaps had.

In the aftermath of his mother's death Archie wrote a candid letter to his brother George telling him about his own affairs. His pay was £3,600 p.a. and he reckoned, taking account that he would receive £3,000 from a life policy due to mature in 1914, he would on his death be worth about £10,000. Earlier savings had all disappeared on doctors' fees and medical expenses incurred when he was wounded in 1885. He had also paid for part of his half-brother Robert's education and for his debts when he died as a young man. If his health failed, or he did not obtain further employment, he would have an income of £1,100 p.a. (wound pension £200, DSO pension £100, half pay £600 and private income £200).[16] When his time in India was up, Archie continued, he thought he would buy a small house near or in London where he could live in 'quiet respectability'. Such a house could be used, until he wanted it permanently for himself, by members of the family.

Family relationships were always important to Archie, and while on leave from India he visited in successive years Abby in France. She had come over from the United States with her four daughters and lived for some years in Europe. As an uncle Archie enjoyed indulging his nieces. He was constantly sending them little presents from India such as jewellery, necklaces and lockets.

India was a country offering in those days wonderful opportunities for shooting. There was plenty of game, and conservation did not exist. Hunter was not one to neglect his chances. His diary in the years 1904–06 is littered with references to going after tiger, panther, cheetah, bear and deer. What appealed to Hunter about big game hunting was the uncertainty of the chase, the danger and the need for decisive action. He found the animals beautiful but this did not inhibit his enjoyment of the sport. Shooting in India also provided Hunter with some contact with Indians of high rank, and gave him another perspective on a land he described as 'little understood by even those who live in it'.[17]

While he was in India there were for Hunter many memorable occasions of high pageantry and ceremony, quite apart from the balls, levées and parties at Government House and elsewhere. One such occasion occurred when the Prince and Princess of Wales arrived in Bombay in 1905 on their state visit. Preceding the Royal party in their open landaulette Hunter rode at the head of his staff, in the words of *The Times of India*, 'mounted on a magnificent black charger, the cynosure of all eyes, the guardian sword arm of the Egyptian army . . .'[18] A few weeks later at the end of December Hunter made a special journey to Calcutta to attend a parade when the Prince of Wales was to present Colours to the first battalion of his old regiment, The King's Own Royal (Lancaster) Regiment. It was Hunter's first visit to Calcutta and he stayed with Kitchener. That same day he wrote in glowing terms to Sir William Cameron, the Colonel of the regiment, to tell him how well everything had gone. After the parade the Prince spoke to Hunter and told him how proud he must be to belong to such a distinguished regiment. The Prince, wrote Hunter, 'had never seen more perfect discipline under arms, no greater steadiness . . .'[19] It was a fitting end to a busy year. Just a few weeks before, Hunter had been promoted to the rank of full General. He was not yet 50. Rarely can a soldier have reached that rank at so young an age. He had travelled far.

Hunter attached great importance to training and to manoeuvres. In the spring of 1906 he offered his divisional commanders some constructive thoughts in a memorandum for the autumn manoeuvres to be held at Quetta. Perhaps somewhat contrary to the C-in-C's general policy, Hunter had not hitherto been disposed to interfere with the training methods employed by his divisional commanders. He liked to encourage them to show some independence of thought, and said that he had been satisfied up to now with the results achieved in training. But now harking to papers produced by the C-in-C on the Russo-Japanese war, he wanted 'to show our men what a real attack on a strongly fortified position means at the present day – illustrating the value of every kind of artillery fire and rifle fire at various ranges. Let them entrench the position, use their ingenuity in strengthening it and its communications, make every kind of obstacle; how many know the use of mines, or countermines or missiles? Mortar fire illuminating or obscuring the illumination of certain points? How many of them have done a night sortie?'[20]

He went on to suggest that attackers should go to ground by day and attack by night. The roles of attackers and defenders should be reversed. All arms should cooperate and he wanted to see that signalling, scouting (as it was still called), and shooting were thoroughly tested. Money on materials, he ventured, would be well spent. All these ideas were highly pertinent to the kind of warfare in which the army would be involved eight years later. Hunter's suggestions for the forthcoming autumn manoeuvres bore fruit and in his autobiography Smith-Dorrien described what happened that autumn at Quetta. A strong defensive position was created having three lines of trenches with connecting trenches, dug-outs, latrines and so on. The attacking forces surged forward in bursts digging in between them, and used shot, shell, hand grenades and mortars. 'Looking back,' wrote Smith-Dorrien, 'it was quite a good forecast of the trench warfare in the Great War.'[21] Smith-Dorrien spoke appreciatively of the interest shown and encouragement given by Hunter in respect of manoeuvres and training, to say nothing of the large grant of money he made available for them that year.

In May 1907 the reorganisation of the Indian army in the field was completed by Kitchener with the abolition of the three army corps commands. Instead, two great army commands were created: a Northern army and a Southern army comprising in all nine divisions and eight cavalry brigades. Hunter now became the Commander of the Southern army with his Headquarters still at Poona. The putative enemy was still Russia and the two armies were organised so that they could both concentrate, using the railway system to maximum advantage, on the Afghan frontier. The Northern army would converge on Peshawar and Hunter's Southern army on Quetta.

Hunter told Wingate in a letter of the enormous area of his new command, which spread from Baluchistan in the west to Burma in the east on a line just 30 miles south of Delhi and a fraction south of Calcutta, at the same time including Aden. He added: 'You have an extensive area yourself! But think of this one of mine. I hope some day it may be yours too.' Hunter always seemed for some reason to keep a kind of semi-fatherly eye on Wingate's career. At the bottom of this letter Wingate – who never threw away even a bus ticket – scribbled: 'I have not the smallest intention of succeeding H!'[22]

One of Kitchener's purposes in creating just two army commands was to decentralise power from the old Corps Headquarters to the divisional Generals, thereby freeing the two army commanders from much administrative work. This left them to concentrate on inspecting their troops, in the manner of an Inspector-General, and to improve their efficiency for war. Now that his area of command encompassed southern India Hunter was able to make in early 1908 an extended tour to attend field days and manoeuvres in Hyderabad, Bangalore and Ootacamund. Burma was then ruled as part of British India and he did not neglect visiting his troops there.

We have taken a look at Hunter as a soldier in India, but what of his private life? Little is known. Was he considered an eligible bachelor? We do not know. His old flame Daisy Low was in India in 1905 and again in the summer of 1908 when she and a companion stayed with Hunter.[23] There was always plenty of social life in which he fully participated. Sometimes the hectic round seemed designed to distract the expatriate community from illness and death. In August 1904, for instance, there was an outbreak of cholera, and Hunter did his best to arrange 'dances, picnics, drives, excursions by boat . . . fancy dress balls, suppers, masque balls . . .'[24] Once he gave a dance after the Poona manoeuvres but was unable to attend it himself being laid low with fever, an illness which, as his diary shows, dogged him on and off during his Indian years.

Hunter's time in India was up in October 1908. He issued his Farewell Order to his army on the 29th of that month. Judging by the fact that during his time he had been promoted to General and then became an army commander, his tour of duty must be considered to have been successful.

NOTES

1. Magnus 196.
2. Fraser *India under Curzon and After* 39.
3. Phillipps 180.
4. Hopkirk *The Great Game* 508; Dilks *Curzon in India* II 69.
5. DHD 254.
6. RA W 3/20.
7. NR AH letterbook 14 Apr. 1905.

8. *Record of Lord Kitchener's Administration of the Army in India 1902–09* (NAM 355 48) 25 et seq. and appendix 1.
9. Magnus 219.
10. Curzon Collection MSS Eur F 111 411 Lovat Fraser–Curzon 26 Jan. 1908.
11. Ibid.
12. Ibid.
13. AHd 1/7/05.
14. Magnus 219.
15. NR loc. cit. AH–Gilmour (family solicitor) 30 Apr. 1905.
16. NR loc. cit. AH–George Hunter 30 Apr. 1905.
17. DHD 254
18. *The Times of India* 10 Nov. 1905.
19. NR loc. cit. 30 Dec. 1905.
20. Ibid. 20 May 1906.
21. Smith-Dorrien 326.
22. SAD WP 280/6/4 AH–Wingate, 11 June 1907.
23. DHD 278.
24. Ibid. 254–5.

CHAPTER 19

Governor of Gibraltar

When he returned to England Hunter found that during the five years he had been away many changes had taken place in army organisation, though no doubt in India he would have been aware of what was going on. In the aftermath of the Boer war a spate of committees of inquiry had been set up to reform the army. One of them considered the War Office and its organisation. This committee under Lord Esher worked quickly and produced within four months or so a set of far-reaching proposals. The most important of these were: the office of Commander-in-Chief should be abolished; the army should be run by an Army Council, the first military member of which should be the Chief of the General Staff; eight new departments with clearly defined functions should be established at the War Office under Major-Generals; and a new General Staff should be set up. Esher set about implementing his committee's proposals. In doing so he had the backing of Balfour, the Prime Minister, and of the King.

By now it had become plain that a new military and naval threat had to be met in Europe. The incoming Liberal government, showing itself to be alive to the dangers posed by the sabre-rattling policies of Germany, initiated in 1906 military discussions with France. It was agreed that if France were attacked by Germany then a British Expeditionary Force (BEF) would go to her assistance. For the first time for nearly 100 years the army had to think hard and prepare itself for campaigning on the continent against European powers.

Many of the younger and abler Generals were now filling important posts, particularly in the War Office. Thus Grierson, Hunter's old school friend, was appointed Director of Military Operations; Hunter wrote him a generous letter of congratulation expressing his pleasure at seeing his old friend at the head of the 'thinking and plotting bureau'.[1] Haig was brought back from India, where he had been Inspector-General of Cavalry, to be Director of Military Training. Rawlinson had become Commandant of the Staff College. Esher, always ready to express a view on the competence of soldiers, considered that the leading Generals in the country included Ian Hamilton now GOC Southern Command, Smith-Dorrien in command at Aldershot and Arthur Paget, all three of whom had served with or under Hunter at one time or another. Perhaps pre-eminent among the military luminaries was French due to become CIGS in 1911 and destined to command the BEF when war broke out some years later.[2]

What place did Hunter have in this new scheme of things? None. It was as he had predicted to Duncan eight years before. He was of course by now very senior. It was almost as if he had been promoted too fast and at too young an age. If in 1908 he had been more junior in rank there would have been more posts open to him. As it was there was only a handful of posts available for full Generals. According to the Army List of 1909 there were 20 full Generals on the active list. Four of them were Royals, three were Marines, and one was Lieutenant of the Tower of London. Seven of the others had jobs: Kitchener in India, O'More Creagh as Military Secretary at the India Office, and Methuen and Lyttleton as C-in-Cs in South Africa and Ireland respectively. The remaining three: Nicholson, the CIGS, Ian Hamilton and French, the Inspector-General, were at home. The other five full Generals, including Hunter, were unemployed. There was nothing for Hunter to do but to wait and hope something would turn up. He may also have known that he had little, if any, chance of becoming C-in-C in India, for Kitchener recommended that he should be succeeded by an Indian army officer.

In the meantime Hunter enjoyed his social life, spending some time in Scotland. In the new year he travelled, in appalling weather, to Switzerland to spend a few days with Abby and his nieces who were living at Territet on the Lake of Geneva.[3] In February 1910, to escape the rest of the winter, he went on a prolonged visit to Tenerife in the Canary Islands. Quite soon after his return home he developed pneumonia. He had been to the Palace to inquire after the health of the very sick King and on his way back received a soaking. He sat up late with a new jigsaw puzzle of 1,250 pieces and went to bed shivering. The next day his servant called a doctor and his temperature was found to be 104 deg F. He had to stay in bed for a fortnight, and missed the King's funeral.

Soon there was good news for Hunter. In June he was offered the post of Governor and Commander-in-Chief of Gibraltar. Willingly he accepted. Apparently he had been promised the post of C-in-C South Africa, but General Botha, the first premier of the new Union of South Africa, had insisted that Lord Methuen, then C-in-C, should stay to finish the work he had begun.[4] As it was, Hunter was quite content with Gibraltar, which was nearer home. He might have been in the running – there seems no way of knowing – for the new post of GOC Mediterranean Command and Inspector General of Overseas Forces, which in 1910 went to Ian Hamilton, after it was turned down by Kitchener. As C-in-C Gibraltar Hunter would in fact now serve under Hamilton to whom he wrote on 24 June saying how he was 'looking forward with great glee to the prospect of more work', and to serving under him. As the post usually went to senior soldiers just before their retirement, Hunter may have assumed this would be his last job.

At this moment Hunter was again chosen by his Sovereign to join a Special Mission. This time it was to announce the Accession of the new King, George V. In August he travelled with the Special Ambassador, the Earl of Granard, and his Mission to the courts of seven monarchs – those of Belgium, Denmark, Holland, Norway, Portugal, Spain and Sweden.

The time had now come, Hunter decided, to marry. The Governor of Gibraltar would need a helpmate and hostess. It may, nonetheless, have been a surprise to most people when on 29 September he announced his engagement to Mary Inverclyde, the widow of the second Lord Inverclyde, formerly Chairman of the Cunard Shipping Company. Like Archie, Mazie, as she was known, was a lowland Scot. Her father was Hickson Fergusson of Ayr, formerly a Glasgow merchant. Mazie was nine years younger than Archie and the couple had known each other for some time. Archie's brother George approved of the match and thought that Mazie was 'sensible, level-headed, and capable. Good to look at though not pretty'. Also she was 'well dowered'.[6] He was relieved too that at long last his elder brother was to be settled. As there was not time for the wedding before Archie went to Gibraltar, the plan was that he would take up his post and then come back for his marriage, which would take place at the beginning of November.

Hunter arrived at Gibraltar on 4 October and was duly sworn in that day by the Chief Justice as Governor of the Crown Colony. As Governor and Commander-in-Chief his salary was £4,500 p.a. with an expenses allowance of £1,000 p.a. His position was one of great authority. This was derived from Letters Patent issued under the Great Seal and signed by the King's own hand, and from the Commission appointing him to his post, also signed by the King. In those days there was no Legislative or Executive Council in Gibraltar (it was not until after Smith-Dorrien became Governor in 1918 that an elected City Council was formed). The Governor was empowered to make laws for 'the peace, order and good government of the City and garrison', and his was the executive authority by which the laws were carried out. There were one or two local organisations, such as the Chamber of Commerce, which he could consult if he so chose. As C-in-C Hunter commanded the troops, including the naval personnel, stationed on the Rock, and thus was responsible for the defence of the fortress. He therefore wore two hats; on the one hand he was accountable for the administration of the Colony to the Secretary of State for the Colonies, and on the other as an army officer he was responsible to the Secretary of State for War through his superior, Sir Ian Hamilton.

The Governor had under him the usual civilian establishment found in a colony. There was the Colonial Secretary, Frederick Evans (a highly experienced official who had been in his post since 1901 and who was knighted in 1912), the Attorney-General, and some other less exalted officials engaged in running various departments, such as the Revenue, Public Works, Medical Department, and so on. A Board of Sanitary Commissioners looked after the water supply and matters of drainage, and exercised some of the functions of a local authority. Gibraltar also had its own civilian police force. There were 13 elementary schools on the Rock and several private schools. According to the 1911 census the population was 25,370. Apart from the British, the population was mixed, with the Genoese remaining prominent in banking and business. It also included Spanish, Portuguese, Maltese, a Jewish community, and some Indians.

Gibraltar in 1910 was a somewhat different place from what it was in 1879 when Hunter had last served there. A modern harbour had been constructed and the naval dockyard extended to serve the naval base. Land had been reclaimed, a new sewage system completed and the water supply much improved by the construction of a water catchment area. There was a large influx of Spaniards every day who found work in the dockyard. Gibraltar, almost a 'free port' for goods,[7] had also become increasingly important as a port of call for shipping passing up and down the Mediterranean. Passenger liners to and from India, the Far East and Australasia, all with coal-fired boilers, stopped there. It is not surprising, therefore, that about 1,200 people were employed in coal depots in the Colony, much of the coal being stored in old hulks anchored in the harbour. Like many seaports the world over, Gibraltar had obtained in the past a somewhat murky reputation and had once been a haunt of smugglers.

Tourism was not yet the industry that it was to become. But the apes, an early attraction for visitors to the Rock since they were the only monkeys native to Europe, were found by Hunter's time to be a nuisance raiding the town for food. So in December 1910 a Fortress Order was passed forbidding the feeding of the apes by the military. One Sapper

Colonel had complained that the apes attacked his children, dug up his potatoes, stole his trousers and slept in his bed!

The very day that Hunter stepped on to the Rock and became Governor, a revolution broke out in Portugal. The young King Manuel was forced to flee the country embarking on the royal yacht *Amalia* at Ericeira. With him went his mother Queen Amélie and his grandmother Queen Maria Pia.[8] The yacht was at first destined for Oporto but the ship's officers refused to proceed to that port owing to the reported disloyalty of the Portuguese navy there, and instead set sail for Gibraltar. On 6 October the yacht arrived late at night at the port of Gibraltar, and anchored inside the mole. Hunter, warned of what was happening, went without delay to see the King whom he had met just three months before. The new Governor at once put himself out to help the unfortunate monarch. For instance he undertook on behalf of King Manuel to find out through the British Minister in Lisbon the fate of certain royalist families and to have relayed to his subjects the King's readiness to place himself at the head of any party in Portugal loyal to his House.[9] Then he made his launch available for the royal family and asked them to dine at Government House. At first they preferred to remain on the hot and uncomfortable little yacht. Later they came ashore and stayed with Hunter. The royal family had arrived with no possessions and only the clothes in which they stood. According to family legend Hunter lent the King a spare pair of pyjamas. Later Hunter's ADC lent him a dinner jacket.

King George V, sympathetic to the deposed monarch's plight, sent the Royal yacht *Victoria and Albert* to Gibraltar to pick him up. Sir Edward Grey, the Foreign Secretary, had with some misgivings agreed to this; but to forestall any possible criticism he at once recognised the new republican government in Lisbon.[10] So on 16 October the King and his mother left the Rock on the British yacht heading for Southampton and exile, while the Italian navy collected Queen Maria Pia. Throughout this unusual baptism of fire as Governor, Hunter had kept George V closely posted of developments, often in lengthy letters written by hand.[11] This was the kind of crisis in which Hunter excelled. He had done everything possible to help King Manuel and his family. He was off to a good start.

On 18 October Hunter left Gibraltar on leave to return home and on 1 November at St George's, Hanover Square, he was married to Mazie. The Archbishop of York officiated and Kitchener was best man. After the wedding Hunter handed his old chief a cheque for £100. It was in settlement of a long-standing bet. The first of the two to marry would forfeit that sum to the other. The newly-weds seemed in no hurry to return to Gibraltar. Finally duty called and they sailed for the Rock on 2 December. Once there the Governor and his wife settled into their routine, both business and social. All now looked set fair for a five-year tour in a not too exacting post, yet one which was important in defence terms at a moment when Europe was entering an uneasy political period. Hunter, it must have been expected, would provide a safe pair of hands. Unaccountably this was not to be so.

Early in 1911 the German government took offence at the despatch by France of a military expedition to Fez in Morocco after the Sultan had appealed for help to put down insurgent tribes. The Germans sent the gunboat *Panther* to Agadir, a small port on the Moroccan coast, ostensibly to protect German residents there. Morocco was regarded as lying within the French sphere of influence, and strong protests to the Germans were made from London and Paris. For a time it was feared there would be war. Precautionary orders were issued to the British fleet and extra guards placed on naval depots. This crisis, which simmered on for some months, must have concentrated Hunter's mind on the need to ensure that the defences of Gibraltar were adequate to cope with the increasing might of the German navy and any other potential enemy. The strategic importance of Gibraltar was still undisputed, standing as it did at the entrance to the Mediterranean and astride the Empire's lines of communication.

King George V's Coronation took place on 22 June 1911. The occasion was celebrated in Gibraltar with a Ball in Government House attended by leading figures of the Colony and their wives, and by the Spanish Governor of nearby Algeciras. In September the Hunters returned home on leave, and Hunter was invested with the GCB at Balmoral. Early in the new year the King and Queen paid an official visit to the Rock, and again Hunter received an award, this time the GCVO. Hunter was always punctilious over his relations with Spain and during his time in Gibraltar he was awarded the Spanish Order of Military Merit by King Alfonso XIII.

During his first two years as Governor Hunter was regarded as being popular with Gibraltarians. On his own admission he was learning about the place, and introduced no real changes. On arrival he had told the Chamber of Commerce that he was worried about the 'depressed state of trade' and wished to assure them that he would do all in his power 'to foster the commercial prosperity of the port and to promote the welfare and happiness of the community'.[12] In June 1912 Hunter converted Empire Day into Empire Week. He mixed with the crowds and took part in the festivities, which pleased the people. Then he was applauded for reopening the theatre, and referred to 'the courteous behaviour and cheerful merriment of the people'. It was only right, he said, that 'Gibraltar and its inhabitants should receive . . . the praise they have so justly earned'.[13] It might be supposed therefore that the Governor had struck up a rapport with the Colony's inhabitants. Any such appearance was misleading.

NOTES

1. Macdiarmid 207.
2. Brett II 302.
3. DHD 280.
4. Acland papers AH–Mrs John Acland, 14 Sep. 1910.
5. AHd 31/7/10–8/9/10.
6. DHD 284.
7. *Colonial Office List, Gibraltar* 1913.
8. Nicolson *King George V, His Life and Reign* 177.
9. RA G V M 75 (1)/31, 36.
10. Nicolson, loc. cit.
11. RA G V M 75 (1)/31, 44, 49, 51, 53 and 57.
12. Harcourt Papers dep 489 F 41–66.
13. Ibid.

CHAPTER 20

Conflict and Resignation

For some time certain matters had been on Hunter's mind and in the winter of 1912 he decided to act. For one thing he was worried that not enough was being done in Gibraltar for the relief of the poor, who relied entirely on charity. He therefore wrote to the Board of Sanitary Commissioners whose responsibility it was. They politely disagreed pointing out that there were four asylums for admitting the poor and orphans, and that there were other methods of dispensing relief. Further distress from unemployment in Gibraltar practically did not exist. Thus they advised against the introduction of a 'poor rate'.[1] Hunter was obstinate and unconvinced.

The hulks, already mentioned, which were anchored in the harbour, bothered Hunter, especially the matter of licensing them. But the main reason he objected to their presence was that they, and certain buildings that had grown up on the harbour's edge, impeded the field of fire of the garrison's artillery. Both the Admiralty and Colonial Office, however, did not want the hulks removed.[2]

Of much greater significance for the people of the Rock and, as it proved, for Hunter's future was the whole question of the movement, within the narrow streets of the town, of the Spanish dockyard workers who, several thousand in number, entered the Colony every day to work in the naval dockyard. They used the chief thoroughfare of Gibraltar, Main Street, both to reach and to leave the dockyard, which was situated south of the town.

After work the men were in the practice of surging down the confines of Main Street to – as Hunter saw it – the inconvenience of passers-by and those who lived in the street. Without consulting the Gibraltarians, he proceeded to issue – as he was perfectly entitled to do – Fortress Order No. 1 dated 24 December 1912 closing to all foot passengers the Landport Gate through which the dockyard workers were accustomed to enter the Colony from Spain. Instead, they were directed to proceed to the dockyard by a slightly longer route, this time via Waterport Gate, Casemates Square and so on down Main Street. The workmen were further directed on leaving the dockyard after work to proceed down Reclamation Road outside the walls of Gibraltar to Waterport Gate.[3] On this occasion they were no longer permitted to walk north along Main Street, where the shops were. If they wished to do any shopping they had to double back from Waterport down Main Street, a much more circuitous route than the one they had formerly used.

Order No. 1 was implemented on 1 January 1913. The immediate effect was that the workers used the shops less, because of the longer walk now involved in visiting them; consequently shopkeepers suffered a loss of trade. In no time they complained to the Chamber of Commerce, who sent a deputation to the Governor under their chairman Mr Porral. Initially Hunter refused to meet the deputation, but Sir Frederick Evans, the Colonial Secretary, persuaded him to change his mind.[4] Accordingly he called a meeting in the garrison lecture room on 31 January to which the deputation was invited as well as the leading members of the naval, military and civil communities including the Sanitary Commissioners. Hunter then went down with 'flu. He was at least partially recovered in time for the meeting, but he had lost his voice. On that last critical day of the month he was probably feeling below par.

The meeting opened at 11 a.m. The Governor welcomed those present and explained about the request from the Chamber of Commerce. He thought that it would save time, 'as well as be fair to myself, in view of the criticism and abuse [sic] I receive in Gibraltar', for his views on certain matters to be heard. He would have to close the meeting, he warned, at 12.45 p.m. First the recent fortress orders were read out by one of Hunter's staff officers. To save his voice, Hunter than asked the Brigade Major to read the 'Notes' which he had prepared for the meeting. These Notes, which became known as the Governor's speech, were lengthy, running to some 8,000 words. By the Governor's order they were published *in extenso* in the *Gibraltar Chronicle and Official Gazette* of 31 January 1913.

Several underlying themes were discernible in Hunter's rather rambling address. The main one was that Gibraltar was a fortress and therefore everybody and everything, including trade, was subordinate to military needs; further that Gibraltar in peacetime should be organised as if for war. Others were: the irritation he felt about the traffic congestion, his desire for order and cleanliness, and his wish to tell the people the truth

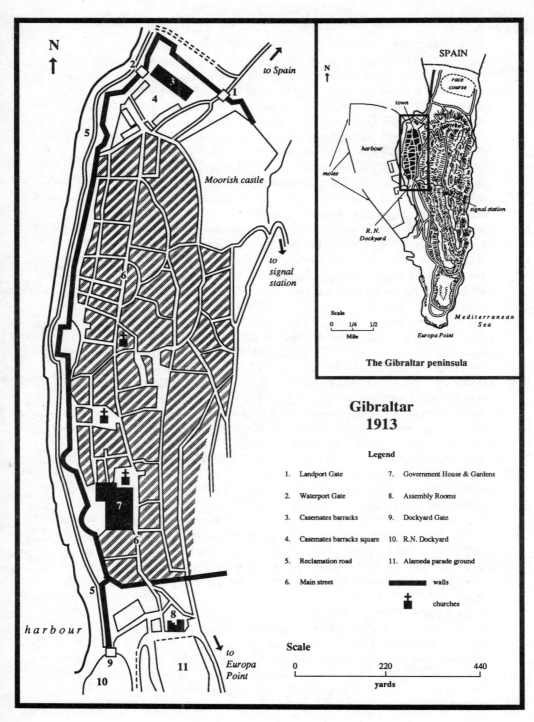

N

to Spain

Moorish castle

to
signal
station

6

5

9

10

11

to
Europa
Point

harbour

SPAIN

N

*race
course*

town

harbour

moles

*R. N.
Dockyard*

signal station

*Mediterranean
Sea*

Europa Point

Scale

0   1/4   1/2
Mile

The Gibraltar peninsula

Gibraltar
1913

Legend

1. Landport Gate
2. Waterport Gate
3. Casemates barracks
4. Casemates barracks square
5. Reclamation road
6. Main street
7. Government House & Gardens
8. Assembly Rooms
9. Dockyard Gate
10. R.N. Dockyard
11. Alameda parade ground

━━━ walls

✝ churches

Scale

0   220   440

yards

about the place. There were here two old fads: his preoccupation with cleanliness and his urge, which at times was irresistible, to get matters off his chest. Whatever the merits of his proposals, and there was much sense in some of them, the whole speech was interspersed with extra comments and asides by Hunter, some of which caused grave offence to the inhabitants of the Rock.

He began by reminding his audience that during the annual mobilisation exercise the Landport Gate was closed and workers were required to return home by way of Reclamation Road, the shortest route back to Spain. He had been urged to make these orders permanent but had refrained for two years while he studied the problem fully. He also made the point that he was anxious to make life in the restricted fortress 'as little irksome' to all the inhabitants as possible, consistent with the safety of the place.

Hunter considered the changes he had made in re-routing the dockyard workers had proved to be a 'public boon'. Before the introduction of the new rules he had himself been 'hustled' off the pavement by the crowds in Main Street. The police, he observed, were either afraid or unable to exercise their authority, though he did not say whether he had taken this up with the Chief of Police. He rejected the argument that local trade had been ruined by the changes, believing that most of the shopping in Gibraltar undertaken by those who lived in Spain was done by women and children and certain middlemen.

Despite what he had said on his arrival in Gibraltar the Governor did not show himself well-disposed to those in trade. He took the view that the Fortress was 'not maintained for purely commercial interests'. For a start there were too many shops, stalls and booths; some of these should be 'swept away'. Although the main market had no right to be where it was, for certain of its buildings infringed military regulations, nonetheless he hoped, seemingly as a concession, that the market could stay where it was. Not so the Jews' market, which attracted an undesirable crowd and 'stuff is exposed for sale [there] which ought to be put in the dust destructor'. Similarly, he was determined to put a stop to the sale of adulterated drink through liquor shops. British Bluejackets and soldiers, he said, needed protecting against harmful liquor.

The Governor made some astringent remarks on the Colony's cleanliness. He referred to public urinals and latrines and commented that some were an outrage to public decency. In a letter to Lewis Harcourt, Secretary of State for the Colonies, he said, by way of expanding on this, that people were 'unbuttoning and beginning before they enter, often not finishing before they leave'.[5] On refuse, he told his audience that people threw their dirt and rubbish from windows, while at the same time admitting there was nowhere else for refuse to go. He, again, expanded for Harcourt's benefit and mentioned 'the unspeakably filthy practice prevalent in Gibraltar of throwing ordure from upper windows on to other people's roofs and courtyards below' (roofs were water-catchment areas in Gibraltar, he explained).

In the same vein, he complained about men in the street who 'spat most effusively and hugely', and had clearly been incensed when 'a lady staying in my house walking with her husband in the street had her dress spat upon by a Gibraltar man'. At this point, he spoke in an aside to Admiral Brock, the Dockyard Superintendent, sitting next to him. Despite his loss of voice what he said was plainly heard in the room. According to the complaint subsequently made by the jurors of Gibraltar to the Secretary of State, he asked the Admiral what *he* would have done if his wife had been spat on. Answering his own rhetorical question Hunter suggested that the offender would have been taken by 'the scruff of his neck' and dealt with appropriately. This would have meant a summons and a fine 'for the jurors are partisans and Gibraltar juries are notoriously unjust in favour of their own'.[6]

Hunter's speech ranged widely over other subjects. He thought he could find a better site for the small-pox hospital. Space for cemeteries was limited and he wanted to build a crematorium. In wartime, workers from Spain would not be available so he favoured bringing into Gibraltar labour from the 'congested districts of India', adding that he could 'find room for them by turning other people out'. Still the authoritarian, he said that press censorship was a duty that he might soon have to undertake.

Turning to public servants, he emphasised that no person should draw British pay from government employment unless he spoke 'intelligible English'. He then instanced the telephone operator at the Colonial hospital as being unable to speak English at all, 'not even', he added, 'the gibberish that passes here for English.' In fact, he thought that English in Gibraltar was spoken no better than by rickshaw-men in Durban and worse than by donkey-boys in Cairo. For some present there would have been a shiver of apprehension when Hunter said he liked the former arrangements whereby the Secretary of the Sanitary Commissioners, the Magistrate and the Colonial Engineer were all military officers.

The Chamber of Commerce, responsible for the meeting being called in the first place, was not let off lightly. Hunter contrasted the way he and the Chamber of Commerce did business. He did nothing without careful thought while the Chamber of Commerce took 'no time for reflection'. Moments later, referring to the time when the hulks were to be removed, he commented 'A "fat lot" the Chamber of Commerce will care'.[7]

On a more positive note Hunter showed that he had given much thought to the question of motor traffic on the Rock and its future development. Thus, he thought roads needed widening in places and their surfaces improving. Some one-way streets might have to be introduced. He then reported the setting up of a commercial wireless station. Finally he hoped soon to see the introduction of compulsory education.

His last words were strong ones. It was almost as if he was throwing down a challenge to Gibraltarians. He said: 'This town is like the Augean stables but it is small, and it is under lock and key whenever, for military reasons, the Fortress Commander chooses to shut it up.'

It was now 12.50 p.m. Hunter thanked his audience for listening to him and rose as if to go. Porral, surprised and pained that the delegation was not to be given a hearing, went up to the Governor and told him how very sore they were at his unwillingness to receive them. The Governor said, 'Well, how do you expect me to receive you when I knew you were coming to give me a wigging.' Porral was taken aback but managed to ask if he was to assume that for the future the doors of Government House were to be closed to any deputation. Hunter to this replied, 'No, no, no, you think of what I have said, you consider it and then you come to me, good-bye.'[8] That was the end of it. Hunter at once left to keep another appointment.

Four days later Hunter sent a copy of the *Gibraltar Chronicle and Official Gazette* reporting his speech to the Secretary of State for the Colonies, Lewis Harcourt. In his covering letter he told Harcourt that 'no body of civilians here has the right to dispute my military orders here: my opinion, as Fortress Commander, is that their doing so is an impropriety.'[9] This line would be his constant theme in defending his action over the closing of the gate and the re-routing of workers. The man Hunter was dealing with, Lewis Harcourt, known to his friends as Lou Lou, was an experienced politician (his father had led the Liberals in the Commons for a time).

The papers received from Gibraltar were fielded by the top civil servant in the Colonial Office, the Under Secretary Sir John Anderson. After he had read the Governor's speech, Anderson lost no time in sending a handwritten minute to Harcourt. He began it by noting that Hunter was going to establish a press censorship (this was not quite accurate) and remove the hulks against the wishes of the Admiralty and Colonial Office. He then went on: 'A man who can talk in this ridiculous and insulting fashion to the civil population is impossible. The people are loyal and proud of being British subjects but if they are hectored *and* treated like coolies or worse, their loyalty will be severely strained ... I really don't see how we can allow such a man to remain and the W.O [War Office] should remove him as soon as possible to some sphere where he can do less mischief.'[10]

The crisis, for such it now was, proceeded to build up apace. On the Rock the jurors of Gibraltar led by Mr Sallust Smith and numbering 21 persons wrote a memorial to Harcourt complaining that they had been 'deeply insulted and aggrieved by His Excellency's words which cast so painful an imputation upon their character, morality, integrity and honesty'.[11]

Harcourt acted quickly and wrote to Colonel Seely (later Lord Mottistone), the Secretary of State for War, on 19 February as follows:

'... What are you going to do about Sir Archibald Hunter? It is quite
clear to me that we can not leave him at Gibraltar after his extraordinary
effusion, which has produced the greatest possible ill feeling amongst
the civilian population and I hear that petitions and remonstrances are
on their way to me ... I should imagine, from the tone and substance
of his recent speech and from some other proceedings of his of which
I have heard, that he can hardly be quite in his right mind.'[12]

Seely replied to this letter on 21 February:

'I have read the papers you sent me about Hunter; there can be no doubt
that he is or was off his head – the references to scripture and to sanitary
matters are similar to the anonymous letters we all receive from lunatics.
On enquiring I find that he has been subject to periods of great excit-
ability in times past . . .'[13]

In fact Hunter's allusion to the scriptures was rather neat, as will presently
be seen. On 'sanitary matters', surely Hunter was justified in referring to
the state of hygiene in Gibraltar? Usually Hunter has been depicted as
cool and calm, not excitable. It is quite possible that Seely received his
information from Ian Hamilton, who was Hunter's superior officer and
who can, therefore, be expected to have been consulted. Hamilton's views
on Hunter's temper have been mentioned earlier.

That week the Cabinet discussed the situation that had arisen in Gibraltar and decided to send out Seely to try and find out the cause of the
trouble, and do what he could to put it right. So Seely took passage in the
cruiser *HMS Hyacinth* about to leave for South Africa.[14] He duly saw
Hunter as planned and came home overland via Madrid, where he called
on the Ambassador Sir Maurice de Bunsen. The War Secretary found the
situation in Gibraltar difficult but commented to Harcourt that any change
in the Governorship would have 'a most unfortunate effect', a view with
which the Ambassador in Madrid 'fully concurs'.[15] This suggests that
Seely may have shifted his ground, and also that some people regarded
Hunter as doing a reasonable job. In addition, the Ambassador may well
have been conscious of the good relations Hunter seemed to have established with the Spanish.

In March two further memorials, as expected, reached Harcourt from
Gibraltar. One was from the Chamber of Commerce and the other from
the Exchange Committee, representing the merchants, landholders, rate-
payers and other inhabitants of the Colony.

The Chamber of Commerce explained at length the damage suffered
by traders in Main Street and adjacent streets as a result of the Fortress
Orders the Governor introduced. Workers now preferred to buy their

goods in Spain. Strong complaint was voiced too about 'the offensive language and allusions' made by the Governor both in his speech and in his verbal remarks. There was now, the memorial stated, a feeling of unrest and uncertainty.

The memorial from the Exchange Committee covered more ground than the other two, and took the Governor to task on various points. They strongly rejected Hunter's view that Gibraltar was dirty and insanitary pointing to favourable reports by the Medical Officer of Health. The Committee challenged the power which the Governor asserted he possessed of arbitrarily deporting people in peacetime; also they were filled with anxiety by the Governor's views on the future of the hulks and of the buildings on the waterfront, and on the liberty of the press; they considered the filling of public offices by officials of the Colonial Service a 'vast improvement' on the former practice of employing military men.[16]

Hunter accompanied each memorial forwarded to London with a letter of his own to Harcourt in which he set out to justify what he had said in his speech. He was not alone in holding the view, he asserted, that Gibraltar juries were partisan. He ended his letter on the jurors' memorial by saying that the whole matter was summed up beautifully in St Paul's Epistle to the Galatians Ch. 4, v. 16, which runs: 'Am I therefore become your enemy, because I tell you the truth?'

Hunter did not believe there were feelings of unrest except among the grog shop owners. If, as he insisted, Gibraltar in peacetime should be ready for war, then the police, he argued, should be organised as an armed force of constabulary. Seely on his visit to the Rock, had twice remarked, Hunter noted, that the dangers to Gibraltar lay on the inside, more than the outside. Rather dramatically Hunter gave his opinion that quite possibly 'bombs exist in Gibraltar. There are many anarchists in the neighbourhood . . .'[17]

On 3 March 1913 a deputation left Gibraltar for London. Its aim, as reported in the press, was 'to plead the cause of the townspeople with the Home Government'. The shops shut at midday and crowds thronged the wharf as the steamer left for Algeciras from where the delegates would depart by rail for England. 800 dockyard workers obtained leave to attend the peaceful demonstration. The great crowds seemed to represent the popular expression of the mood on the Rock in favour of their delegation and against Hunter.

Harcourt saw the deputation, which consisted of Mr Porral and Mr Sallust Smith, on 20 March. He had with him Lord Emmot, Under Secretary of State for the Colonies and Sir John Anderson his senior civil servant. The deputation was given a full hearing. They lost no time in going into the fine detail of their grievances against Hunter.[18] Up to the eve of the meeting held by the Governor at the end of January, Porral told Harcourt, Hunter had been popular in Gibraltar, and went so far as to say

213

he was regarded as the most popular Governor they had ever had. He was at a complete loss to account for Hunter's behaviour.

The two Gibraltarians made it clear that they considered Hunter unjustified in the view he took of the inconvenience caused by the workmen swarming down Main Street after work. They seemed to accept some nuisance was caused but that it only lasted half an hour. They rejected Hunter's view that there were too many shops and that the markets were not clean. Criticisms of other contentious matters were rejected equally. They did, however, broadly welcome the Governor's proposal to introduce compulsory education.

At the conclusion of the meeting Harcourt, quite improperly, indicated to the two delegates that he was taking their side in this dispute. For instance, he used the words: '. . . if the Governor had acted sensibly' and 'if the Governor had acted judiciously'. More explicitly, he told the deputation that the Governor's language at the meeting in Gibraltar could not be countenanced by the government.[19] He said that he was going to see Hunter.

Hunter was summoned back to London to meet Harcourt. He left Gibraltar on 25 March. The King had been briefed about the crisis. A decision was made that Lord Grenfell, formerly Sirdar of the Egyptian army and now a Field-Marshal, should see the King at Windsor Castle and be asked to meet Hunter as some kind of intermediary.[20] We do not know what precisely Grenfell had been asked to do, but on 29 March he duly saw Hunter. He had had a difficult job, he reported the next day to Lord Stamfordham, the King's Private Secretary. This was because Hunter – naturally in Grenfell's view – was much annoyed at Harcourt's action in accepting the statements of the deputation before hearing his side of the question. Grenfell had an hour's discussion with Hunter and eventually Hunter agreed to a course of action proposed by Grenfell. This envisaged that he would be ready to resign should Harcourt not accept his explanation of what had occurred.[21]

The stage was now set for Hunter to see both Harcourt and Seely at 4.15 p.m. on Monday 31 March in Harcourt's room at the Colonial Office. There can be little doubt that Harcourt entered the meeting determined to have Hunter removed as Governor, hoping that Grenfell had prepared the ground satisfactorily. It was more a question of how this was done. Would he resign quietly or would he have to be dismissed?

The meeting lasted an hour and a half, and was described by Harcourt, who took the lead from Seely, to Stamfordham as 'very painful'. Hunter had been in a fighting mood and was given two days to consider the situation. He had been treated with 'great consideration'.[22] Immediately after the meeting, which could not have gone entirely to plan for Harcourt, it looked as if Hunter was not prepared to give in, despite his earlier undertaking to Grenfell, and was ready to challenge the Government's attempt to seek his resignation. Grenfell was again called upon to intervene, but he was now in Brighton and it was too late apparently for him to tackle Hunter again in person. He did, however, send him an express letter.[23] We don't know its contents but can only guess that Grenfell urged Hunter to agree to go quietly. He would have pointed out that since the Government was determined that Hunter should not return to Gibraltar, any course challenging the Government's decision could involve messy publicity including possible publication of the memorials and more. This letter may have helped him to make up his mind. By 4 April Harcourt could report to Stamfordham that Hunter had asked for three months' leave of absence and had accepted that his resignation would take effect at the end of that period.[24] Hunter always disliked publicity. Did the possibility of a public airing of the whole dispute weigh with him? It may have done. There is no telling. He did, however, say to Grenfell that he hoped there would be no questions asked in Parliament about the affair. He may also have realised that publicity might embarrass the army.

In an interesting comment to Harcourt, Grenfell said that Hunter 'was a curious mixture – a good soldier but obstinate and not quite normal in his actions when (as French said to me yesterday) he sees red'.[25] French may well have obtained his information about Hunter from Ian Hamilton, who could have been, as suggested earlier, Seely's source. This does not, of course, mean that Grenfell's comment was necessarily inaccurate.

Some news of what had been happening in Gibraltar had come to the ears of the British press but had not attracted much attention. One newspaper, however, wrote that the gallant 'Sir Archie', famed throughout the Army for his caustic utterances, was 'in hot water' again. He had done the people of Gibraltar a real service by 'telling them off' in his own straight-from-the-shoulder style. Further he showed great moral courage in speaking his mind whenever occasion demanded it. Overoptimistically, from Hunter's point of view, the paper added that it would not be surprised to see the vacant baton of a Field-Marshal conferred upon Sir Archie, in spite of the popular idea that it was to go to General French.[26] Hunter may still have been held in warm regard by the public and the army but the baton, in the event, went to French.

Towards the end of his three months' leave of absence Harcourt wrote to Hunter giving him the proposed wording of the announcement of his successor. It was brief and merely referred to the King approving the appointment of Lieutenant-General Sir Herbert Miles as Governor of Gibraltar 'in place of General Sir Archibald Hunter who has resigned his appointment from the termination of his leave of absence on June 30'. Hunter replied to Harcourt writing from the Hunters' house in Upper Grosvenor Street:

'Dear Mr Harcourt,
I have received your very courteous letter of this day's date by hand.
As regard to the wording of the announcement you propose to make I
am debarred by the sense of discipline which has always regulated my
conduct in the army from offering any criticism whatever.
                        Very sincerely yours . . .'[27]

In the press there was some anodyne mention of Hunter's departure, but
awkward publicity was avoided.

After this disaster Hunter could hardly hope, at least for the moment,
for another job, but he had the gratification of being appointed Colonel
of his regiment after the death in March 1913 of Sir William Cameron. He
loved the regiment and was its Colonel, a very good one, for 13 years.
The war, however, came to the rescue of his career, as will shortly be seen.

But what had gone wrong at Gibraltar? Hitherto Hunter's career had
been pretty well an uninterrupted success story. How had he come to lose
his job in such an extraordinary fashion?

In trying to find some explanation for what happened, if indeed this is
possible, we must understand that, for Hunter, Gibraltar was first and foremost a fortress. His first duty, as he saw it, was to ensure that the defences
of this important base were in good order. The civilian population was a
secondary consideration. With the increasing tensions in the political situation in Europe, this prime duty would have become, for him, most
pressing. At the same time the matter was made worse, unhappily, by some
antipathy Hunter developed for the people of Gibraltar. Any lack of cleanliness and order irritated him. As a man of action he wanted to improve matters, but being authoritarian in temperament, he felt no need to consult the
people. The military under him would almost certainly have agreed with
much of what he proposed to do. Probably he was too strong a personality
for his civilian officials to remonstrate effectively about some of his more
contentious ideas. Nor would it have been his way to seek advice from the
Colonial Office. The ingredients present were combustible and the scene, at
least viewed from our vantage point, looks as if it was set for an inevitable
clash between the Governor and the people for whom he was responsible.

In deciding to close the Landport Gate and to re-route the dockyard
workers, to be fair to Hunter, he was only carrying out what he had been
asked to do by the military a long time before. His proposals were not
unreasonable provided acceptable alternatives could be found. And
indeed his mind was not closed. Thus, following the issue of the controversial Orders, the dockyard workers complained to the Admiral about
their access to the centre of the town. Accordingly Hunter made a concession to them and allowed the opening of another gate so that they
could more easily reach the shops.

Some of his ideas for reform made good sense. Others such as the scrapping of the hulks and wharf-side buildings and the threat to introduce press censorship were highly controversial and unsettling for the people. But these ideas were not cast in concrete and there may have been an element of kite-flying in them. Again, representations could have been made to him whenever the population felt threatened. Nonetheless, it must have been worrying to Gibraltarians that the Governor could even contemplate imposing censorship, deporting people and so on.

To call a meeting, in the absence of any formal consultative process, to present his ideas had some merit, though not all the Gibraltar community were represented at it, for example, the Exchange Committee. But not to receive or hear the Chamber of Commerce delegation, either at the meeting or on some other occasion, was both a tactical blunder and a discourtesy. Normally Hunter was a polite man who took pride in the fair treatment he meted out to people whatever their rank and station.

What is difficult to defend is Hunter's rudeness during the meeting to the people of Gibraltar as a whole, and to both the jurors and to the Chamber of Commerce in particular. Many of his comments and asides were ill-considered and boorish. Nor was there any sign of Hunter apologising or climbing down. Indeed he continued to believe that he was in the right. For he was just as intemperate in his views in the letters he wrote Harcourt in the following weeks when he had had time to reflect and was aware of the reaction he had caused on the Rock.

The explanation for his seemingly uncharacteristic conduct is elusive. Did his wife have a hand in what happened, goading him to take action on the local people or on dockyard workers surging past her front door? There is no information about Mazie's views on Gibraltar and its people. But Hunter is unlikely to have allowed women, even his wife, to influence his handling of affairs. Was he ill? It is true he had recently had influenza. It is also true that he often had pain from his old wound, which might have made him tetchy at times. These conditions, however, hardly seem to offer adequate explanations. Discounting the rather woolly rumours that had come to the ears of Harcourt and Seely, there is no evidence that he was ill with any serious disorder, physical or mental, during or after his tenure as Governor. If there had been something really wrong then it would surely have come out later.

The key to this mystery surely lies in Hunter's character. As we have seen in his story he suffered at certain moments from an uncontrollable impulse to tell the truth, as he saw it, about certain events or situations. He would then take the line: 'This is what my duty tells me needs to be said. I will say it and be damned.' The matter would be compounded if he was angry and if he believed fervently that he was right. On these occasions – perhaps they were few in number, we can't be sure – there was no holding him and his judgement, normally exceptionally sound, left him. His outward conduct then defied rational analysis.

NOTES

1. *Gibraltar Chronicle and Official Gazette (Gib Gaz)* No. 23336, 31 Jan. 1913.
2. CO 91/452 minute Anderson–Harcourt 12 Feb. 1913.
3. *Gib Gaz* loc. cit.
4. Harcourt Papers dep 489 F 41–66.
5. CO loc. cit. AH–Harcourt 13 Feb. 1913.
6. CO loc. cit. Jurors' memorial to Harcourt, 10 Feb. 1913.
7. *Gib Gaz* loc. cit.
8. Harcourt Papers loc. cit.
9. CO loc. cit. AH–Harcourt 4 Feb. 1913.
10. CO loc. cit. minute Anderson–Harcourt, 12 Feb. 1913.
11. CO loc. cit. Jurors' memorial.
12. Mottistone Papers 20 166.
13. Harcourt Papers loc. cit. F 5–6.
14. Seely *Adventure* 148–9.
15. Harcourt Papers loc. cit. F 6.
16. CO loc. cit. Exchange Committee's memorial received in the Colonial Office on 12 Mar. 1913.
17. CO loc. cit. AH–Harcourt 13 Feb., 24 Feb. and 5 Mar. 1913.
18. Harcourt Papers loc. cit. proceedings of deputation F 41–66.
19. Ibid.
20. Harcourt Papers loc. cit. F 8.
21. RA G V L521/4; Harcourt Papers loc. cit. F 12.
22. RA G V L521/7.
23. Harcourt Papers loc. cit. F 17.
24. RA loc. cit.
25. Harcourt Papers loc. cit. F 14.
26. NR unidentifiable press cutting, from almost certainly a London paper, in the spring of 1913 (French became a Field-Marshal on 3 Jun. 1913).
27. Harcourt Papers loc. cit. F 29 and 31 exchange of letters between Harcourt and AH, both letters written on 23 Jun. 1913.

CHAPTER 21

Aldershot – Ambitions Denied

The murder at Sarajevo on 28 June 1914 of the heir to the Austro-Hungarian throne, the Archduke Ferdinand, by a Bosnian fanatic set in motion a chain of events that led to the outbreak of World War I. On 4 August, the German army invaded Belgium, and at the end of that day Britain, standing firm with her allies France and Russia, was drawn into war with Germany and Austria. The British Cabinet responded quickly to the military needs of the moment. Kitchener, about to return to his position in

Egypt, was summoned from Dover to London by the Prime Minister and appointed Minister of War. Almost overnight he virtually assumed the role of a warlord, taking charge of the military apparatus and gearing up the country for a long war.

The start of the war found Hunter in Scotland, living with Mazie at Monkton on the Ayrshire coast. Four days after Kitchener took up his new appointment, Hunter, now the senior General on the active list, wrote from Scotland to his old chief as follows:

> 'My dear Lord Kitchener,
>
> I live in hopes of your giving me a command.
>
> I shall come to London tomorrow night to 11 Upper Grosvenor Street. If you see your way I wish you would bring me back to the full pay list and give me some idea of what work is likely to fall to my lot, so that I may prepare a staff and set to work to study the matter. My French is quite good enough for practical purposes. I am ready to go anywhere and do anything at a moment's notice. Is it asking too much that someone should send me a wire tomorrow here to say if you have anything in prospect for me?
>
> Very sincerely from
> Archibald Hunter.'[1]

Two days later on 11 August from London he again wrote to Kitchener in urgent terms asking for work.

Hunter's persistence was rewarded. On 17 August he was appointed to command the new 13th (Western) Division to be based on Salisbury plain.

The organisation at the top level of the army was in a state of some flux. Sir John French had, as was expected, assumed command of the British Expeditionary Force. Under him French had initially four infantry divisions and a cavalry division, divided into two corps (later to expand and become armies) under Lieutenant-Generals, one under Haig who had been GOC Aldershot, and the other under Grierson. Lt.-Gen. Edmund Allenby commanded the cavalry. Smith-Dorrien (from Southern Command at Salisbury) took Haig's place at Aldershot.

These arrangements were momentarily thrown into confusion when the unfortunate Grierson on his way to the front had a heart attack in the train near Amiens and died. Smith-Dorrien took over command of the 2nd corps in France (French wanted Plumer). This meant the post at Aldershot was again vacant. Kitchener now decided that Hunter should fill it, and set up there a new centre to train the huge armies being raised. Hunter wrote to Kitchener on 21 August to thank him 'very cordially' for giving him the command.[2] He was also given at the same time command of the new 8th Light division and the new 9th (Scottish) division. Ever since his early promotion to Major-General he had had a horror of serving at Aldershot. But these were circumstances which he had not foreseen and he began work with all his old enthusiasm. Unlike many of his military contemporaries he predicted the war would last three years. He told Abby Hunter that it was the 'duty of civilisation to crush the overbearing Prussians and to relieve the world of the constant worry of her menaces and tempers. And we shall do it, or die in the attempt'.[3]

In response for calls by Kitchener to join his new armies, hundreds of thousands of men came flooding into the recruitment offices all over the country. By the end of September 750,000 volunteers had enrolled. These numbers produced enormous administrative and training problems for the regular army. Somehow they were surmounted. First, the recruits were formed locally into battalions. They were then placed in brigades and divisions, being moved in due course to the training centres of which Aldershot was far and away the most important.

In the early days of the war there were no uniforms or boots for many recruits, who continued to wear civilian clothes. When Asquith the Prime Minister motored down to Aldershot one Sunday in September he noted that the streets were 'swarming with K's new army – some in regulation khaki but the vast majority loafing about in Eastend costumes: such a rabble as has been rarely seen'.[4] Equipment was in equally short supply and there was a chronic shortage of rifles. Many volunteers drilled with brooms and sticks. Schools, halls, churches were used to house the recruits. Army huts designed for 20 men had to take 50. A crash building programme was instituted but there was a shortage of seasoned timber and it was many months before enough huts had been constructed for the new troops.

It was laid down that infantry for the new armies should be given six months' training for war, ten weeks of which was to comprise basic training. This consisted of physical training to get the men fit, and drill to instil discipline. Next would come instruction in musketry. Training on machine guns, signalling and exercises in the field would come later. Overall, training in the early days was for a type of open warfare which bore little resemblance to what was happening on the western front where before the end of the year there was deadlock between the opposing forces. A more realistic type of training was introduced later on in 1915. Certain special qualities were demanded of those responsible for training Kitchener's armies. Apart from administrative skills and energy there was a need, early on, for some flair at improvisation. Above all, though, a great knowledge of the profession of arms in the broadest sense was required, combined with an understanding of people. Hunter, a highly practical soldier, seemed well suited to the task he had been given, and was soon making himself, by his application to it, indispensable to Kitchener.

Hunter determined to lead, as had always been his wont, by example. He set himself rigorous standards. He was always up before his men's reveille which was at 5.50 a.m. and he never went to bed before 'lights out'. Government House, the name by which his official residence in Aldershot was known, became a teetotal establishment following the example set by the King. The *Daily Mirror* reported that, in covering his Command, Hunter preferred his horse to his motor car except when visiting outlying parts. Often he seemed to be on horseback all day long.[5] He had not lost his touch with the common soldier, and the same paper reported his great popularity among the men. Hunter's wartime world of Aldershot and its surroundings hummed with military activity of every kind. Never, wrote a correspondent of the *Westminster Gazette*, had the town been 'more orderly, cleaner and more disciplined'. Hunter would have found it all a great change from his last posting, and it has to be said, more to his liking. But he was already hankering about serving overseas. With his seniority and record as a front-line soldier, his claims to command an army in the field could hardly be disputed.

In early December he told Abby that he hoped to go to France 'early next year' with the troops he was training. On Christmas Eve he told her that he expected 'to go abroad in about ten weeks time'. This fits with the original programme of giving the infantry six months' training. Christmas that year was an austere affair. It was not, Hunter felt, a year for festivities or attempts at merriment. The Hunters sent out no cards and limited themselves to a children's party and a servants' dinner.[6]

King George V and his consort gave staunch support to the training of the new armies. They came down regularly to Aldershot to review and inspect the troops. The King's first visit was in late September 1914, when he saw the staggering total – or so it was estimated by the press – of some 130,000 men training in the area. Invariably Hunter accompanied the King. Often he and Mazie would lunch with the King and Queen, or dine with them when they stayed overnight. According to Hunter's diary the King visited Aldershot on no less than seven occasions in 1915. On one of their visits the Royal pair were instructed by Hunter on the Rushmoor rifle range into the mysteries of firing a machine gun. The Queen was startled by the first few rounds she fired but 'finished the magazine with composed interest' according to one observer! By early 1915 five out of six of the new divisions so far raised were located at Aldershot. Intensive training before leaving for the front always took place under Hunter's professional eye. His Training Centre had become the anvil on which the raw material for the volunteer armies was hammered into shape.

There is no record of Hunter paying an early visit to the Western Front. He was too busy at Aldershot. But it was clearly important for the chief trainer to see for himself at first hand conditions in France. He made his first visit to the front at the end of December, 1914. First he went to see the C-in-C, Sir John French, carrying a message from Kitchener. French's diary for 30 December states that 'Hunter and six other officers came "to look on". I had some rather warm words over a message he brought from Kitchener. However I gave him a piece of my mind.'[7] From this it does not sound as if Hunter received much of a welcome. But then many of the top brass at the front were at each other's throats and the atmosphere at GHQ must have been strained. French himself was a mercurial character and had strong likes and dislikes. For instance, he loathed Kitchener and once said that he would gladly put the War Minister up against a wall and shoot him.[8] French also hated Smith-Dorrien the commander of the 2nd army and eventually, and unfairly, sacked him.

On 30 December 1914 it was announced in an Army Order that the organisation of the Land Forces was to be 'further developed by the creation of armies, each of which will consist generally of three army corps'. Altogether there were to be six armies (two were already in the field). The 3rd army, presumably the next one due to take its place in the line, was to be commanded by Hunter. The 4th, 5th and 6th armies were to be commanded respectively by Ian Hamilton, Rundle and Bruce Hamilton. The announcement received wide press coverage with pen pictures of all six army commanders.[9] Hunter must have been delighted with the news of his appointment. It was confirmation that he was still recognised as one of the nation's leading soldiers and at 58 was not considered too old to command an army in France. Further, it surely indicated that he was back in favour after Gibraltar. No wonder Hunter expected to be in France within a few months. Of course the four new armies were paper ones and did not yet properly exist.

At that time the War Office seemed to be thinking that, when trained and ready, the new armies would move, more or less as whole units with their appointed commanders, from England to the western front. The War Office had gone so far as to designate the particular divisions which would make up each new army. For example the third army would be composed of the 21st, 22nd, 23rd, 24th, 25th and 26th divisions.[10] This may have all looked neat and tidy in the War Office. What no one had bargained for were the heavy casualties taken by the BEF and the consequent need to reinforce its formations on a somewhat *ad hoc* basis.

French did not respond well to the new Army Order. On 3 January 1915 he wrote to the War Office giving his view that the size of the BEF should be increased by the 'augmentation' of existing divisions.[11] The influential Haig shared French's view. He noted in his war diary on 15 January that new units should be drafted into the existing BEF formations by battalions and brigades, instead of forming new army corps or armies in England under commanders inexperienced in trench warfare. He thought each corps in France should have a new division attached to it, and advocated the BEF being divided into three armies.[12] The Army Council replied to French on 20 January in a communication which is not easy at this distance to understand. The Council seemed to be saying that it had not yet decided how to incorporate the new armies in the country's Land Forces. But French could, if he wished, produce new army corps by combining brigades from current BEF formations with those coming out from England.[13] This seemed to be giving French what he wanted.

There is an interesting reference to French and Hunter by Asquith in a letter he wrote to his close friend and confidante, Venetia Stanley, on 26 January 1915. He was talking about the health of French's Chief of Staff Sir Archibald Murray and saying that French wanted him back in France to command the third army when he had recovered. But French, Asquith felt, 'had a considerable dread lest Hunter should be sent out'.[14] Clearly French would not have welcomed Hunter as one of his army commanders. Both men had strong personalities and they might have clashed. Nevertheless, French had a respect for Hunter's professional qualities and tried to do him a good turn later in the war.

In the event the policy advocated by French and Haig was finally adopted. The original 3rd, 4th, 5th and 6th new armies were never in fact formed in England. Except for Ian Hamilton, their designated commanders, that is Hunter, Rundle and Bruce Hamilton, were never destined to command an army at the front. In July 1915 the BEF was divided into three armies. The command of the 3rd army was entrusted to Sir Charles Monro, a rising man in the BEF and four years younger than Hunter. If French had wanted to keep Hunter away from France then he had succeeded. Kitchener, still a powerful figure must, though, have concurred.

In the first year of the war Hunter was constantly begging Kitchener to send him to the front. On 4 April 1915 he wrote to his chief '. . . of course it is a disappointment. But I still hope something may turn up yet to give you an opportunity of employing me in the field . . .' We do not know what this particular disappointment was, unless he had just been told, against his hopes, he was not to have command of the third army in France. Later in the same month, when writing to Kitchener on training matters, Hunter said that he still hoped to see the new armies fight. 'They all say quite openly they hope to go with me.' Yet again in May in a postscript to a letter he told Kitchener '. . . I still cling to the hope that I may get abroad with [the new armies]'.[15] The impression must not, however, be given that Hunter was only concerned with his own ambitions. On the contrary he was highly motivated to do the training job which he had been given.

An opportunity to command a field force had occurred in 1915 which was almost tailor-made for Hunter. With the stalemate on the western front plans were discussed in January of that year to force the Dardanelles, capture Constantinople and knock Turkey out of the war. At first it was thought that the operation could be carried out solely by the Royal Navy, who would reduce by gunfire the forts on the Gallipoli peninsula and opposite. But the navy's bombardment did not succeed in its object. So it was agreed early in March to send the army in. As commander of the force Kitchener's eye first alighted on Rundle,[16] but he changed his mind and instead decided on Ian Hamilton. It was all a hurriedly arranged and badly organised affair with Hamilton leaving London for the Mediterranean the day after being told of his appointment. We have no idea whether Hunter was ever considered for the command.

Opportunities were undoubtedly missed in the Gallipoli campaign. For instance after the landings in August at Suvla bay there are grounds for believing the Allied troops, forcefully led, might have gained the commanding heights before these were occupied by the Turks. Unfortunately the troops did not push on vigorously inland and up into the hills. Part of the blame must lie with the commander, Ian Hamilton, even if he was not served well by some of his subordinates.

What was wanted for the campaign was a resolute and decisive commander, a real leader of men. Hunter was surely the man for this job, his record and character ideally suiting him for it. The chances of succeeding at Gallipoli would have greatly increased if he had been appointed C-in-C. He would have driven his subordinates hard and controlled the battle. The tough Australians and New Zealanders would have responded to him. He was raring to go overseas and his days in the saddle had made him fit. Interestingly, the family – no doubt biased about him – felt he should have gone. A letter written in February 1916 by May von Dumreicher, Hunter's niece, to Abby Hunter has survived. She said that 'Archie . . . is sad at not getting to the front. Every time he asked to be sent, his age was cast up in his teeth. Almost everyone said from the beginning that he ought to have gone to the Dardanelles instead of Ian Hamilton.'[17]

At the end of 1915 there were changes of command in France with Haig replacing French as C-in-C. The BEF had been greatly expanded and the year had been one of intense activity for the trainers at Aldershot. Some 19 divisions of the new armies, most of which had passed through Hunter's hands at Aldershot, were in France, while two were in Macedonia and one was in Egypt. In retrospect that year was a critical year for Hunter's career. If he was to command in France or somewhere else overseas, he would surely have been sent out in 1915 or at the latest early in 1916. He was too senior for a corps (Kitchener was a great stickler in these matters); either he would have had to command an army or a theatre.

Apart from France and later Italy, the possibilities of commanding overseas were limited. Hunter might usefully have been sent to Egypt at the end of 1915 instead of the mediocre Murray who replaced the cautious John Maxwell. Hunter would have been suited to campaigning in the desert terrain and would surely have done better against the enemy than these two men. With his Indian background the command in Mesopotamia might have been a suitable alternative possibility for him, for the War Office took over responsibility there from the Indian army early in 1916.

There were two other theatres which might have benefited from Hunter's drive: Salonika and East Africa, though the latter was a relatively minor affair. The four overseas expeditionary forces involved in these four theatres comprised in all over 1,000,000 men,[18] so there was scope for talented soldiers to be employed in commanding them. Maybe Kitchener never considered Hunter for an overseas post, believing that he was too successful as a trainer. Or perhaps after all he was thought to be too old when he turned 59 in September 1915. Or was it, which may be more likely, that after Gibraltar there were still lingering doubts about Hunter's competence to hold an independent command overseas?

By the end of 1915 Kitchener's reputation with his Cabinet colleagues had begun to decline. He was sent off in the summer of 1916 on a mission to Russia. On 5 June *HMS Hampshire* the cruiser carrying him to Archangel struck a mine off the Orkneys and quickly sank. Some dozen men survived and Kitchener was not one of them. Hunter went to his Memorial Service in St Paul's on 13 June. In his diary he noted that he and Mazie sat at the back 'behind all the civilian clerks and nobodies!'

With Kitchener's death there is one inevitable question which must be asked and answered. How much in his career, or obversely how little, did Hunter owe to Kitchener? When Kitchener became Sirdar in 1892, and was therefore in a position to promote his subordinates, Hunter was already well established and marked out for further advancement. By giving Hunter command of the Egyptian division at the start of the Dongola campaign in 1896 Kitchener was doing no more than acknowledge the position. After Omdurman it was Wolseley who took Hunter under his wing sending him first to India and then seeing him transferred to South Africa. In the Boer War Hunter owed his early promotion to Lieutenant-General to Roberts. In 1903 Hunter certainly owed his transfer to India from his less than welcome posting in Scotland to his old chief; in the same way his promotion to General at the early age of 49 was Kitchener's doing. On Hunter's return to England the paths of the two men did not cross for six years. In World War I Kitchener turned Hunter into a trainer and proposed at one time to give him command of an army. So what is the balance sheet? Hunter had unusual ability and would have made his way without Kitchener. But in World War I from Hunter's point of view Kitchener was found wanting. Hunter's former chief was unwilling to see him entrusted with the command he coveted beyond all others.

A sequence of events now took place, which involved Hunter and his career, without his being aware of them at all, at least at the time. French, now commanding the Home Forces, had an interview with Asquith on 16 June. During it he asked the Prime Minister (who, after Kitchener's death, acted as War Minister until Lloyd George accepted that post in July) to remember Hunter's name when selecting a new Field-Marshal.[19]

This was surely a somewhat surprising move by French. Could he have had a slightly guilty conscience about Hunter? So favourably did the Prime Minister receive this suggestion that he wrote that very day a letter to Lord Stamfordham, the King's Private Secretary. There were, he said, two vacancies for Field-Marshal. One only should be filled. He went on to say that he hoped the King might favourably consider the claims of Hunter, the senior General on the active list, who had done 'excellent though unadvertised work' at Aldershot since the beginning of the war. The King at once approved the proposal to make Hunter a Field-Marshal.[20]

On 29 June Stamfordham who had not heard again from Asquith wrote to the Prime Minister from the Royal Pavilion at Aldershot where the King was staying while inspecting his troops. He said that the King would like to make the appointment while he was present in Hunter's command, and asked the Prime Minister to send the formal submission for the King's signature. The same day there came a reply from Bonham Carter, Asquith's Principal Private Secretary, writing from 10 Downing Street. He said that the Prime Minister, since speaking to the King, had begun to have considerable doubts about the advisability of promoting Hunter, and would prefer it, if the King had no objection, that no announcement was made for the present. He then gave his reasons. Apparently the Prime Minister 'was inclined to think that Sir A. Hunter had not quite got the record which in these times should be demanded of an officer holding that rank'.[21] Stamfordham wrote back the next day to say that the King was sorry to hear about the Prime Minister's doubts. Hunter's record, the King felt, compared 'very favourably' with that of any other General on the active list and that he had done good service at Aldershot. Also, he reminded the Prime Minister that at one time Kitchener 'was inclined to send him in command of an army at the front'.[22]

So there it was. The King, who liked Hunter, thought he should become a Field-Marshal, and had done his level best for him. Someone or something had made Asquith change his mind. It would in the circumstances have to be an argument which carried weight. The Gibraltar episode may have been resurrected or it may have been suggested that service at the front was a prerequisite in war-time for promotion to Field-Marshal. On 27 June French lunched with Asquith and Lloyd George, then Minister of Munitions, at No. 10. After lunch French strolled down to the House of Commons with Lloyd George and had a talk with him. Could Hunter's imminent promotion have at some stage that day been discussed, and perhaps discouraged by Lloyd George? According to King George V's biographer, Harold Nicolson, the King suggested in August that the time had come to make Haig a Field-Marshal. Asquith thought this was premature and Lloyd George thought it better to await the outcome of the battle of the Somme then in progress.[23] It is interesting that the decision seems to have effectively rested with Asquith and Lloyd George. Haig was promoted to Field-Marshal on 1 January 1917, the only man in the British army promoted to that rank during the war.

Two weeks after the exchanges between the Palace and No. 10 just described, Duff Cooper, then a young man at the Foreign Office, dined at No. 10. A friend of the Asquiths, he had been required by the Prime Minister to make up a four at bridge, the other two being Lord Crewe and Lord Robert Cecil, both members of the government. Asquith liked talking about instances of miscalculation by the military and the talk turned to the Dardanelles, and how Kitchener would not consent to the recall of Ian Hamilton. Crewe said, and Asquith agreed, that the failure of the Dardanelles was the failure of one man – Ian Hamilton. They then all agreed in praising Archibald Hunter whom Asquith described as 'the most sensible soldier he had ever met. He had won the battle of Omdurman in spite of Kitchener and defended Ladysmith in spite of White. But he had fits of insanity . . .'[24] The last observation was in obvious reference to his time on the Rock. The word 'insanity' should not though be taken too literally. Tantalisingly, we are not told by Duff Cooper whether there was any discussion of whether Hunter should have gone to Gallipoli instead of Hamilton. We are, however, left wanting to know more about that fascinating conversation over bridge at No. 10.

The King had one more shot at achieving promotion for Hunter. On 21 December 1917, three months after Hunter had relinquished his command at Aldershot, Stamfordham wrote to Lord Derby, the Secretary of State for War (Lloyd George had become Prime Minister a year before). As the King understood that Derby could now recommend two supernumerary Field-Marshals, His Majesty was inquiring whether he, Derby, had considered promoting Hunter to that rank in the new year.[25] Stamfordham was ready to come and see Derby on the subject. An interim reply from the War Office was received a few days later saying the addition to the establishment of Field Marshals was still under discussion. On 2 January 1918 came the final reply under Derby's own signature. It was short. His idea of creating supernumerary Field-Marshals had met with 'very violent opposition from Military Members'. He was obliged therefore to 'hang the matter up' until he had discussed it with them.[26]

So, to his great regret, Hunter never achieved his ambition of becoming a Field-Marshal. But it was a near miss. There can be few soldiers who have been recommended for promotion to that rank by both Sovereign and Prime Minister, and yet have not achieved it.

The war dragged on into 1917 with mounting casualty lists, a matter which must have caused Hunter the greatest concern, though we have no knowledge of what he thought about the tactics employed on the Western Front, and of the competence of the senior British Generals. In January 1917 he became ADC General to the King, and was elevated to the position

Orders by General Sir Archibald Hunter, G.C.B., G.C.V.O., D.S.O., A.D.C.Gen., Commanding-in-Chief, Aldershot Command.

ALDERSHOT, SATURDAY, SEPTEMBER 29, 1917.

FAREWELL ORDER.

1. Field-Marshal Lord Kitchener ordered me on 22nd August, 1914, to proceed to Aldershot to train New Armies for service against the enemy, without waste of an hour. I started the Aldershot Training Centre on 23rd August, 1914.

2. My command at Aldershot has happened at a crisis in our Empire's history when all loyal subjects of His Majesty have given, ungrudgingly, of the best that is in them for the King's service.

Looking back on the last three years, I can say that officers and all ranks who have worked under me here, have done their duty faithfully in that respect.

3. Hundreds of thousands of soldiers have undergone war training in this Command since August, 1914. I take pride to place on record, here and now, that, to the lasting honour of the New Armies, the British soldier's name for steady discipline, and for correct and kindly relations with our neighbours, has never stood higher at Aldershot than it does to-day.

It is no secret when the New Armies took the field; nor where they have fought; nor how they have acquitted themselves.

4. In matters relating to the comfort of the wounded and sick, to the entertainment and social welfare of all ranks and their relatives, many ladies have given their services, contributing in a marked degree to the recovery of the patients, and to the genuine happiness and well-being of the duty troops. These ladies may rest assured that their efforts in the soldiers' interests are greatly appreciated.

5. In many Departments of the Command, in various ways, the work of men has been performed by women substitutes. This is a novel feature which so far has been marked with promising results. Hundreds of soldiers have been released for the service abroad they hankered after; the fighting strength of drafts has been favourably affected in consequence.

6. The one regret that I shall carry to my grave is that I have not been privileged to fight with the men I have helped to train.

7. To friends and neighbours, to soldiers of all ranks who have served as comrades with me in this Command, Good-bye.

ARCHIBALD HUNTER, GENERAL,
Commanding-in-Chief, Aldershot Command.

of General Officer Commanding-in-Chief Aldershot Command, not that this title changed anything. He held this post until the end of September 1917 when after a three-year tour of duty he made way for the lesser figure of Sir Archibald Murray.

During their three years in Aldershot the Hunters had entertained a steady flow of visitors at Government House. Mazie played a full part in the life of the garrison town as the General's wife. When the Hunters came to leave, there was a special presentation made to her by the Chairman of the Aldershot District Council. This must have warmed the heart of Hunter. He, too, was thanked for the many courtesies he had shown to the town and for the way he had sent military bands to play in the municipal gardens during the summer. He must have been especially gratified to hear how the town had welcomed the strong leadership provided by Government House.

Hunter issued his Farewell Order to the troops under his command on Saturday, 29 September. In it he took pride in the high standing of the British soldier's name and in how the new armies trained at Aldershot had acquitted themselves in the field. Nor did he omit to mention all those in his Command who had been involved in the welfare of the troops and of the wounded. He ended his message, which was later published in *The Times*, on a slightly sad note:

'The one regret that I shall carry to my grave is that I have not been privileged to fight with the men I have helped to train. To friends and neighbours, to soldiers of all ranks who have served as comrades with me in this Command, Good-bye.'[27]

It was, after 43 years, service, the last order he issued to troops. With a kind of *cri de coeur* he tells us in it how his ambition has not been fulfilled. He had not fought in France. It is difficult to resist the temptation to speculate how he would have fared had he commanded there, or in some other theatre. In December 1988 Henry Keown-Boyd, who some years before published an illuminating book on the Sudan campaigns wrote a letter to the *Sunday Telegraph*. A reviewer of a biography on Haig had written that Lloyd George had no alternative candidate to Haig as C-in-C in France. Keown-Boyd disagreed. There was Allenby. But also:

'. . . waiting vainly in Aldershot was perhaps the most outstanding "front-line" soldier of his day, General Sir Archibald Hunter . . . his powers of leadership and tactical sense were unrivalled in his generation. One can not imagine him sitting in a *château* miles behind the lines . . . His absence from the battlefields of the First World War is as extraordinary as the lack of any comment upon it, or him, from military historians.'[28]

This is a generous tribute. We are still waiting for the military historians to pronounce.

NOTES

1. Kitchener Papers 30/57 WV 40 83 AH–Kitchener 9 Aug. 1914.
2. Ibid. 90 AH–Kitchener 21 Aug. 1914.
3. DHD 306.
4. Brock *H. H. Asquith's Letters to Venetia Stanley* 153.
5. *Daily Mirror* 6 Nov. 1915.
6. DHD 307–9.
7. French's Diary PP/MCR/C32, 30 Dec. 1914.
8. Wilson's Diary 27 Jan. 1915.
9. *Morning Post* 2 Jan. 1915.
10. Westlake *Kitchener's Army* 12.
11. CAB 37/123/9 memorandum by French 3 Jan. 1915.
12. Haig Papers Acc 3155 No. 100 11 Jan. 1915.
13. CAB 37/123/34 Army Council to French 20 Jan. 1915.
14. Brock 397.
15. Kitchener Papers 30/57 AH–Kitchener 4 and 9 Apr. and 3 May 1915.
16. Duff Cooper *Old Men Forget* 56.
17. DHD 314.
18. Cruttwell *A History of the Great War 1914–1918* 235.
19. G. French *Some War Diaries, Addresses and Correspondence of the Earl of Ypres* 252.
20. RA G V F 930/2.
21. RA G V F 930/3 and F 930/5.
22. RA G V F 930/6.
23. Nicolson 277.
24. Duff Cooper loc. cit.
25. RA G V F 930/7.
26. RA G V F 930/9.
27. *The Times* 10 Oct. 1917.
28. *Sunday Telegraph* 4 Dec. 1988.

CHAPTER 22

Parliament, Retirement & Retrospect

When Hunter left his command at Aldershot in September 1917 the war still had a little more than a year to run. He was now 61. No job, or no job he wanted – we cannot tell which – was offered to him by the War Office.

Many people after so active a life would be beginning to run out of steam. Not Hunter. A new interest, even career, surprisingly, caught his attention: politics. Years before, he had been asked if he would stand for parliament. Twice he declined.[1] We don't know which party approached him but, unlike his father, he was not radically-minded. Despite the reforming tendencies we have sometimes detected along the path of his story, his political instincts were conservative.

Once again the politicians, this time in Lancaster, approached Hunter. As a potential candidate he had attractions. His straightforward resolute manner would appeal to the electorate. With his distinguished record of military service and his love of country pursuits, he might have seemed the ideal man to represent a shire or county town.[2] The Unionists were persistent. Lancaster was the home of his regiment. He was its Colonel. He was a Freeman of Lancaster, and knew its people. Eventually, as the long war was coming to its end, he gave way and agreed to stand in the next election as a Coalition Unionist candidate against the Liberal Member Sir Norval Helme. Hunter was undoubtedly motivated by his strong sense of duty. He must have believed that he would have a role to play in seeing that soldiers returning from the war received a fair deal. At the same time he may have been looking for some useful activity with which to occupy himself. Also he loved a challenge. On the other hand his dealings with politicians in 1913 had not been happy ones, and he must have known well enough that they looked at problems in a different way from soldiers.

On 19 October 1918 Hunter was adopted at a meeting of the Lancaster Unionist Association. On the 23rd he was writing in his diary: 'Politics from the Unionist point of view have been shamefully neglected. I have an uphill game to fight. There is apathy and negligence rampant. A few keen supporters who deserve due praise but the bulk are useless . . .' It seemed to be a bleak prospect and for a time he admitted he was 'in despair'. In contrast the Liberals had an effective party machine and had triumphed in the last four elections in Lancaster. Nonetheless Hunter set to work to breathe life into his local party and was soon attracting new supporters. He wrote, unashamedly, to the Officers Commanding eleven of the battalions of the King's Own regiment[3] about his candidature. Afterwards he was to say that these letters did not secure him a single vote, but he could hardly have known!

There is something endearing about this man's enthusiasm for a new cause and willingness in late middle age to risk his reputation in such an unexpected venture. Nobody could have quarrelled with the lofty aspirations expressed in his election address even if they were couched in banal platitudes.

'I am a champion for fairplay for all our fighting men and seamen with a special care for the widow and orphan, for the maimed and blind . . . I insist on good wages, healthy conditions of living and working, the support of British farming and of key industries . . . No taxing of our

231

daily bread ... I have no axe to grind and only seek to serve my country ...'

Towards the vanquished enemy he lived up to his reputation for toughness, reflecting the mood of the electorate. 'I am dead against pro-Germans, Bolshevists and such like elements of disorder and ruin ... we must exact payment from the enemy of our war costs.'[4]

It is not easy to imagine Hunter stumping round the hustings. But he did. This was the election when women, for the first time, had the vote. Hunter was quick to spot their importance and, with Mazie playing her part, took pains to canvass them.

Polling took place, in glorious weather, on 14 December 1918; this ensured a good turn-out. The votes were recorded as having been cast as follows:

Gen Sir A. Hunter	14,403
Sir N. W. Helme	9,778
majority	4,625

It was a handsome victory. Hunter put it down to the women's vote claiming they all voted for him!

In the country the coalition was swept to power gaining 533 seats in the House of Commons. Lloyd George was again Prime Minister but had become trapped as a prisoner of the Unionists. The new parliament has been much criticised. Baldwin called its members hard-faced men who had done well out of the war. Given the validity of this comment Hunter would have been uncomfortable with many of his fellow members.

During his slightly less than four years in the House, Hunter was never much more than a passive observer of the parliamentary scene. He made no real impact as a Member. He diligently attended the debates and listened to the speeches. He voted in the lobbies, and once during an all-night sitting in December 1920 cast his vote in no fewer than 24 divisions.[5] But he never once spoke in the House, though this was not in those days unusual. Sir George Younger, a powerful figure on the government side, asked Hunter in January 1920 if he would move or second the Address in reply to the King's speech on the opening of parliament. The invitation might have been regarded as an honour, the two members involved appearing in levée dress, and calculated to appeal to Hunter. But he refused.[6] Instead he preferred to attend King George V as his ADC General. Nor did Hunter sit on any of the committees of the House except for the Select Committee which inquired in 1921 into the organisation and administration of the telephone service.[7]

But he was ready to help old friends. For example in November 1920 he held a meeting at his house attended by Wingate, then High Commissioner in Cairo, to which various Lancashire MPs were invited to discuss the promotion of cotton-growing in the Sudan. The plan was to prepare for a meeting with the Prime Minister on the matter. Duly, three weeks afterwards Hunter had an interview about the project with Lloyd George and the Chancellor of the Exchequer, Sir Austen Chamberlain.

As a constituency MP Hunter was much more at home. He travelled to Lancaster with fair regularity to give lunches to the great and the good, to attend fetes and to open bazaars, and perform all the other social duties expected of the sitting MP. Hunter made speeches at these functions but they were always short. Nor did he forget the problems of his constituents. Thus he attended to the Post Office workers in respect of their queries over a minimum wages bill and to the fishermen who felt threatened by the import of Dutch shrimps.[8]

Probably what gave Hunter as much pleasure as anything during his time as an MP was hosting a dinner in the House of Commons in July 1922 in honour of the 96-year-old General Sir George Higginson, a veteran of the Crimean War. Some 79 attended the dinner including the Duke of Connaught, the last Royal Duke to command an army unit on the battle-field (at Tel-el-Kebir in Egypt in 1882), Asquith, Bonar Law and Stanley Baldwin. In proposing Higginson's health Hunter told the assembled company that this was his maiden speech in the House of Commons (there were cries of 'shame'). Revealingly, as if to explain why he had not spoken in the House, he went on to say 'I do not waste your time.'[9] Perhaps Hunter on arrival at the House of Commons realised soon enough with his quick instinct that he would have no real political contribution to make as a debater on the floor of the House, and did not wish to pretend otherwise.

During his parliamentary years Hunter found himself much involved in charitable work. Thus he was elected to the Executive of the Gordon Memorial College in Khartoum. In January 1921 he chaired a huge meeting attended by some 10,000 people at the Albert Hall in aid of Dr Barnardo's Homes. In July 1922 he presided at the Jubilee festival of the College for the Blind. These were all charities which provided an outlet for a side of his character, glimpsed from time to time in these pages, when his compassion for those in need was expressed.

He attended, too, during these years to certain military duties of a mainly ceremonial kind for both his Sovereign and his regiment. In 1921 he unveiled the West Window in the King's Own Memorial chapel of the beautiful Lancaster Priory, the town's parish church, in memory of nearly 7,000 men of the regiment who were killed during World War I. Years later after his death a window in the chapel was unveiled in his memory. A major landmark was reached for Hunter in October 1920 when, having been unemployed for three years, he finally retired from the army after 46 years' service.

While Hunter was an MP, Mazie's health had begun to decline. She had developed a heart complaint which became serious in the autumn of 1922. It may have been exacerbated by drinking. Her illness coincided with the decision of the Conservative and Unionist party to withdraw its support from Lloyd George; the party was dissatisfied with the Prime Minister's pro-Greek policy in the conflict between the Turks and the Greeks. A meeting was called at the Carlton Club on 19 October. Bonar Law moved that at the next election, the Conservative party should stand as an independent party with its own leader and programme. The motion was passed by 187 votes to 87. Hunter voted with the majority. This was the end of the road for Lloyd George, for he had lost the vital support he needed to keep him in power. Parliament was dissolved a week later and a general election was held. Hunter had already decided not to stand again. Mazie's health may possibly have provided a pretext, but he was wholly content to ring down the curtain on his parliamentary career. When he was asked privately why he was not continuing his career as an MP he replied: 'Because I wish to die an honest man.'[10]

After he had shaken the dust from off his parliamentary feet Hunter wondered for an idle moment whether he should not follow the urgings of his sister-in-law, Abby Hunter, and write a book of reminiscences.[11] He had kept despatch boxes and tins full of papers, so he had the material and his memory was good. But it was not to be. For one thing the horror of blowing his own trumpet was strong. Hunter has been described as a disappointed man in these later years, sad that his career had not ended more successfully. This too could have inhibited the would-be author. But it is a pity that Hunter never put pen to paper, for had he done so, the attention of military historians could have been attracted to his story and he would probably have suffered less from neglect.

Mazie's heart condition did not improve. But perfectly well able to cope without her husband's presence, she did not begrudge him making two long sea journeys on his own. Hunter loved travel and was a good sailor. In January 1924 he visited South Africa, calling on the Premier Jan Smuts, in Cape Town. The other journey, a more ambitious one, took him 16,000 miles to Valparaiso in Chile and back via the Panama canal.

The month after he returned from the Pacific Hunter went to Lancaster to attend on 27 November the unveiling of the War Memorial Shrine and the Roll of Honour by Field-Marshal Earl Haig. Hunter's visit to the north was interrupted. He was urgently summoned back to London by a serious deterioration in Mazie's condition. Three days later, on 30 November 1924, she died.

After fourteen years of marriage, Hunter was once again on his own. His union with Mazie had not been a love match. Both had made no bones about it – theirs had been a marriage of convenience. Nonetheless Mazie had been supportive to Hunter at Aldershot and while he was an MP. She had been very well off, and Hunter could look forward to a comfortable retirement. But her will stipulated that if he remarried then he would lose the income from her estate.

Without children of his own he took, as a widower, a keen and generous interest in his young relations. He was pleased that George's younger son Anthony had become a soldier, and gave him £50 towards getting kitted out on being commissioned. He also gave his two young Hunter nephews a handsome gift of ICI shares. Hunter invited his Grahame cousins, twenty-year-old twin sisters, to stay with him when they were taken to the Sandhurst Ball. On returning to London in the early hours the twins found their host anxious about them and awaiting their return sitting on his own doorstep!

Very much the genial uncle he happily entertained his fourteen-year-old great-nephew Hugo von Dumreicher, grandson of his deceased twin Nellie, at the start of the school holidays by taking him to the London zoo. Hunter's young relations found the elderly General tolerant and good-humoured with a distinct sense of fun. He was even at times not averse to playing the mimic.

In 1926 Hunter's long term as Colonel of the regiment came to an end. His attention to regimental duties had been assiduous. For over half a century his life had revolved around the army. Now the cord was loosed.

What kind of overall assessment can we make of Archie Hunter, the soldier? Was Hunter just a good fighting General, effective in colonial-type wars, but never tested in a more demanding arena? Or were his talents greater?

Judged by any standard, Hunter had a highly successful military career. That cannot be in dispute. No one who had reached the rank of full General before he was 50 could be considered not to have done very well. As a battlefield commander he had always emerged victorious against the only two opponents with whom he fought – the Dervishes and the Boers. In the Sudan it is easy enough to belittle the Dervishes, Hunter's adversaries in war for 14 years, if only because of their antiquated equipment. But often numerically and always in terms of courage, as Hunter well knew, they were formidable, as commanders of earlier expeditions had learnt to their cost. In South Africa he quickly demonstrated an ability to adapt to a new set of circumstances and in particular to appreciate the military capacity of his wily Boer opponents

There are perhaps four aspects of Hunter's qualities as a fighting General which stand out.

First, his undisputed capacity for leadership; he was invariably cool and confident. Men looked to him to lead them.

Second, his ability to plan a battle, be it an offensive or defensive one;

in this he had a meticulous eye for detail and paid careful attention to intelligence.

Third, his command of tactics on the field demonstrated in varied terrain. He was bold and decisive, yet cautious when necessary. He could be imaginative and had an ability to surprise the enemy. He also understood how the different arms should combine to achieve maximum effect.

Fourth, his concern for the well-being of his troops and the need whenever possible to avoid casualties. On the latter point he was ahead of his time.

But Hunter had military talents other than those displayed on the battlefield. For example he had undoubted abilities as a staff officer. He thought a good deal about his profession and it is fair to say he was a student of warfare. For instance, he was ready to analyse and learn from his and other campaigns. His evidence to the Royal Commission on the South African war shows how his mind ranged freely over many of the contemporary problems facing the army. We have referred earlier to the praise Liddell Hart bestowed on Hunter. Hunter also showed himself to be, at the time of Prinsloo's surrender in South Africa, a tough but fair-minded negotiator.

As a trainer of troops Hunter must be judged to have been highly successful. The Aldershot command was unrewarding and trainers can be forgotten. A handsome tribute to his work at Aldershot is paid by A. J. Smithers in *The Fighting Nation: Lord Kitchener and his armies,* in which he underlines Hunter's great authority and sheer professionalism.[12]

There are only two military misjudgements of any significance discernible during Hunter's career as a General. The first turned out to be of little consequence. This was at Omdurman in 1898 when clearly he has to bear some share of the responsibility for the gap which opened up between MacDonald's and Lewis's brigades, thus allowing the Dervishes the opportunity – which they failed to take – to exploit what could have become a dangerous situation. The other was more grave and occurred when he failed to seal properly Slabbert's Nek pass in July 1900 and so allowed de Wet to escape from the Brandwater Basin.

Hunter's principal faults lay off the battlefield. He could be outspoken, as we have seen, to the point of foolhardiness. When he was determined, fearlessly, to speak out, he was often right in what he had to say but wrong in how he said it. But sometimes, as happened at Gibraltar, his judgment left him and his consequent behaviour defied all reason. This apparent flaw in his character may have weighed with Kitchener, and others, in deciding whether or not to give him command of an army in World War I.

How would Hunter himself have looked back over his career? He would surely have been satisfied with its course up to the end of his time in India. Possibly had he been more of an 'insider' or an overtly ambitious 'thruster', he might have had less time to wait for reemployment. It would not have been lost on him that during those critical years before World War I contemporaries like French and Ian Hamilton, as well as his juniors, were surging past him in the race to the top. After the fiasco of Gibraltar he saw himself presented on the outbreak of the war with one great final opportunity for soldiering. He must have believed, and with good cause, that he was uniquely qualified to lead armies in the field against Germany.

For Hunter there were certain matters in World War I which must have upset him in varying degrees. First and foremost there was the way he had been singled out at the end of 1914 to command the 3rd army, but was then denied the post and any succeeding field command.

Second, he can hardly have been unmoved by the shattering losses of men at the front. The soldiers he had seen trained at Aldershot were decimated in repeated and senseless attacks such as those which began in the Somme offensive on 1 July 1916, and which continued for month after pointless month until October of that year. We do not know whether or not Hunter accepted the thinking and tactics which made these losses inevitable, but we do know his long-held view that unnecessary casualties should be avoided. Had he been an army commander at the front it is inconceivable – so he would have argued to himself as he brooded over the war – that, with his prestige, independent thinking and above all moral courage, he would have allowed such crippling losses of infantry to take place with so little to show for the sacrifice. Hunter might be forgiven for believing that as a front-line army commander he would have saved the lives of thousands of men. Asquith, remember, had called him the most sensible soldier he ever knew.

Third, there was the question of how he had narrowly failed to become a Field-Marshal. It seems unlikely that Hunter could have been entirely ignorant of what had happened. He may not have been aware of all the details just as we today are not in possession of them all. But the probability is that he knew, or came to know in time, that he had been within an ace of being promoted to Field-Marshal. It need hardly be stated that such promotion would have helped to compensate him for his failure to attain a field command.

So on several grounds Hunter might with some justice have felt aggrieved at the unkind way fate had treated him during those vital war years. No ordinary soldier, Hunter believed that he could have commanded an army at the front in World War I with distinction. It was the country's loss that he did not.

After Mazie's death Hunter wished to be near his brother George. So he took a house, Glaston Hill House, in the depths of the north Hampshire countryside in Eversley, opposite the church where Charles Kingsley had been rector. George and Hylda were two and a half miles away near

Bramshill. Hunter may have found time lying heavily on his hands at Eversley, for as far as we know, he did not become involved in local affairs or sporting activities. Nor did he have any absorbing pastimes. Once he had amused himself by collecting the autographs of famous people, but he gave away his collection, and, a curiosity, it now resides in Lancaster City library.

When George died in the autumn of 1930 there seemed nothing to keep Archie in Hampshire. So he returned to London and took a flat high up in Queen Anne's Mansions overlooking St James's Park. Later he moved to Drayton Gardens in Chelsea. Apart from his half-sister Clemence, he was at 74 the sole survivor of Mary Jane's 11 children. Hunter's great energy was now noticeably running down. Also he had for some time, sadly, been finding consolation in drink. He was also lonely. Some years after Mazie's death, wanting companionship, he took up with a middle-aged Irish widow, Mrs Sinclair Westcott. Even if he had wished to marry her and she had been willing, the terms of Mazie's will inhibited him from taking this step. Several times he went with his new-found friend to winter abroad, usually to Jamaica. The family did not care much for Mrs Westcott, but she was kind and did her best to see that Hunter did not over-indulge.

In the early 1930s Hugo von Dumreicher stayed for a time with his great-uncle. Hugo had fond memories of Hunter in old age as a wise and generous man, always immaculately turned out. The presence was still there and he could, probably unknowingly, fix the person to whom he was talking with an intimidating glower. He was ready to speak of the past, though on his own terms, and was willing to answer questions but not to put them. He read *The Times* carefully but did not often open a book. He suffered from gout and so rarely went out except occasionally to dine at the Carlton club. He saw a few old friends like the Rundles. Once a former Sergeant-Major visited him. Immediately another place was laid for lunch, and the two old soldiers were soon immersed in their memories. Years before, Daisy Low had said Hunter concealed his emotions. Yet in some ways he was a sentimental man. Hugo recollected that the news of a mining accident came through on the wireless. There was no more hope for the men. Hunter was speaking of this and he had to stop. Tears came into his eyes.

On 20 January 1936 King George V, who had tried so signally all those years before to have Hunter made a Field-Marshal, died. He at least had known Hunter's worth. Edward VIII was now King. The storm clouds were again gathering over Europe, and the world would soon be plunged into nearly six years of horrific war. But Archie Hunter did not live to see this conflict. For him the fighting was over, and on 28 June he died at his home in London.

NOTES

1. DHD 319.
2. Ibid. 320.
3. AHd 26 and 27/10/18.
4. Lancaster Central Library for information held on AH.
5. AHd 22/12/20.
6. AHd 15/1/20.
7. *Hansard* 10 Mar. 1921 col 834.
8. Lancaster Central Library loc. cit.
9. AHd 25/7/22; DHD 318–9.
10. Family information.
11. DHD 319.
12. Smithers *The Fighting Nations: Lord Kitchener and his Armies* 124, 125 and 148–9.

Select Bibliography

Books are published in London unless otherwise stated

Alford, H. and Sword, W., *The Egyptian Soudan: its Loss and Recovery*, 1898
Amery, L. S. (ed.), *The Times History of the War in South Africa*, 1900–1909
Arthur, Sir George, *Life of Lord Kitchener*, 1920
Barthorpe, M., *The British Army on Campaign 4 1882–1902*, 1988
Birdwood, Lord, *Khakhi and Gown: An Autobiography*, 1941
Bond, Brian, *The Victorian Army and the Staff College*, 1972
Bradford, Ernle, *Gibraltar*, 1971
Brett, M. V. (ed.), *Journals and Letters of Reginald Viscount Esher*, 1934
Brock, M. and E. (ed.), *H. H. Asquith's Letters to Venetia Stanley*, 1982
Calwell, Maj-Gen. Sir C. E., *Field-Marshal Sir Henry Wilson: Life and Diaries*, 1927
Cecil, Lord Edward, *Leisure of an Egyptian Official*, 1921
Chenevix-Trench, Charles, *The Indian Army and the King's Enemies 1900–1947*, 1988
Chisholm, Ruari, *Ladysmith*, 1979
Churchill, Winston S., *The River War*, Sceptre paperback ed. 1987
Churchill, Winston S., *London to Ladysmith*, 1900
Cooper, A. Duff, *Old Men Forget*, 1953
Cowper, L. I., *The King's Own: The Story of a Royal Regiment*, 1939
Cromer, Earl of, *Modern Egypt*, 1908
Crutwell, C., *A History of the Great War 1914–1918*, 1936
De Groot, G. J., *Douglas Haig 1861–1928*, 1988
De Wet, C. R., *Three Years War*, 1902
Dilks, David, *Curzon in India*, 1970
Doolittle, Duncan H., *A Soldier's Hero: General Sir Archibald Hunter*, Narragansett, Rhode Island, U.S.A., 1991 (privately printed)
Doyle, A. Conan, *The Great Boer War*, 1903
Duncan, J. S. R., *The Sudan*, 1952
Durand, Sir Mortimer, *The Life of Field-Marshal Sir George White*, 1915
Eastwood, S. A., *Lions of England: A Pictorial History of the King's Own Royal Regiment (Lancaster) 1680–1980*, 1991
Farwell, Byron, *Queen Victoria's Little Wars*, 1973
Fraser, Lovat, *India under Curzon and After*, 1911
Fraser, Peter, *Lord Esher*, 1973
French, Major the Hon. Gerald, *Some War Diaries, Addresses and Correspondence of the Earl of Ypres*, 1937

240

Gibson, G. F., *The Story of the Imperial Light Horse in the South African War 1899–1902*, 1937
Gleichen, Count A. E., *With the Camel Corps up the Nile*, 1889
Griffith, Kenneth, *Thank God we kept the Flag flying*, 1974
Haggard, Lt-Col. Andrew, *Under Crescent and Star*, 1895
Hamilton, I., *The Happy Warrior: A Life of General Sir Ian Hamilton*, 1966
Harries-Jenkins, G., *The Army in Victorian Society*, 1977
Hopkirk, P., *The Great Game*, 1990
James, D., *Lord Roberts*, 1954
Jeal, Tim, *Baden-Powell*, 1989
Kenyon, E. R., *Gibraltar under Moor, Spaniard and Briton*, 1911
Keown-Boyd, Henry, *A Good Dusting: The Sudan Campaigns 1883–1899*, 1986
King, Peter, *The Viceroy's Fall*, 1986
Liddell Hart, B. H., *History of the First World War*, Pan Books paperback ed. 1973
Lines, G. W., *The Ladysmith Siege*, Maritzburg, 1900
Macdiarmid, D. S., *The Life of Lieutenant-General Sir J. M. Grierson*, 1923
Magnus, Philip, *Kitchener: Portrait of an Imperialist*, 1958
Magnus, Philip, *King Edward the Seventh*, 1964
Maurice, Lt-Col. F. M., *Sir Frederick Maurice: a Record of Essays*, 1913
Maurice, Maj-Gen. Sir Frederick M., *The Life of General Lord Rawlinson of Trent*, 1928 (the author is identical with Lt-Col. F. M. Maurice)
Maurice, Maj-Gen. Sir Frederick and Grant, M. H., *Official History of the War in South Africa 1899–1902*
Milner, Alfred, *England in Egypt*, 1892
Mockler-Ferryman, A. F., *Annals of Sandhurst*, 1900
Moorehead, A., *Gallipoli*, 1956
Moorehead, A., *The White Nile*, 1960
Neville, H. L., *Campaigns on the North–West Frontier*, 1912
Nicolson, Harold, *King George V*, 1952
Officer, an, *Sudan Campaign 1896–99*, 1899 (this work was anonymous)
Pakenham, Thomas, *The Boer War*, Futura paperback ed. 1988
Pakenham, Thomas, *The Scramble for Africa*, Abacus paperback ed. 1992
Pemberton, W. B., *Battles of the Boer War*, 1964
Phillipps, L. March, *With Rimington*, 1901
Preston, Adrian, (ed.), *In Relief of Gordon: Lord Wolseley's Campaign Journal*, 1967
Repington, Colonel Charles à Court, *Vestigia*, 1919
Robertson, Field-Marshal Sir William, *From Private to Field-Marshal*, 1921
Royle, Charles, *The Egyptian Campaigns*, 1900
Royle, Trevor, *The Kitchener Enigma*, 1985
Sandes, E. W. C., *The Royal Engineers in Egypt and the Sudan*, 1937
Seely, J. E. B., *Adventure*, 1930

Sharp, G., *The Siege of Ladysmith*, 1976

Shultz, G. D., and Lawrence, D. G., *Lady from Savannah*, Philadelphia, U.S.A., 1958

Simkins, Peter, *Kitchener's Army, the Raising of the new Armies 1914–16*, 1988

Slatin, R., *Fire and Sword in the Sudan*, 1987

Smith-Dorrien, General Sir Horace, *Memories of Forty-Eight Years Service*, 1925

Smithers, A. J., *The Fighting Nation: Lord Kitchener's Armies*, 1994

Steevens, G. W., *With Kitchener to Khartum*, 1899

Stewart, John, *A Subaltern in the Sudan 1898*, from *The Stewart Society Journal*, v. xvii no. 4, 1987

Symons, Julian, *Buller's Campaign*, 1963

Taylor, A. J. P., *English History 1914–1945*, 1965

Ternan, Brig-Gen. Trevor, *Some Experiences of an Old Bromsgrovian*, Birmingham, 1930

Terraine, John, *Douglas Haig: the Educated Soldier*, 1963

Travers, T. H. E., *The Killing Ground*, 1987

Warner, P., *Dervish: Rise and Fall of an African Empire*, 1973

Watkins, Owen, *With Kitchener's Army*, 1899

Watkins-Pitchford, H., *Besieged in Ladysmith*, Pietermaritzburg, 1964

Westlake, Roy, *Kitchener's Army*, 1989

Wilson, H. W., *With the Flag to Pretoria*, 1901

Wilson, H. W., *After Pretoria: the Guerrilla War*, 1902

Wingate, F. R., *Mahdiism and the Egyptian Sudan*, 1891

Wingate, Sir Ronald, *Wingate of the Sudan*, 1955

Wolseley, Field-Marshal Lord, *Story of a Soldier's Life*, 1903

Wood, Field-Marshal Sir Evelyn, *From Midshipman to Field-Marshal*, 1906

Young, Brigadier Peter, and Lawford, Lt-Col. J. P., (eds.), *The History of the British Army*, 1970

Ziegler, Philip, *Omdurman*, 1973

Sources

A. Unpublished

Acland Papers, Dorchester
CAB 37, Cabinet Papers, PRO
Lord Edward Cecil's Diary 1896, Hatfield House, Hatfield
CO 91, Colonial Office, PRO
Lord Curzon Collection, O and IO, BL, MSS Eur F 111
Field-Marshal Earl Haig Papers and Diaries, NLS, Acc 3155
Gen. Sir Ian Hamilton Collection, LHC, 24/7/11
Lord Harcourt Papers, Bodleian Library, University of Oxford, Oxford
Field-Marshal Lord Kitchener Papers, PRO 30/57
Lancaster City Library, information held on Hunter
Maj-Gen. Sir Frederick Maurice Collection, LHC, 2/1
Gen. Sir Ivor Maxse Papers, West Sussex Record Office, 334
Lord Mottistone Papers, Nuffield College, Oxford, 20
Gen. Lord Rawlinson Collection, NAM 5201
RA, G V L521, QVJ, P5/55, W 3, W 38, W 56, G V M75, G V F930
Field-Marshal Lord Roberts Papers and telegrams, NAM 7101-23-114-1
SAD, 110/11 and Staff diary and intelligence reports 1889
Field-Marshal Sir George White Collection, I and IO, BL, MSS Eur F 108
Field-Marshal Sir Henry Wilson Diary, IWM,
Gen. Sir Reginald Wingate Papers, SAD 102/1, 257/1, 258/1, 267/1, WP280
WO 105, 108, and 175, War Office, PRO
Field-Marshal Earl of Ypres' Diary, IWM, PP/MRC/C 32 30

B. Published

DHD   Duncan H. Doolittle, *A Soldier's Hero: General Sir Archibald Hunter*
OH   *Official History of the War in South Africa 1899–1902*
RCSAW   *Royal Commission on the War in South Africa*, Cmnd 1789–92
TH   *The Times History of the War in South Africa*

Index

In subheadings, Hunter's name is abbreviated to AH. When the names of his relatives appear as main headings, then their relationship to him is put in brackets.

Edward VIII, King, 238
Edwards, Lt-Col. A.H.M., 131, 146
Egeiga, 92, 93, 94, 96
Egypt, 10, 12, 14, 24, 72, 105, 224; British
 intervention in, 10; AH arrives in, 15;
 AH departs from, 109; AH visits,
 111, 181
Egyptian army, 17, 49, 54; before
 British reforms, 10, 11–12;
 conditions in, for British officers,
 12–13; strength of, 13, 44, 55, 70, 75,
 91; and Wolseley's expedition, 21;
 improvement in, 43; casualties at
 Omdurman, 102–3; *see also under*
 Egyptian army units,
Egyptian army units,
 infantry
  1st Egyptian: 23, 31, 88
  2nd Egyptian: 83, 103
  3rd Egyptian: 48, 62, 66
  7th Egyptian: 86, 99, 103
  8th Egyptian: 83
  15th Egyptian: 99
  9th Sudanese: 181; AH as OC, 15,
   17–18, 22–4, 27, 106; on the
   frontier, 28, 29, 31; and
   reconquest campaign, 62, 66,
   68, 83, 106
  10th Sudanese: 29, 31, 62, 66, 83,
   86
  11th Sudanese: 27, 62, 66, 71, 83,
   86, 103
  12th Sudanese: 28, 47, 48, 83
  13th Sudanese: 29, 31, 83, 97, 102,
   103
  14th Sudanese: 83
 cavalry, 13, 28, 29, 47, 62, 80, 82, 94,
  96, 100, 102
 camel corps, 13; on the frontier, 23, 28,
  29; and reconquest campaign, 47,
  70, 71, 72, 86, 91, 94, 96, 100
 artillery, 13, 62, 66, 70, 71, 75, 91; at
  Omdurman, 94, 96, 100
Elandslaagte, 122, 140; and battle of
 (1899), 123, 124
El Kab, 65
El Obeid, 18, 102
Elgin, Lord, 181
Elles, Maj-Gen. Sir Edmond, 194
Emmot, Lord, 213
Erasmus, General Daniel, 121
Ericeira, 204
Eritrea, 43
Esher, Lord, 174–5, 181–2, 200, 201
Evans, Sir Frederick, 203, 207

Eversley, 237
Exchange Committee (Gibraltar), 212,
 213, 217

Fareeg, 52
Farquhars Farm, 124
Fashoda, 105
Fergusson, Hickson, 202
Ferreira, General J.S., 141
Fez (Morocco), 205
Ficksburg, 150, 153, 154, 155, 157;
 command 164
*Fighting Nation, The: Lord Kitchener and
 his armies*, 236
Finch Smith, Sgt. (later Lieut), 131
Fire and Sword in the Sudan, 70
Firket, village and battle of (1896),
 45–9, 52, 54, 86, 106
Fisher, Admiral Sir John (later Admiral
 of the Fleet Lord), 184
Fitton, Capt. H.G., 80, 83, 103
Fitzclarence, Lieut. Edward, 66, 67, 181
Fitzherbert, Col., 111
Fleetwood, 9
Fort Atbara, 69, 75, 79, 89, 91; defences
 at, 77, 128
Ford Sandeman, 191
Fortress Orders, Gibraltar, 203, 207,
 212, 216
Fourie, Commandant Christiaan, 169,
 171
Fouriesburg, 153, 157, 160, 162;
 advance on and capture of, 161
Fourteen Streams, 143, 145, 146
Fowke, Capt., 131
France, 10, 197, 205, 221, 229; and the
 upper Nile, 104, 105; as an ally, 200,
 218
Frankfort, 151, 169, 172
Franz Ferdinand, Archduke, 218
Fraser, Lovat, 195
freemasons, 7
French, Field-Marshal Lord, 237; in
 Natal, 123, 124, 126; commands at
 Aldershot, 179, 188; CIGS 201; and
 opinion of AH, 215; C-in-C, BEF, 219,
 221–3; replaced, 224; suggests AH
 becomes a Field-Marshal 225–6
Froneman, General C., 169

Gallipoli, 223, 224, 227
Gardner machine gun, 62
Gatacre, Maj-Gen. Sir William, 75, 81,
 83; at battle of Atbara, 85, 87; at
 battle of Omdurman, 93